Exam Ref MD-101 Managing Modern Desktops

D1407554

Andrew Bettany
Andrew Warren

Exam Ref MD-101 Managing Modern Desktops

Published with the authorization of Microsoft Corporation by:
Pearson Education, Inc.

Copyright © 2020 by Pearson Education

ISBN-13: 978-0-13-556083-9
ISBN-10: 0-13-556083-7

Library of Congress Control Number is on file.

2 2019

Editor-in-Chief	Brett Bartow
Executive Editor	Loretta Yates
Assistant Sponsoring Editor	Charvi Arora
Development Editor	Rick Kughen
Managing Editor	Sandra Schroeder
Project Editor	Tracey Croom
Copy Editor	Rick Kughen
Indexer	Tim Wright
Proofreader	Abigail Manheim
Technical Editors	Boyd Nolan, Chris Rhodes
Editorial Assistant	Cindy Teeters
Cover Designer	Twist Creative, Seattle

I would like to dedicate this book to Annette and Tommy, for being hugely supportive and encouraging whenever I work on projects that sometimes eat into our quality time together. This book is also for the reader. Having taught thousands of IT Professionals over my career, I hope this book reaches a greater audience and helps you achieve your career aspirations. Work hard and aim for the stars!

—Andrew Bettany

Any book is a collaborative effort, and I'd like to thank my co-author, Andrew, and the team at Microsoft Press for helping get this book out there. It seems I've always been the sort of person that needs a deadline. At school, my homework deadline was the sound of the school bus brakes as we pulled in to the campus. So, I'd also like to thank my daughter, Amelia, for occasionally popping through to my office to say, "The school bus is almost in, Dad," and for bringing me an espresso to help sharpen my writing.

—Andrew Warren

portal. office. com — Office 365 Portal

add. portal. azure. com — Azure admin center

endpoint. microsoft. com — Endpoint admin center

Contents at a glance

Introduction   *xv*

CHAPTER 1   **Deploy and Update Operating Systems**   1

CHAPTER 2   **Manage Policies and Profiles**   95

CHAPTER 3   **Manage and protect devices**   153

CHAPTER 4   **Manage Apps and Data**   217

Index   *285*

Contents

Introduction   xv

Organization of this book   xv

Microsoft certifications   xv

Errata, updates, & book support   xvi

Stay in touch   xvi

Chapter 1   Deploy and Update Operating Systems   1

Skill 1.1: Plan and implement Windows 10 by using dynamic
    deployment...1

      Evaluate and select an appropriate deployment option   2

      Manage pilot deployment   10

      Manage and troubleshoot provisioning packages   14

Skill 1.2: Plan and implement Windows 10 by using
    Windows Autopilot...17

      Evaluate and select an appropriate deployment option   17

      Implement pilot deployment   20

      Create, validate, and assign deployment profiles   22

      Extract device hardware information   25

      Import device hardware information to cloud service   26

      Troubleshoot deployment   28

Skill 1.3: Upgrade devices to Windows 10.............................30

      Identify upgrade and downgrade paths   31

      Manage in-place upgrades   36

      Configure a Windows Analytics environment   36

      Perform Upgrade Readiness assessment   42

      Migrate user profiles   44

Skill 1.4: Manage updates 47

      Configure Windows 10 delivery optimization   48

      Configure Windows Update for Business   51

      Deploy Windows Updates   54

Implement feature updates   60

Monitor Windows 10   61

Skill 1.5: Manage device authentication 65

Manage authentication policies   65

Manage sign-in options   73

Perform Azure AD join   83

Thought experiments. 87

Scenario 1   87

Scenario 2   88

Scenario 3   88

Scenario 4   89

Scenario 5   89

Thought experiment answers 90

Scenario 1   90

Scenario 2   90

Scenario 3   90

Scenario 4   91

Scenario 5   91

Chapter summary 92

Chapter 2   **Manage Policies and Profiles**   **95**

Skill 2.1: Plan and implement co-management 95

Implement co-management precedence   96

Migrate group policy to MDM policies   98

Recommend a co-management strategy   100

Skill 2.2: Implement conditional access and compliance
policies for devices 102

Plan conditional access policies   103

Implement conditional access policies   106

Manage conditional access policies   109

Plan device compliance policies   110

Implement device compliance policies   115

Manage device compliance policies   117

Skill 2.3: Configure device profiles 119

    Plan device profiles   119

    Implement device profiles   122

    Manage device profiles   126

Skill 2.4: Manage user profiles 131

    Configure user profiles   131

    Configure sync settings   135

    Implement Folder Redirection   140

    Implement OneDrive Known Folder Move   141

    Configure Enterprise State Roaming in Azure AD   144

Thought experiments 146

    Scenario 1   146

    Scenario 2   147

    Scenario 3   147

    Scenario 4   148

Thought experiment answers 149

    Scenario 1   149

    Scenario 2   149

    Scenario 3   149

    Scenario 4   150

Chapter summary 150

Chapter 3   **Manage and protect devices**   **153**

Skill 3.1: Manage Windows Defender. 153

    Implement and manage Windows Defender
    Credential Guard   153

    Implement and manage Windows Defender Exploit Guard   155

    Implement and manage Windows Defender Application
    Guard   165

    Implement Windows Defender Advanced Threat Protection   167

    Integrate Windows Defender Application Control   168

    Manage Windows Defender Antivirus   170

    Configure Windows Defender Advanced Threat Detection   173

    Using Microsoft Intune for Endpoint Protection   173

Skill 3.2: Manage Intune Device Enrollment and inventory 175

    Configure enrollment settings   176

    Enable Device Enrollment   186

    Configure Intune automatic enrollment   187

    Enroll Windows devices   188

    Enroll non-Windows devices   196

    Generate custom device inventory reports and
review device inventory   198

Skill 3.3: Monitor devices 204

    Monitor device health   204

    Monitor device security   212

Thought experiments 214

    Scenario 1   214

    Scenario 2   215

    Scenario 3   215

Thought experiment answers 215

    Scenario 1   215

    Scenario 2   215

    Scenario 3   216

Chapter summary 216

Chapter 4   Manage Apps and Data   217

Skill 4.1: Deploy and update applications 217

    Deploy apps by using Intune and assign apps to groups   218

    Adding a Windows store app   221

    Deploy apps by using Microsoft Store for Business   229

    Enable sideloading of apps into images   243

    Using Windows Configuration Designer to deploy apps   245

    Configure and implement assigned access or
public devices   248

    Deploy Office 365 ProPlus   253

    Gather Office readiness data   255

    Configure Internet Explorer Enterprise mode   257

Skill 4.2: Implement Mobile Application Management 259

    Plan MAM   260

    Implement and manage MAM policies   261

    Securing data by using Intune   268

    Configure Windows Information Protection   273

    Implement Azure Information Protection templates   278

Thought experiments 281

    Scenario 1   281

    Scenario 2   282

Thought experiment answers 282

    Scenario 1   282

    Scenario 2   282

Chapter summary 283

Index   *285*

About the Authors

ANDREW BETTANY is a Microsoft Most Valuable Professional (Windows and Devices for IT), dad, IT Geek, training mentor and consultant, entrepreneur, and author.

As a Microsoft MVP, Andrew is recognized for his Windows expertise, and he is the author of many publications, including several Windows exam certification prep guides and Microsoft official training materials. He is the author of video training materials for LinkedIn Learning and Pluralsight. As a Microsoft Certified Trainer, Andrew delivers learning and consultancy to businesses on many technical areas, including Microsoft 365, Azure, and Windows.

He has co-founded the "IT Masterclasses" series of short intensive technical courses (see www.itmasterclasses.com), and he is passionate about helping others learn technology. He is a frequent speaker at Microsoft Ignite and other technical conferences worldwide.

Andrew is active on social media and can be found on LinkedIn, Facebook, and Twitter. He lives in a village just outside the beautiful city of York in Yorkshire, England.

ANDREW WARREN MCT, has been writing for Microsoft for many years, helping to develop their official curriculum of instructor-led training material. He has served as a subject matter expert on many of the current Windows Server 2016 courses, was technical lead on several of the Windows 10 titles, and was involved in Microsoft 365, Azure, and Intune course development. When not writing about Microsoft technologies, he can be found in the classroom, teaching other IT professionals what they need to know to manage their organization's IT infrastructure.

Introduction

With the new Microsoft 365 Certified: Modern Desktop Administrator Associate certification, Microsoft has changed the way that IT Pro certifications work. Rather than being based on a technology area, they are focused on a specific job role. The Microsoft MD-101 Managing Modern Desktops exam provides the foundation of this new Modern Desktop Administrator Associate certification.

This book covers every major topic area found on the exam, but it does not cover every exam question. Only the Microsoft exam team has access to the exam questions, and Microsoft regularly adds new questions to the exam, making it impossible to cover specific questions. You should consider this book a supplement to your relevant real-world experience and other study materials. If you encounter a topic in this book that you do not feel completely comfortable with, use the "Need more review?" links you'll find in the text to find more information and take the time to research and study the topic. Great information is available on the Microsoft Learn website at docs.microsoft.com.

Organization of this book

This book is organized by the "Skills measured" list published for the exam. The "Skills measured" list is available for each exam on the Microsoft Learn website: http://microsoft.com/learn. Each chapter in this book corresponds to a major topic area in the list, and the technical tasks in each topic area determine a chapter's organization. If an exam covers six major topic areas, for example, the book will contain six chapters.

Microsoft certifications

Microsoft certifications distinguish you by proving your command of a broad set of skills and experience with current Microsoft products and technologies. The exams and corresponding certifications are developed to validate your mastery of critical competencies as you design and develop, or implement and support, solutions with Microsoft products and technologies both on-premises and in the cloud. Certification brings a variety of benefits to the individual and to employers and organizations.

> **MORE INFO**   **ALL MICROSOFT CERTIFICATIONS**
>
> For information about Microsoft certifications, including a full list of available certifications, go to *http://www.microsoft.com/learn*.

Errata, updates, & book support

We've made every effort to ensure the accuracy of this book and its companion content. You can access updates to this book—in the form of a list of submitted errata and their related corrections—at:

http://www.microsoftpressstore.com/examrefmd101/errata

If you discover an error that is not already listed, please submit it to us at the same page.

For additional book support and information, please visit *MicrosoftPressStore.com/Support*.

Please note that product support for Microsoft software and hardware is not offered through the previous addresses. For help with Microsoft software or hardware, go to *http://support.microsoft.com*.

Stay in touch

Let's keep the conversation going! We're on Twitter: *http://twitter.com/MicrosoftPress*.

CHAPTER 1

Deploy and Update Operating Systems

The MD-101 Windows 10 exam focuses on how to deploy and update Windows 10 in the most efficient manner, with the least amount of administrative effort, and by using modern tools and technologies. You need to understand how to plan and deploy Windows 10 and be able to choose the most appropriate method. Once deployed, you'll need to manage Windows 10, join the device to Azure Active Directory, and auto-enroll it in Microsoft Intune. You will keep Windows 10 up to date and secured, manage Windows updates, and ensure that updates are aligned with organizational requirements. You will need to understand how modern devices are joined or registered to Azure Active Directory and how to manage authentication of devices and users using the cloud.

Skills covered in this chapter:

- Skill 1.1: Plan and implement Windows 10 by using dynamic deployment
- Skill 1.2: Plan and implement Windows 10 by using Windows Autopilot
- Skill 1.3: Upgrade devices to Windows 10
- Skill 1.4: Manage updates
- Skill 1.5: Manage device authentication

Skill 1.1: Plan and implement Windows 10 by using dynamic deployment

Windows 10 offers organizations new and exciting methods for deploying the operating system to users. Legacy image creation-based deployment methods will continue to be supported and used. You can expect that the adoption of the new dynamic deployment methods will gain traction in the modern workplace and will be featured in the MD-101 exam. You need to understand when these methods should be implemented over traditional methods.

> **This skill covers how to:**
> - Evaluate and select an appropriate deployment option
> - Manage pilot deployment
> - Manage and troubleshoot provisioning packages

Evaluate and select an appropriate deployment option

Dynamic provisioning of Windows 10 using modern tools including mobile device management solutions offers organizations new deployment choices. Many of these options were not available when deploying previous versions of Windows using traditional deployment methods. Table 1-1 provides a summary comparison between modern dynamic provisioning and traditional deployment methods, which can also incorporate image creation.

TABLE 1-1 Provisioning Methods

DYNAMIC PROVISIONING METHODS	TRADITIONAL DEPLOYMENT METHODS
Enrollment into Azure Active Directory and Mobile Device Management (such as Microsoft Intune)	On-premises deployment tools using Windows ADK, Windows Deployment Services, Microsoft Deployment Toolkit, or System Center Configuration Manager
Provisioning packages using Windows Configuration Designer	Bare-metal install
Subscription Activation	In-place upgrade
Windows Autopilot	Wipe-and-load upgrade

> **NOTE TRADITIONAL DEPLOYMENT METHODS**
>
> The traditional deployment methods are covered in *Exam Ref MD-100 Windows 10* by Microsoft Press. This book focuses on the modern deployment methods because these are most likely to be examined on the MD-101 exam.

The deployment choices available to an organization may be skewed by the existing investment it has made in traditional deployment methods and infrastructure. This may include reliance upon on-premises tools and procedures, such as using Microsoft Deployment Toolkit (MDT) and System Center Configuration Manager (SCCM) for Windows 7 and newer versions. These tools will continue to be supported and can be used to support traditional deployment methods, such as bare metal, refresh, and replace scenarios.

You should understand the modern alternatives to the traditional methods, and these will be emphasized throughout this book and tested extensively on the MD-101 exam.

Deploying Windows 10 using modern cloud-based deployment and dynamic provisioning methods includes using subscription activation, Windows Autopilot, and Azure Active Directory (Azure AD) join. Ongoing management of Window 10 is then undertaken using Mobile Device Management (MDM), such as Microsoft Intune.

Dynamic provisioning

You should see a theme throughout this book, which is to recommend an alternative method of provisioning client devices to the traditional approach, which would typically include the following stages:

- Purchase or re-provision a device.
- Wipe the device.
- Replace the preinstalled operating system with a customized image.
- Join an on-premises Active Directory.
- Apply Group Policy settings.
- Manage apps using Configuration Manager.

With a cloud-based deployment approach, the stages are simplified to the following:

- Purchase or re-provision a device.
- Apply a transformation to the preinstalled operating system.
- Join Azure AD.
- Manage the use of Mobile Device Management.
- Use MDM to enforce compliance with corporate policies and to add or remove apps.

There is a significant difference between the two approaches. Dynamic provisioning seeks to avoid the need for on-premises infrastructure and resource intensive reimaging procedures.

Because Windows 10 is updated twice a year to a newer version—with each new version supported for a maximum of 18 months (30 months for Enterprise and Education editions)—maintaining customized deployment images becomes a costly process and burdensome for the IT department.

The types of transformations that are currently available using dynamic provisioning include:

- **Provisioning packages** A provisioning package is created using the Windows Configuration Designer and can be used to send one or more configurations to apps and settings on a device.
- **Subscription Activation** Windows 10 Subscription Activation allows you to automatically upgrade devices with Windows 10 Pro to Windows 10 Enterprise without needing to enter a product key or perform a restart.
- **Azure AD join with automatic MDM enrollment** A device can be joined to Azure AD and automatically enrolled into the organizational MDM solution by having users enter their work or school account details. Once enrolled, MDM will configure the device to the organization's policies.

The transforms outlined above will be discussed in more detail in later stages of this chapter.

Provisioning packages

Provisioning packages are created using the Windows Configuration Designer (WCD), which is included in the Windows Assessment and Deployment Kit (Windows ADK). You can also download the standalone Windows Configuration Designer app from the Microsoft Store.

> **NOTE DOWNLOAD WINDOWS ADK**
>
> You can download the Windows ADK from the Microsoft website at *https://docs.microsoft.com/windows-hardware/get-started/adk-install*. Ensure that you download the version of the Windows ADK that matches the version of Windows 10 that you intend to deploy.

If you are used to using Group Policy Objects (GPOs), you could draw some similarities between GPOs and provisioning packages, such as they use very small configuration files and they are used to modify existing Windows 10 installations and configure their runtime settings.

A provisioning package can perform a variety of functions, such as:

- Configure the computer name and user accounts.
- Add the computer to a domain.
- Upgrade the Windows 10 version, such as Windows 10 Home to Windows 10 Enterprise.
- Configure the Windows user interface.
- Add additional files or install apps.
- Remove installed software.
- Configure network connectivity settings.
- Install certificates.
- Implement security settings.
- Reset Windows 10.
- Run PowerShell scripts.

To create a provisioning package, you should complete the installation process of Windows Configuration Designer using either the Windows ADK or the Microsoft Store. Once you have done so, you are ready to create and deploy your provisioning packages. Start by opening Windows Configuration Designer. On the Start page shown in Figure 1-1, click the option that best describes the type of provisioning that you want to do. If you are uncertain, choose the Advanced Provisioning tile.

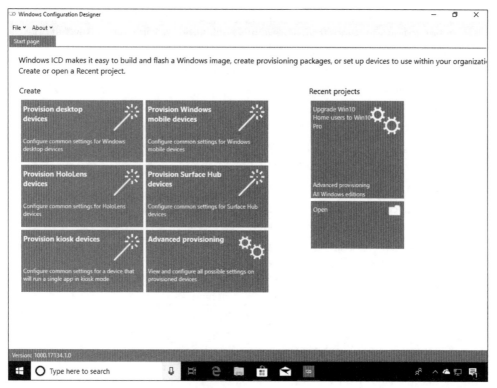

FIGURE 1-1 Creating a new provisioning package

> **NOTE WINDOWS CONFIGURATION DESIGNER USER INTERFACE**
>
> In earlier versions of the Windows Configuration Designer—previously called the Windows Imaging and Configuration Designer (Windows ICD)—you could create deployment packages with which you could deploy Windows 10. This functionality has been removed from the WCD, though the user interface still references the Windows ICD name.

Use the following procedure to create your provisioning package to deploy a universal line of business (LOB) app:

1. Click Advanced Provisioning.

2. In the New Project wizard, on the Enter Project Details page, in the Name box, type the name for your provisioning package and a meaningful description. For example, type **Deploy LOB App1** and then click Next.

3. On the Choose Which Settings To View And Configure page, choose All Windows Desktop Editions and click Next.

4. On the Import A Provisioning Package (Optional) page, click Finish. (You can use this option to import settings from a previously configured package that mostly, but not entirely, meets your needs.)

5. On the Available Customizations page, in View, click All Settings, and then expand Runtime Settings (see Figure 1-2).

6. On the Available Customizations page, in the navigation pane, expand UniversalApp-Install, and then click DeviceContextApp.

7. In the details pane, in the PackageFamilyName text box, type a name for this collection of apps. For example, type **LOB App1**.

8. Select the PackageFamilyName: LOB App1 node.

9. In the ApplicationFile text box, click Browse, and navigate to the .appx file that represents your app, and select it, as shown in Figure 1-2.

10. In the File menu, click Save and note the location of the saved provisioning package file.

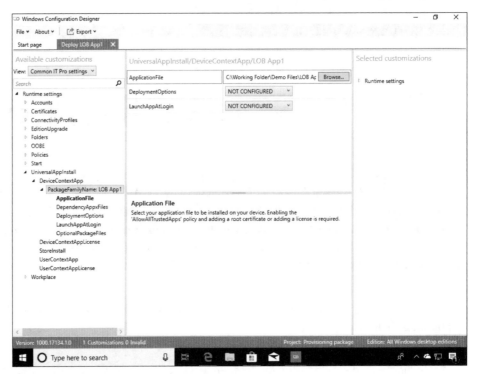

FIGURE 1-2 Available customizations for your provisioning package

You have created a customization for your app, and you are now ready to deploy this customization by applying the provisioning package.

NOTE   **DEPLOY POWERSHELL SCRIPTS FROM PROVISIONING PACKAGES**

If you want to use PowerShell scripts with provisioning packages, you need to select All Windows Desktop Editions on the Choose Which Settings To View And Configure page within Advanced Provisioning. You can then add command line files in the Runtime Settings\ProvisioningCommands\DeviceContext area of the available customizations. To view detailed information about using scripts in provisioning packages, visit this Microsoft website at *https://docs.microsoft.com/en-us/windows/configuration/provisioning-packages/provisioning-script-to-install-app.*

Apply provisioning packages

To apply a provisioning package, you must start by exporting the package. To export your provisioning package, in the Windows Configuration Designer, use the following procedure:

1. Select the project file from the Recent Projects area of the Start Page or select File and locate the project file. (It should use the name of the project and have an .icdproj file extension.)

2. On the menu bar, click Export > Provisioning Package.

3. In the Build wizard, on the Describe The Provisioning Package page, the Name box is already complete with the project name. You can now specify the package version number and vendor information, such as **IT Admin**. Complete this information and click Next.

4. On the Select Security Details For The Provisioning Package page, choose whether you want to encrypt or sign your package (or both) and then click Next. (To digitally sign your package, you must have an appropriate digital certificate that users of your package trust.)

5. On the Select Where To Save The Provisioning Package page, specify where you want to store the package and then click Next.

6. On the Build The Provisioning Package page, click Build. Your provisioning package is exported to your specified location.

7. The All Done page appears. Make a note of the package details and then click Finish.

8. You can now apply the package to client devices and run the .ppkg file.

Once you have configured the settings within the Windows Configuration Designer, you export the provisioning package to a .ppkg file. To secure the .ppkg file, you can optionally choose to encrypt the package and digitally sign it. Once signed, only packages that are trusted can be applied on a client computer.

You can deploy the provisioning package to users by any method, such as email, physical media, or by sharing the file using OneDrive for Business. The settings are applied to the target device by one of the following methods:

- Running the .ppkg file
- Adding the provisioning package using the Settings app
- Use the **Add-ProvisioningPackage** Windows PowerShell cmdlet

Provisioning packages can be applied to a device during the first-run experience when a device is first turned on by using a USB drive containing the provisioning package or after the out-of-box experience (or "OOBE") has been completed.

> **NEED MORE REVIEW?** **PROVISIONING PACKAGES FOR WINDOWS 10**
>
> To review further details about provisioning packages, refer to the Microsoft website at *https://docs.microsoft.com/en-us/windows/configuration/provisioning-packages/provisioning-packages.*

Windows 10 Subscription Activation

Windows 10 requires activation to unlock all the features of the operating system and to comply with the licensing requirements.

Once activated, Windows 10 devices can:

- Receive updates
- Access all Window 10 features
- Access support

There are several types of activation that register the installation of Windows on a device with a standalone or corporate Windows 10 product key.

The three main methods of activation are:

- Retail
- OEM
- Microsoft Volume Licensing (volume activation)

> **NOTE** **MORE ABOUT RETAIL AND OEM ACTIVATION**
>
> Both retail and OEM activation are outside the scope of this book and are part of the MD-100 Windows 10 exam. (See *Exam Ref MD-100 Windows 10*, published by Microsoft Press.)

Organizations with Enterprise Agreements (EA) can use volume activation methods. These provide tools and services that allow activation to be automated and deployed at scale. These tools and services include

- **Active Directory–based activation** This is an automated service that, once installed, uses Active Directory Directory Services (AD DS) to store activation objects. This simplifies the maintenance of volume activation services for an enterprise. Activation requests are processed automatically as devices authenticate to the Active Directory domain.
- **Key Management Service (KMS)** This is an automated service that is hosted on a computer within your domain-based network. All volume editions of Windows 10 periodically connect to the KMS host to request activation.

- **Multiple activation key (MAK)** Enterprises purchase product keys that allow a specific number of Windows 10 devices to be activated using the Microsoft activation servers on the internet.

All the above enterprise activation methods utilize services found within traditional on-premises, domain-based environments. An alternative method of activation is required to meet the needs of devices that are registered to cloud-based authentication and identity services, such as Azure Active Directory.

Subscription Activation allows your organization's Azure AD tenant to be associated with an existing Enterprise Agreement; all valid devices that are connected to that tenant will be automatically activated.

Eligible licenses that can use Subscription Activation include

- Windows 10 Enterprise E3 or E5 licenses obtained as part of an Enterprise Agreement
- Devices containing a firmware-embedded activation key
- Windows 10 Enterprise E3 in CSP (Cloud Solution Provider), which is offered as a subscription for small- and medium-sized organizations, from one to hundreds of users

> **NOTE FIRMWARE-EMBEDDED ACTIVATION KEY**
>
> Most OEM-provided devices designed to run Windows 8 or later will have a firmware-embedded key. You can read more information about firmware-embedded activation key licensing on the Microsoft website at *https://docs.microsoft.com/en-us/windows/deployment/deploy-enterprise-licenses*.

Organizations must meet the following requirements to implement Subscription Activation:

- Enterprise Agreement or a Microsoft Products and Services Agreement (MPSA) associated with the organization's Azure AD tenant.
- Windows 10 Pro or Windows 10 Enterprise is installed on the devices you want to upgrade.
- Azure AD for identity management.
- All devices are either Azure AD–joined or are members of an AD DS domain that is synchronized to Azure AD using Azure AD Connect.

If all the requirements are met, when a licensed user signs in using his or her Azure AD credentials using a device, the operating system switches from Windows 10 Pro to Windows 10 Enterprise and all Windows 10 Enterprise features are then available. This process takes place without entering a product key and without requiring that users restart their computers.

> **NOTE GRACE PERIOD**
>
> Devices that have been upgraded using Subscription Activation must be able to connect to the Azure AD tenant at least every 90 days to remain licensed. If the Azure AD tenant expires or the user license is unassigned, then the device will revert to Windows 10 Pro.

Azure AD Join with automatic MDM enrollment

You can dynamically provision Windows 10 devices using Azure AD and a Mobile Device Management (MDM) solution, such as Microsoft Intune. Once a device is enrolled into management, Microsoft Intune can deploy compliance and corporate security policies to the device in a similar way (but not the same) as Group Policy objects are used within a domain-based environment to configure computers.

MDM can be used to add or remove apps, restrict device features, and more. Through the application of MDM policies, Azure AD can block or allow access to corporate resources or applications based on the status of the device compliance.

To benefit from the cloud-based dynamic provisioning, you need the following requirements:

- Windows 10 Pro or Windows 10 Enterprise Version 1703 (or later)
- Azure AD for identity management
- A Mobile Device Management solution, such as Microsoft Intune

Manage pilot deployment

Embarking on any new project should be carefully planned ahead of time so that the delivery can be given every chance of success. This is especially applicable when deploying Windows 10 within an enterprise environment.

There are several tools and services available to help evaluate, learn, and implement Windows 10. By following best practices and avoiding making deployment mistakes, you can ensure that your users are productive and that the project is delivered on schedule.

Windows 10 is released using a continuous delivery model known as Windows as a Service, with a new version of Windows 10 available every six months. Therefore, the skills you learn in deploying Windows 10 to your users will be reused again, and often.

It is recommended that administrators choose a group of users and deploy Windows 10 into focused pilot projects to test each version of Windows 10 within their organizations prior to rolling out the operating system to larger cohorts of users.

Plan pilot deployments

In this book, we have focused on the modern deployment technologies that are likely to be tested on the MD-101 exam. Each organization is different, and therefore, you need to determine which deployment method (or methods) you will use. For example, you may choose to deploy new devices to your remote sales force using Windows Autopilot and perform an in-place upgrade of your head office computers using the in-place upgrade method.

To make effective decisions relating to the deployment method, you should perform testing in a non-production environment, and if you are successful, you should proceed to roll out Windows 10 to a small group of users.

By breaking down your Windows 10 deployment project into multiple stages, you can identify any possible issues and determine solutions where available. This will involve documenting and obtaining feedback from stakeholders at each stage. The first stage of deploying the operating system will be with a pilot deployment.

As part of the pilot, it is important to determine the following:

- Production hardware, including PCs, laptops, and tablets, meets the minimum hardware requirements for Windows 10.

- Peripherals, such as printers, scanners, projectors, and other devices, are compatible with Windows 10.

- All required device drivers are available.

- All apps required following the deployment will work on Windows 10.

- Any existing third-party disk encryption will work with Windows 10 (alternatively replaced with BitLocker Drive Encryption).

- Your IT support staff has the necessary skills to support Windows 10.

The pilot is essential because it can be useful to ensure compatibility with existing hardware, apps, and infrastructure, and it provides you with an insight to the gains and potential pitfalls that you are likely to encounter during the later stages of the roll-out program. By reviewing and implementing feedback gained during the pilot phase, you can seek to minimize the future impact of any problems encountered.

If you find that your existing IT support staff does not have the necessary skills to support Windows 10, you may use the pilot deployment phase to identify any training needs; doing so gives you time to implement the recommendations before a larger roll-out. You should also consider your non-technical users, who may require information relating to the new operating system so that their day-to-day productivity is not affected by the adoption of the new operating system.

You can also use the pilot to help to determine user readiness for Windows 10 and to identify any training needs—for both users and IT support staff.

Identify hardware requirements for Windows 10

As part of your planning considerations, you should review the system requirements for installing Windows 10. Windows 10 can run adequately on hardware of a similar specification that supports Windows 8.1. Consequently, most of the computers in use within organizations today are Windows 10–capable. However, to get the best from Windows 10, you might consider installing the operating system on the computers and devices that exceed the minimum specifications described in Table 1-2.

TABLE 1-2 Minimum Hardware Requirements for Windows 10

COMPONENT	REQUIREMENT
Processor	A 1 GHz or faster processor or System on a Chip (SoC).
Memory	1 GB RAM on 32-bit versions and 2 GB for 64-bit versions.
Hard disk space	16 GB for 32-bit versions and 32 GB for 64-bit versions.
Graphics card	DirectX 9 or later with a Windows Display Driver Model (WDDM) 1.0 driver.
Display resolution	800x600 pixels.
Internet Connection	Internet connectivity is required to perform updates and to take advantage of some features.

> **NOTE EVALUATE WINDOWS 10 ENTERPRISE**
>
> You can access a 90-day evaluation of Windows 10 Enterprise through the Microsoft Evaluation Center. The evaluation is available in the latest released version, in 64-bit and 32-bit versions, and in multiple languages. The Evaluation Center and Windows 10 Enterprise can be downloaded from *https://www.microsoft.com/evalcenter/evaluate-windows-10-enterprise*.

Determine hardware compatibility for Windows 10

After you have verified that any new or existing computers on which you intend to install Windows 10 meet the minimum hardware requirements, you need to verify that the operating system also supports any existing hardware devices and peripherals.

If you are purchasing new computers preinstalled with Windows 10, take no further action. However, if you are using existing computers, or you want to attach existing hardware peripherals to your new computers, you must verify compatibility of these older computers and peripherals.

If you have only one or two computers and a few peripheral devices to check, the easiest—and probably quickest—solution is to visit the hardware vendor's website and check for compatibility of these devices and peripherals. You can then download any required drivers for the version of Windows 10 (32-bit or 64-bit) that you may need to install.

VERIFY HARDWARE COMPATIBILITY FOR MULTIPLE DEVICES

When you have many computers to install or upgrade to Windows 10, it is not feasible to visit each computer and verify device and peripheral compatibility. In this situation, consider using a tool to help determine compatibility.

If you have a traditional on-premises infrastructure, you can use the Microsoft Assessment and Planning Toolkit (MAP) to assess the computer devices attached to your network. MAP can be used to

- Determine feasibility to upgrade scanned devices to Windows 10
- Determine your organization's readiness to move to Microsoft Azure, Office 365, or Azure AD
- Plan for virtualizing workloads to Hyper-V

Windows Analytics overview

Windows Analytics is a set of tools, solutions, and services that you can use to collate and evaluate data about the state of devices in your environment. These services can be useful when undertaking an enterprise-wide deployment. Windows Analytics includes three solutions, as shown in Table 1-3.

TABLE 1-3 Windows Analytics Solutions

SOLUTION	DESCRIPTION
Device Health	Extracts the device health history, providing ■ Identification of devices that crash frequently ■ Identification of device drivers that cause device crashes ■ Notification of Windows Information Protection misconfigurations that result in prompts to users (See *https://docs.microsoft.com/en-us/windows/deployment/update/device-health-get-started.*)
Update Compliance	Extracts the state of your devices with respect to the following: ■ Windows Update status ■ Allows drill-downs for devices that might need attention ■ Comprehensive inventory of devices and their update statuses ■ Track protection and threat status for Windows Defender Antivirus – enabled devices ■ Overview of Windows Update for Business deferral configurations ■ Built-in log analytics to create custom queries on enrolled devices ■ Access to Windows 10 diagnostic data via the cloud (See *https://docs.microsoft.com/en-us/windows/deployment/update/update-compliance-get-started.*)
Upgrade Readiness	Supports upgrade management from Windows 7 and Windows 8.1 to Windows 10 and the Windows as a service model. Upgrade Readiness provides: ■ A set of tools to plan and manage device upgrades ■ A visual workflow to guide you from pilot to production ■ Detailed computer and application inventory ■ Computer-level search and drill-downs ■ Guidance and insights into application and driver compatibility issues, with suggested fixes ■ Data-driven application rationalization tools ■ Application usage information ■ Data export features (See *https://docs.microsoft.com/en-us/windows/deployment/upgrade/upgrade-readiness-get-started.*)

Windows Analytics requires that devices are enrolled in the service so that Windows Analytics can then collect data directly from the device. Other requirements include

- An Azure subscription.
- Windows Analytics uses Azure Log Analytics, which is deployed in your Azure subscription and accessed using the Azure portal.
- A unique commercial ID key is used to link your devices to the Windows Analytics solutions.
- Windows 7 SP1, Windows 8.1, or Windows 10 is installed on devices.
- Each device needs to have the diagnostic data level configured by using the Upgrade Readiness deployment script or by a policy, which can be deployed using Group Policy or Mobile Device Management.

Manage and troubleshoot provisioning packages

You have already seen how using provisioning packages as part of your dynamic provisioning of Windows 10 can simplify your deployment processes.

The Windows Configuration Designer tool can be installed from the Microsoft Store as an app, which allows it to be regularly updated. Alternatively, you can install the Windows Configuration Designer tool as part of the Windows ADK.

The WCD interface is simple, and common tasks are offered using the available wizards, which can be used to create a provisioning package that can be used in the following environments:

- **Provision desktop devices**   Provides the typical settings for Windows 10 desktop devices.
- **Provision kiosk devices**   Provides the typical settings for a device that will run a single app.
- **Provision Windows mobile devices**   Provides the typical settings for Windows 10 mobile devices.
- **Provision IoT devices**   Provides the typical settings for Windows 10 IoT devices.
- **Provision Surface Hub devices**   Provides the typical settings for Surface Hub devices.
- **Provision Holographic devices**   Provides the typical settings for Windows 10 Holographic devices, such as HoloLens headsets.
- **Advanced provisioning**   Enables you to view and configure all available settings. Choose this option if you are unsure which specific package type to use.

Most provisioning packages will be aimed at provisioning Windows 10 desktop devices and will use the advanced configuration option because this allows the greatest customization.

Provisioning packages offer administrators a quick and simplified mechanism to securely configure devices. Once created, the settings within a .ppkg file can be viewed using the WCD and edited using the built-in wizards or by using the advanced editor. When provisioning packages that need to be deployed to remote devices, they can be protected using encryption and signed.

Several usage scenarios for provisioning packages are shown in Table 1-4.

TABLE 1-4 Usage Scenarios for Provisioning Packages

SCENARIO	PHASE	DESCRIPTION
New devices with Windows 10 need to have apps deployed to the devices.	New device	Provisioning packages can be used to deploy apps to devices.
Existing Windows 10 Pro devices need to be upgraded to Windows 10 Enterprise.	Upgrade	Provisioning packages can be used to change the Windows edition by deploying product keys or licenses using the Edition Upgrade settings.
You must update device drivers on Windows 10 devices.	Maintain	Provisioning packages can be used to deploy device drivers to devices.

Troubleshoot provisioning packages

When using provisioning packages, you may need to troubleshoot them if devices are not configured as expected.

There are several areas on which you can focus your attention when troubleshooting provisioning packages, as follows:

- Configuration errors and missing customizations
- Expired Azure AD Token
- Export errors including encryption & signing issues
- User issues
- Advanced troubleshooting

If you have deployed the .ppkg file to multiple devices, and they have all failed to process the required changes, then you should first inspect the provisioning package. Locate the project file (with the .icdproj file extension) and open it using the WCD. You should then inspect the settings and confirm that they match your expectations and the design specification or change documentation for the provisioning package.

If you use the configuration wizard to configure automatic enrollment into Azure AD, as shown in Figure 1-3, you should ensure that the Bulk Token embedded inside the provisioning package has not expired. By default, this token is set to expire one month after creation, though you can manually set the token expiry date to 180 days after the creation date. If the package is used after the Bulk AAD Token has expired, the package will fail to install. You will need to edit the package, apply for a new Bulk AAD Token, and re-export the package.

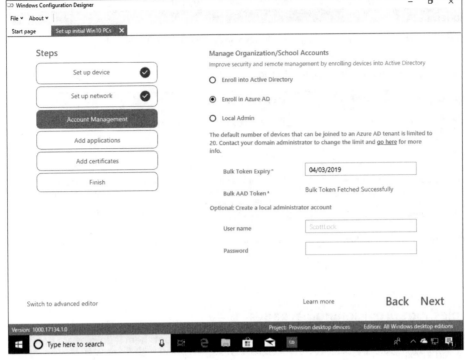

FIGURE 1-3 Set up Bulk AAD Token to enroll in Azure AD

Once the customization settings have been verified as correct, you should export the package again. Increment the version number to avoid confusion with the previous version of the package. Packages with the same versioning number will not be applied to the same target device twice.

If issues are suspected with either the encryption or signing of the package, you can export without these enhancements and re-deploy to your test machine to determine whether the issue remains.

For users, devices can be configured by placing the provisioning package on a USB drive and inserting it during the initial OOBE setup phase. Windows Setup should automatically recognize the drive and ask the user if he or she wants to install the provisioning package. If the package is not recognized, check that the file is in the root directory of the USB drive.

There are several tools that you can use to perform advanced troubleshooting for provisioning packages on user devices, including:

- **Windows Mobile devices** The Field Medic app, which is available from the Microsoft Store, can create and export reports.
- **Desktop devices** The Windows Performance Recorder, which is contained in the Windows Performance Toolkit, offers advanced Event Tracing for Windows. The system events recorded by this tool can be analyzed by using Windows Performance Analyzer, which is available from the Microsoft Store.

Skill 1.2: Plan and implement Windows 10 by using Windows Autopilot

Within a domain-based environment, deploying new devices to users has become increasingly complex. There are many "moving" parts and components, and each one needs to work precisely to ensure devices are compliant, secure, and usable. This is partly due to the granular nature of the tooling used to ensure that devices comply with strict organizational security requirements. Windows Autopilot is a solution that radically changes this approach while allowing IT administrators to deploy secure and compliant devices.

You need to understand how to plan and implement Windows 10 within an organization using Windows Autopilot. This skill explores the planning, example scenarios, and installation requirements for the application of Windows Autopilot.

> **This skill covers how to:**
> - Evaluate and select an appropriate deployment option
> - Implement pilot deployment
> - Create, validate, and assign deployment profiles
> - Extract device hardware information
> - Import device hardware information to a cloud service
> - Troubleshoot deployment

Evaluate and select an appropriate deployment option

Windows Autopilot offers a new method of provisioning Windows 10 within an enterprise. Of course, it is not the only deployment choice, and indeed, there will be scenarios in which using Autopilot would be folly.

You need to explore each of the available deployment options. These options include technology such as MDT or Configuration Manager that may be currently used within your organization. Other methods, such as using Windows Autopilot or Microsoft Intune, may be worth employing to achieve your Windows 10 deployment goals.

Listed in Table 1-5 are many different methods that you can use to deploy and configure Windows 10. You need to understand when to use each deployment method.

TABLE 1-5 Methods for Deploying and Configuring Windows 10

METHOD	DESCRIPTION
Windows Autopilot	Transform an existing Windows 10 installation, join the device to Azure AD, and enroll it into a Mobile Device Management solution to complete configuration. Deploy Windows 10 on an existing Windows 7 or 8.1 device.
Windows 10 Subscription Activation	Upgrade the Windows edition seamlessly without requiring intervention or rebooting of the device.
Azure AD / MDM	Cloud-based identity and management solution offering device, app, and security configuration.
Provisioning Packages	Small distributable .appx files that securely transform devices to meet organizational requirements.
In-place Upgrade	Upgrade an earlier version of Windows to Windows 10 while retaining all apps, user data, and settings.
Bare-metal	Deploy Windows 10 to newly built devices or wipe existing devices and deploy fresh Windows 10 images to them.
Refresh (wipe and load)	Re-use existing devices. Retain user state (user data, Windows, and app settings). Wipe devices, deploy Windows 10 images to them, and finally, restore the user state.
Replace	Purchase new devices. Back up the user state from the current device. Transform or wipe a pre-installed Windows 10 installation and restore the user state.

Windows Autopilot deployment scenarios

Windows Autopilot simplifies and automates the customization of the Out-Of-Box Experience (OOBE) and seamlessly enrolls your devices to management. Once enrolled into Microsoft Intune, devices are secured, configured, and further managed.

There are several usage scenarios currently available with Windows Autopilot, and additional functionality will be added in the future. You should understand the scenarios shown in Table 1-6 that show when you would use Windows Autopilot as part of your Windows 10 deployment strategy.

TABLE 1-6 Windows Autopilot Scenarios

SCENARIO	DESCRIPTION
Windows Autopilot for existing devices	Deploy Windows 10 Version 1809 or later on an existing Windows 7 or Windows 8.1 device. Requires System Center Configuration Manager Current Branch (1806 or later) to replace the operating system and then allow Windows Autopilot to continue.
Windows Autopilot user-driven mode	Provision Windows 10 on a new Windows 10 device. Devices will be set up by a member of the organization and configured for that person to use.
Windows Autopilot self-deploying mode	Used for transforming Windows 10 devices that will be automatically configured for use as a kiosk terminal, shared computer, or as a digital signage device. Requires Windows 10 Version 1809 or later, and can be performed locally by an administrator or via MDM.
Windows Autopilot Reset	Used to redeploy a Windows 10 device. The reset process removes personal files, apps, and settings, and it reapplies a device's original settings. The connection to Azure AD and Microsoft Intune is retained. A user can sign in to the device using his or her Azure AD credentials and be productive immediately.

When comparing Autopilot to traditional on-premises deployment methods, such as imaging, there are clear advantages.

- Windows images are not required.

- Drivers are included with Windows 10 and are pre-installed on the device.

- No on-premises deployment infrastructure is required (except if using Windows Autopilot for existing devices).

In the next section, you will learn that devices must have a connection to the internet to use Window Autopilot. If internet access is not available for the Windows Autopilot deployment, then you will need to select an alternative deployment method.

So long as an organization uses cloud-based services—such as Microsoft 365, which includes Azure AD and Microsoft Intune—they will be able to benefit from

- Joining devices to Azure AD automatically.

- Auto-enrolling your devices into Microsoft Intune.

- Lower provisioning costs.

- Restricted Administrator account creation during OOBE.

- Agile deployment of Windows 10 devices.

- Users will be productive more quickly.

Windows Autopilot requirements

There are several requirements and prerequisites that you need to put in place before you can use Windows Autopilot with your Windows 10 devices. If your organization already has a Microsoft 365 subscription, then you will already meet the licensing requirements:

LICENSING REQUIREMENTS

The following licensing requirements must be met:

- Devices must be pre-installed with Windows 10 Pro, Pro Education, Pro for Workstations, Enterprise, or Education Version 1703 or higher.

- Azure AD Premium P1 or P2.

- Microsoft Intune or another MDM solution to manage your devices.

NETWORKING CONFIGURATION

The following network configuration requirements must be met:

- Devices must have access to the internet.

- Devices must be able to access cloud services used by Windows Autopilot:

  - Using DNS name resolution.

  - Firewall access through port 80 (for HTTP), port 443 (for HTTPS) and port 123 (for UDP and NTP).

- The following URLs need to be accessible:
  - *https://go.microsoft.com*
  - *https://login.microsoftonline.com*
  - *https://login.live.com*
  - *https://account.live.com*
  - *https://signup.live.com*
  - *https://licensing.mp.microsoft.com*
  - *https://licensing.md.mp.microsoft.com*
  - *https://ztd.dds.microsoft.com*
  - *https://cs.dds.microsoft.com*
  - *ctldl.windowsupdate.com*
  - *download.windowsupdate.com*

AZURE AD CONFIGURATION PREREQUISITES

The following Azure AD configuration prerequisites must be met:

- Azure AD company branding must be configured.
- Azure AD automatic enrollment needs to be configured.
- A device must be registered with Azure AD.
- Users must have permissions to join devices into Azure AD.

WINDOWS AUTOPILOT CONFIGURATION

The following Windows Autopilot configuration prerequisites must be met:

- Devices must have their device hardware IDs known by Windows Autopilot.
- Devices must have a Windows Autopilot deployment profile assigned.

Implement pilot deployment

Windows Autopilot is not complex to configure and use, though there are several services that need to work together for your users to see a seamless out-of-box experience. After completing the prerequisites needed for Windows Autopilot, you may want to practice using Windows Autopilot to provision Windows 10 in test lab using virtual machines.

Once you have the basic functionality working, you can explore the additional features that are available; these features can be used to streamline the deployment process or personalize the experience for the user. These enhancements currently include:

- **Device Groups**   Creating device groups with Azure AD allows you to separate devices into logical groupings.
- **Dynamic Groups**   You can use Azure AD Dynamic Groups to simplify device group management. Devices are automatically added to the dynamic group if they meet the group membership criteria outlined in the rules.

- **Deployment Profiles**   You can create a single default deployment profile for your whole organization, or you can create additional deployment profiles and assign them to device groups.

- **Personalization**   Windows Autopilot allows you to assign a username and a friendly name to a specific device. During OOBE, the friendly name is then shown to the user. This feature requires Windows 10 Version 1809 or newer.

- **Enrollment Status Page**   During device enrollment into Microsoft Intune, users will be shown a progress status page, as shown in Figure 1-4.

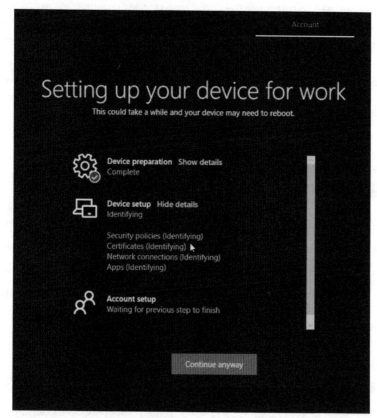

FIGURE 1-4 Enrollment Status Page

Once you have configured your Windows Autopilot processes and successfully provisioned devices in your test lab, you are ready to deploy Windows Autopilot in your production environment. You should follow best practices for any new technology deployment, and you should first pilot the processes to a small group of new devices and their users.

The pilot phase of the Windows Autopilot rollout should be closely monitored, and feedback should be sought from all stakeholders. Any problems with the pilot deployment should be thoroughly resolved before proceeding to a larger scale rollout.

Create, validate, and assign deployment profiles

Deployment Profiles are used to customize the OOBE for a device or group of devices when using Windows Autopilot. You can create a single default deployment profile of settings for your whole organization, or you can create additional deployment profiles and assign them to device groups.

New functionality has been added to Windows Autopilot with each release of Windows, and this is likely to continue. In Table 1-7, you can see how each version of Windows 10 since Version 1703 has introduced changes to how the Autopilot profile is downloaded.

TABLE 1-7 Windows Autopilot Profile Download

WINDOWS 10 VERSION	PROFILE DOWNLOAD BEHAVIOR
1703 or 1709	The profile is downloaded during OOBE at the network connection page when using a wireless connection. When using a wired connection, the network page is hidden, and the profile is downloaded just prior to the EULA screen (if shown).
1803	The Autopilot profile is downloaded as soon as possible. When using a wired connection, this is downloaded at the start of OOBE. If wireless, it is downloaded after the network connection page is displayed.
1809	The Autopilot profile is downloaded as soon as possible, and it is downloaded again after each reboot.

At the time of this writing, the available profile settings that you can configure within a Windows Autopilot deployment profile are shown in Table 1-8.

TABLE 1-8 Windows Autopilot Deployment Profile Settings

PROFILE SETTING	DESCRIPTION
Convert All Targeted Devices To Autopilot	Allows you to convert existing non-Autopilot Intune devices to Windows Autopilot. Devices running Windows 10 Version 1709 can then receive deployment profiles.
Deployment Mode	User-driven devices are devices that are associated with the user enrolling the device. Self-Deploying (preview) devices have no user affinity; an example is a kiosk device. If this setting is chosen, the following settings are enabled: ■ Skip Work Or Home Usage Selection ■ Skip OEM Registration And OneDrive Configuration ■ Skip User Authentication In OOBE
Join To Azure AD As	Azure AD–joined = Cloud-only Hybrid Azure AD–joined (Preview) = Cloud and on-premises Windows Server Active Directory
End User License Agreement (EULA)	Windows 10 Version 1709 allows organizations to skip the EULA page during the OOBE. Effectively, this means that organizations accept the EULA terms on behalf of their users.
Privacy Settings	Organizations can choose not to ask users about Microsoft-related privacy settings during the OOBE process.
Hide Change Account Options	Removes the option for users to restart the OOBE process with a different account. (Requires Windows 10 1809 or later.)
User Account Type	Typically, during the OOBE process, a device will automatically be set up with administrator access. This option can be disabled when using Windows Autopilot as you can choose a Standard or Administrator account type.
Apply Device Name Template	Allows you to specify a naming convention to automatically name devices. For example, **Cycle-%RAND:4%** will generate a device name such as **Cycle-2432**. Windows 10 Version 1809 and later is required.

> **NOTE COMPANY BRANDING IS REQUIRED FOR AUTOPILOT**
>
> You will notice that Autopilot profiles allow you to choose whether a user is presented with the company branding during OOBE. This setting is optional in each profile you create. Regardless of how you configure deployment profiles, you must configure Azure Active Directory Company Branding.

Use the following procedure to create a deployment profile using Microsoft Intune for a user-driven device that is to be joined to Azure AD:

1. Open the Microsoft 365 Device Management portal (at *https://devicemanagement. microsoft.com*) and sign in with a Global Administrator account.

2. Navigate to the Device Enrollment node and then select Windows Enrollment.

3. Select Deployment Profiles under Windows Autopilot Deployment Program.

4. On the Windows Autopilot Deployment Profiles page, click Create Profile.

5. On the Create Profile page, enter a profile name and optional description.

6. Set the Deployment Mode option to **User-Driven.**

7. Set the Join To Azure AD option as **Azure AD Joined.**

8. Click the Out-Of-Box-Experience (OOBE) item to show the Out-Of-Box-Experience (OOBE) blade.

9. On the Out-Of-Box-Experience (OOBE) blade, configure the required settings. An example of a configured Out-of-Box-Experience (OOBE) blade is shown Figure 1-5.

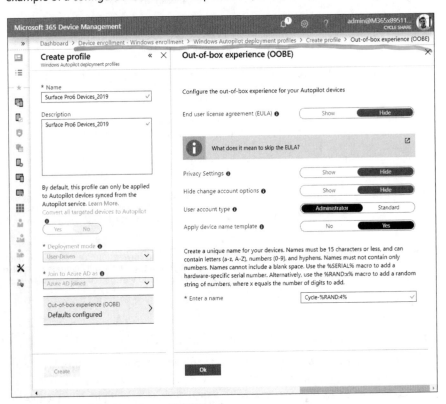

FIGURE 1-5 Out-of-Box Experience (OOBE) blade

10. On the Out-Of-Box-Experience (OOBE) blade, click OK.

11. On the Create Profile blade, click Create.

Once a deployment profile has been created, it needs to be assigned to a device or group of devices for it to be used. Once assigned, devices will be allocated to the profile during the Windows Autopilot process. To assign the device profile, perform the following steps:

1. On the Windows Autopilot Deployment Profiles page, select the deployment profile that you want to assign to devices.

2. On the profile page, under the Manage heading, select Assignments.

3. On the Assignments page, click Select Groups To Include.

4. On the Select Groups To Include page, use the Search facility at the top of the page to search for a specific group, or select the group(s) from the list. You can add more than one group by selecting additional groups.

5. Click Select.

6. On the Assignments page, you can optionally exclude groups by clicking Exclude and then selecting device groups to exclude.

7. On the Assignments page, click Save.

8. On the profile page, select Overview. In the results pane, you will see that the profile has been assigned to several groups; also, you can see if any devices have been included in this assignment.

9. If no devices have been assigned to the profile, after you have configured the assignments, you should check that selected groups have device members within Azure Active Directory.

Extract device hardware information

The next stage of configuring Windows Autopilot is to extract the device hardware information so that the Autopilot service can recognize devices that will be provisioned using Windows Autopilot.

The device-specific information, which includes hardware device IDs of the devices, needs to be uploaded to Microsoft Intune or to Microsoft Store for Business, and then synchronized to the Windows Autopilot Deployment Service. You will learn how to upload this information in the next section.

Typically, the hardware vendor that supplied the new devices will upload the device-specific information and associate that information with your organization's Microsoft 365 tenant. If an organization works closely with a Cloud Solution Provider (CSP) partner, then the vendor may pass the file to it for subsequent uploading via the Partner Center.

Alternatively, the vendor can provide you with a list of the required device information in .csv file format so that you can upload the information.

Another useful method is for the organization to extract the device-specific information from devices by running a Windows PowerShell script. This is especially useful if you are deploying a small number of devices using Windows Autopilot (for example, in a test lab environment or if you are reusing existing devices).

You can extract the hardware ID (or hardware hash) from any existing device that device is running Windows 10 Version 1703 or later. Use the **Get-WindowsAutoPilotInfo.ps1** Power-Shell script, which has been published to the PowerShell Gallery website at *https://www.powershellgallery.com/packages/Get-WindowsAutoPilotInfo*.

The following script needs to be run on each computer from an elevated Windows Power-Shell prompt:

```
md c:\HWID
Set-Location c:\HWID
Set-ExecutionPolicy Unrestricted
Install-Script -Name Get-WindowsAutoPilotInfo
Get-WindowsAutoPilotInfo.ps1 -OutputFile DeviceID.csv
```

Once the output file has been created, it can be saved to a location such as a USB drive or network share. The file then needs to be imported to the organization's preferred cloud service as discussed in the following section.

> **NOTE** **SYSTEM CENTER CONFIGURATION MANAGER**
>
> It is possible to collect the hardware ID from existing devices running Windows 10 Version 1703 (and higher) by using System Center Configuration Manager, Current Branch Version 1802 or later. This information is automatically collected by Configuration Manager and made available in a new report called Windows Autopilot Device Information. Visit the Microsoft website to understand how to access this report. See *https://docs.microsoft.com/sccm/core/plan-design/changes/whats-new-in-version-1802#report-on-windows-autopilot-device-information*.

Import device hardware information to cloud service

With the hardware ID for each device, you need to import the information into one of the cloud-based administration centers and then synchronize this information to the Windows Autopilot deployment service.

Devices must be known to Azure AD and registered to your tenant before you can provision the devices using Autopilot.

The following administrative portals can be used to import the device hardware information:

- Microsoft Intune or Microsoft 365 Device Management
- Microsoft Store for Business
- Microsoft 365 Business Admin Center
- Office 365 Admin Center
- Partner Center

Depending on the subscription used, there are multiple admin portals that you can use to import the device information. Both Microsoft Intune and Microsoft 365 Device Management offer the same functionality, though they are accessed using different website addresses:

- **Microsoft Intune**: *https://portal.azure.com*
- **Microsoft 365 Device Management**: *https://devicemanagement.microsoft.com*

Use the following procedure to add Windows Autopilot devices to a Microsoft 365 tenant by importing a CSV file with its information:

1. Open the Microsoft 365 Device Management portal and sign in with a Global Administrator account.

2. Navigate to the Device Enrollment node and select Windows Enrollment.

3. Under the Windows Autopilot Deployment Program heading, click Devices.

4. On the Windows Autopilot Devices page, click Import.

5. On the Add Windows Autopilot Devices page, browse to a .csv file containing the hardware IDs of the devices you want to add, and click Open.

6. On the Add Windows Autopilot Devices page, the file formatting will be validated; if the rows are formatted correctly, as shown in Figure 1-6, you should click Import.

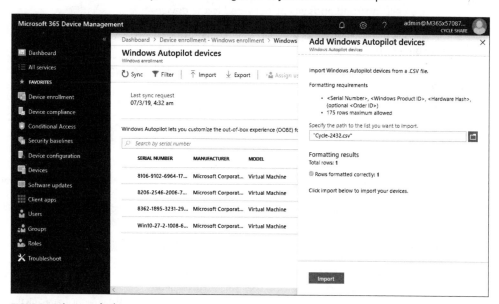

FIGURE 1-6 Import devices

7. On the Windows Autopilot Devices page, the banner should indicate that the import is in progress and show the elapsed time. Importing can take several minutes to complete depending on how many devices are being imported.

8. When the import process has completed, click Sync on the menu bar. A banner should indicate that the synchronization is in progress. The process might take a few minutes to complete, depending on how many devices are being synchronized.

9. Once the sync process has been completed, you will see a notification indicating whether the sync was successful and whether some devices have not been imported. Click Refresh to see the new devices that have been added.

Troubleshoot deployment

Before you can resolve an issue with Windows Autopilot, you need to identify in which part of the overall process the problem is occurring. The Windows Autopilot process can be broken down into logical stages.

- **Network connectivity** Establish an internet connection and connect to the Windows Autopilot service.

- **Deployment profile and OOBE** A deployment profile will be delivered to the device to manage the Out-Of-Box Experience (or OOBE). The OOBE will complete using the settings within the deployment profile.

- **Azure AD** Has Azure AD been configured correctly? For user-driven deployments, users need to enter their Azure AD credentials to join the device to Azure AD.

- **MDM enrollment issues** After being auto enrolled into the MDM service, any policies, settings, and apps will be delivered to the device.

The whole process should result in the device being set up, configured, and ready for the user to be productive.

For a summary of possible troubleshooting areas within these stages, review Table 1-9.

TABLE 1-9 Windows Autopilot Process Flow

PROCESS	TROUBLESHOOTING
Network connectivity	Can the device access the Windows Autopilot services? ■ Windows Autopilot requires internet access. ■ Ensure that specific network requirements are met, including firewall port settings and DNS name resolution. ■ Only Windows 10 Version 1703 or later can connect to the Windows Autopilot deployment service.
Deployment Profile & OOBE	There are settings in the deployment profile that configure the Out-Of-Box Experience. You should focus your troubleshooting on whether ■ The device has received its deployment profile. ■ A deployment profile has been assigned to the device. ■ The correct deployment profile type has been assigned to the device; for example, is the device a kiosk? ■ The assigned deployment profile settings are correct; for example, has the Administrator account creation been configured by accident?

(Continued)

PROCESS	TROUBLESHOOTING
Azure AD	Azure AD needs to be configured prior to deploying devices with Windows Autopilot. Focus your troubleshooting on the following things: ■ Ensure that MDM auto enrollment in Azure AD is correctly configured. ■ Ensure that the MDM discovery URL is correctly configured, so devices can find the MDM service. ■ Ensure that Azure AD custom branding is in place. ■ Ensure that device hardware IDs have been successfully synchronized to the Windows Autopilot deployment service. ■ Ensure that the user has a valid Azure AD account. ■ Ensure that user has not exceeded the maximum number of devices allowed to be joined to Azure AD. ■ If a third-party MDM solution is being used, make sure it has been correctly authorized in Azure AD.
MDM enrollment issues	In the final stage of the Windows Autopilot process, the device will be enrolled into Mobile Device Management. If MDM fails, then policies, settings, and apps will not be deployed to the device. You should focus your troubleshooting on the following things: ■ The Enrollment Status Page is useful for troubleshooting MDM issues. ■ Has the user been assigned an Intune license? ■ Ensure that users have not exceeded their device enrollment limits.

> **NOTE TIME**
>
> If you have ensured that the configuration is correct, then wait. Maybe go grab a coffee. Nearly all issues that I have experienced, such as the new device not being recognized by the Autopilot service, can be resolved by waiting 15 minutes and rebooting the device. Remember that Autopilot uses the cloud, and Azure AD group membership propagation or device ID synchronization can sometimes take a little longer to update.

Error Codes

Whenever a major issue occurs when using Windows Autopilot, an error code will be generated. Some error codes can be viewed on the device whenever a problem occurs during setup. Also, error codes can be viewed using the Event Trace for Windows tool.

Some common error codes relating to Windows Autopilot are shown in Table 1-10.

TABLE 1-10 Windows Autopilot Error Codes

ERROR CODE	DESCRIPTION
0x800705B4	This error is caused by the device being either a virtual machine or not having TPM 2.0; therefore, the device is not capable of running Autopilot in self-deploying mode.
0x801c03ea	This error means that the device is TPM 2.0 capable but that the TPM still needs to be upgraded from 1.2 to 2.0.
0x801c0003	The error page will report this error code with a message reading, "Something went wrong," which indicates that the Azure AD join failed.

(Continued)

ERROR CODE	DESCRIPTION
0x80180018	The error page will report this error code with a message reading, "Something went wrong," which indicates the MDM enrollment failed.
0x80070032	When Windows Autopilot Reset is used to prepare existing devices to become business ready, you should confirm that the Windows Recovery Environment (WinRE) is correctly configured and enabled on the device; otherwise, you will get this error.

When troubleshooting, other sources of information include looking in the Event Viewer for issues relating to the deployment profile settings and the OOBE. The relevant logs are located at

```
Application and Services Logs -> Microsoft -> Windows -> Provisioning-Diagnostics-
Provider -> AutoPilot.
```

An example log entry might read, "Autopilot policy name not found."

NEED MORE REVIEW? **REVIEWING EVENT LOG ENTRIES**

If you want to know more about the event log entries related to troubleshooting Autopilot profile settings and OOBE flow, visit the Microsoft website at *https://docs.microsoft.com/ en-us/windows/deployment/windows-autopilot/troubleshooting*.

You can also look in the registry to find evidence of Windows Autopilot failures. The Autopilot deployment service will record information in the registry at this location:

```
HKLM\SOFTWARE\Microsoft\Provisioning\Diagnostics\AutoPilot.
```

An example of a problem recorded in the registry would read, "The device has not been registered with Autopilot."

For more advanced troubleshooting, administrators can use the Event Tracing for Windows (ETW) tool to capture detailed information from Autopilot. This will generate trace files, which can be viewed using the Windows Performance Analyzer.

NOTE **SUPPORT CASE FOR WINDOWS AUTOPILOT**

If you have an issue that you cannot resolve, you can obtain help by contacting Microsoft Support and opening a support case for Windows Autopilot at *https://docs.microsoft.com/en-us/ windows/deployment/windows-autopilot/autopilot-support*.

Skill 1.3: Upgrade devices to Windows 10

In situations where organizations have an existing environment of Windows 7 and/or Windows 8.1 devices that are fully working and supported, Microsoft recommends using an in-place upgrade strategy to deploy Windows 10 to these devices.

The upgrade process takes care of updating the operating system while retaining the apps, user data, and user settings. Utilizing in-place upgrades can offer a low-risk, quick, and reliable method of transforming devices and enabling users to be productive once the upgrade has completed.

If administrators fear that an existing installation is "old" or not a reliable candidate to upgrade to Windows 10, they could redeploy the legacy operating system—complete with apps, policies, and settings—and then perform the in-place upgrade shortly afterward. Another benefit of using an in-place upgrade approach is that driver and app compatibility issues are minimized.

By using the cloud-based Windows Analytics environment, administrators can quickly assess the status of their entire estate of installed Windows devices. The Upgrade Readiness tool allows you to see a detailed inventory of all devices and installed apps, and you can use this information to help plan and implement your Windows 10 deployment.

> **This skill covers how to:**
> - Identify upgrade and downgrade paths
> - Manage in-place upgrades
> - Configure a Windows analytics environment
> - Perform an Upgrade Readiness assessment
> - Migrate user profiles

Identify upgrade and downgrade paths

When planning to deploy Windows 10, you should consider whether your existing version of Windows can be directly upgraded to Windows 10 and whether you can migrate from one edition of Windows 10 to a different edition of the same release.

So long as you are running Windows 7 or a later operating system, you can upgrade to Windows 10. This includes upgrading from one release of Windows 10, such as Version 1703, to a later release, such as Windows 10 Version 1903.

When upgrading from one version of Windows to a later version, the upgrade process can preserve personal data, settings, and applications.

In a few situations, you can perform an edition downgrade. In these situations, you should note that all personal data is maintained; however, any incompatible applications and settings will be removed.

> **NOTE   WINDOWS 10 LTSC**
>
> An in-place upgrade from Windows 7, Windows 8.1, or Windows 10 Semi-Annual Channel to Windows 10 Long Term Servicing Channel (LTSC) version is not supported. For more information relating to Windows 10 LTSC and how it should be used, visit *https://docs.microsoft.com/en-us/windows/deployment/update/waas-overview#long-term-servicing-channel.*

You should review the information shown in Table 1-11, which shows the various upgrade and downgrade paths available in Windows 10. The Windows 10 Mobile and Windows 10 Mobile Enterprise editions have been omitted from the table because these versions are nearing the end of support from Microsoft at the time of this printing.

When reviewing the table, use the following key:

- **X**   The upgrade path is supported.
- **D**   The downgrade path is supported.

TABLE 1-11 Windows 10 Upgrade and Downgrade Paths

		DESTINATION EDITION				
		WINDOWS 10 HOME	WINDOWS 10 PRO	WINDOWS 10 PRO EDUCATION	WINDOWS 10 EDUCATION	WINDOWS 10 ENTERPRISE
Windows 7	Starter	X	X	X	X	
	Home Basic	X	X	X	X	
	Home Premium	X	X	X	X	
	Professional	D	X	X	X	X
	Ultimate	D	X	X	X	X
	Enterprise				X	X
Windows 8.1	(Core)	X	X	X	X	
	Connected	X	X	X	X	
	Pro	D	X	X	X	X
	Pro Student	D	X	X	X	X
	Pro WMC	D	X	X	X	X
	Enterprise				X	X
	Embedded Industry					X
	Windows RT					
	Windows Phone 8.1					
Windows 10	Home	X	X	X	X	
	Pro	D	X	X	X	X
	Education				X	D
	Enterprise				X	X

STARTING EDITION

Downgrade paths due to license expiration

Organizations with an expired or expiring volume license agreement can opt to downgrade their edition of Windows 10 to an edition with an active license.

Like the options for performing an edition upgrade, if a downgrade path is supported, then the user's apps and settings will be available in the downgraded version of Windows 10.

You cannot downgrade from any edition of Windows 10 to Windows 7, 8, or 8.1. You also cannot downgrade from a later version of Windows 10 to an earlier version of the same edition (for example, Windows 10 Pro Version 1809 to Version 1803) unless you use the built-in rollback process.

Review the supported Windows 10 downgrade paths shown in Table 1-12. If a path is not supported, then you will need to perform a clean installation.

When reviewing the table, use the following key:

- **X** = The downgrade path is supported.
- **S** = Supported but path is not considered a downgrade or an upgrade
- [blank] = Not supported or not a downgrade option

TABLE 1-12 Windows 10 Upgrade and Downgrade Paths

		DESTINATION EDITION						
		HOME	PRO	WINDOWS 10 PRO FOR WORKSTATION	PRO EDUCATION	EDUCATION	ENTERPRISE LTSC	ENTERPRISE
STARTING EDITION	Home							
	Pro							
	Pro for Workstation							
	Pro Education							
	Education	X	X	X				S
	Enterprise LTSC							
	Enterprise		X	X	X	S		

Upgrading from Windows 10 in S Mode

If you have devices that ship with Windows 10 in S Mode, the edition of Windows can be upgraded at any time using the Microsoft Store. The switch from S Mode to Windows 10 Home, Pro, Pro Education, or Enterprise is a one-time switch, and the device cannot be reverted to Windows 10 in S Mode without a complete wipe and reload of the operating system.

Table 1-13 shows several methods you can use to switch devices out of Windows 10 in S Mode.

> **NOTE** **SWITCHING DEVICES RUNNING WINDOWS 10 IN S MODE**
>
> You can only upgrade or switch devices running Windows 10 (Version 1709 or later) from Windows 10 in S Mode to Windows 10 Home, Pro, or Enterprise.

TABLE 1-13 Windows 10 in S Mode Switch Methods

TOOL	DESCRIPTION
Settings app	Unless it's been disabled, this app allows you to configure one device at a time.
Microsoft Store	Unless it's been disabled, the Microsoft Store allows you to configure one device at a time; a Microsoft account is required.
Microsoft Intune	Allows you to configure a group of devices that are known to Azure AD.

To switch one device at a time, you can use the Settings app and then perform Activation on the device. Alternatively, a user with a Microsoft account can use the Microsoft Store.

Follow this procedure to use the Microsoft Store to perform the switch from Windows 10 in S mode to Windows 10:

1. On the device running Windows 10 in S Mode, sign in to the Microsoft Store using your Microsoft account.
2. Search for **S Mode**.
3. In the offer displayed on screen select Buy.
4. You'll be prompted to make a back up of your files before the switch starts. After backing up your files, follow the on-screen prompts to switch to Windows 10 Pro.

Organizations can use the following procedure to switch multiple devices in bulk using Microsoft Intune or Microsoft 365 Device Management:

1. Open the Microsoft 365 Device Management portal and sign in with a Global Administrator account.

2. Navigate to Device Configuration

3. On the Device Configuration page, under Manage, select Profiles.

4. On the Device Configuration—Profiles page, click Create Profile.

5. On the Create Profile blade, enter a descriptive name for the new profile, such as **Windows 10 switch off S Mode**.

6. Enter a description for the profile.

7. On the Platform drop-down menu, select Windows 10 And Later.

8. On the Profile Type drop-down menu, select Edition Upgrade And Mode Switch.

9. Click Settings.

10. On the Edition Upgrade And Mode Switch blade, click Mode Switch (Windows Insider Only) and select one of the available options shown in Figure 1-7.

NOTE   SWITCHING OUT OF WINDOWS 10 IN S MODE

At the time of this writing, the option to switch out of Windows 10 in S Mode by using Device Management is only available for Windows Insider devices.

FIGURE 1-7 Select Edition Upgrade And Mode Switch settings

11. Click OK twice, and then click Create to save the new profile.

12. The profile is created and will need to be assigned to your Azure AD device groups to take effect.

> **NOTE   BLOCK SWITCHING OUT OF WINDOWS 10 IN S MODE**
>
> You can control the ability of which devices or users can switch out of Windows 10 in S Mode by using Group Policy. Review the GPO at Device Configuration\Profiles\Windows 10 And Later\Edition Upgrade And Mode Switch In Microsoft Intune.

Manage in-place upgrades

In previous versions of Windows, you could use several tools to help you assess, perform, and manage the task of upgrading to a new operating system. This process includes tools, such as the Microsoft Assessment and Planning (MAP) toolkit and the Application Compatibility Toolkit (ACT), which are included in Windows Assessment and Deployment Kit (Windows ADK). These tools assist in discovering applications and device drivers and then testing them for potential compatibility issues with the new OS. All these tools and processes require specialist knowledge and often add significant time and cost to the rollout project.

Many large enterprises use System Center Configuration Manager (SCCM), which is a powerful, yet complex, tool to manage devices, apps, and upgrades within an organization. System Center Configuration Manager (Current Branch) continues to be supported by Microsoft and can be used to upgrade a Windows 7 or later operating system to Windows 10.

To simplify the process of upgrading to Windows 10, Microsoft has released Upgrade Readiness, which is part of Windows Analytics. Windows Analytics offers free tools for enterprises to plan and manage the upgrade process end to end.

In addition to providing help with upgrading from Windows 7 and later to Windows 10, Upgrade Readiness allows businesses to respond to how they will manage Windows releases that are being released multiple times a year; these multiple releases are known as the Windows as a service model.

If you already use System Center Configuration Manager (Current Branch) in your organization, you can allow Upgrade Readiness to export captured analytic data directly to SCCM.

For the MD-101 exam, you should focus your learning on the new solutions within Windows Analytics because these provide the most up-to-date, cost effective, and flexible management tools. You will need an Azure subscription (or a free trial) to use the service. By default, using Windows Analytics does not generate Microsoft Operations Management Suite (OMS)/Azure costs.

Configure a Windows Analytics environment

Windows Analytics is a cloud-based service hosted within Microsoft Azure that offers organizations a new modern method of assessing and reporting on the state of deployed devices in your organization.

There are three solutions provided by Windows Analytics:

- Device Health
- Update Compliance
- Upgrade Readiness

These solutions, in their default configurations, are offered at no cost and have no on-premises infrastructure requirements. Because the services are hosted within Microsoft Azure, you will need to create an Azure subscription if the organization does not already have one.

> **NOTE   FREE MICROSOFT AZURE TRIAL**
>
> If you do not have an existing Azure subscription, you can use this Microsoft website to sign up for a free trial. It is recommended that you create and use a newly created Microsoft account for use with the Azure trial, which is not associated with your business or personal account. See *https://azure.microsoft.com/free/*.

Table 1-14 provides a summary of the key features of the three solutions within Windows Analytics and the solution name that you will see in Azure.

TABLE 1-14 Windows Analytics Components

SOLUTION (AND AZURE NAME)	DESCRIPTION
Device Health (DeviceHealthProd)	■ Identify devices that crash often, which allows you to take corrective action, such as refresh or replace. ■ Identify device drivers that are causing device crashes. ■ Report Windows Information Protection misconfigurations.
Update Compliance (WaaSUpdateInsights)	■ Identify Windows 10 devices that might need attention. ■ Report on the Windows Update state of your devices. ■ Create an inventory of your devices, including the current Windows version and current update status. ■ Report protection and threat status for devices. ■ Create custom reporting queries within the log analytics workspace.
Upgrade Readiness (CompatiblityAssesment)	■ Plan and manage your Windows 10 upgrade process. Supports upgrade management from Windows 7 and Windows 8.1 to Windows 10. ■ Supports Windows as a service upgrades. ■ View workflows to guide you from pilot to production deployments. ■ Report detailed inventory on devices and apps. ■ Gain insights into app and driver compatibility issues, together with suggested fixes. ■ Report app usage information across devices. ■ Export analytic data to software deployment tools, including SCCM.

To create a Windows Analytics workspace, perform this procedure:

1. Sign in to the Azure portal at *https://portal.azure.com* using a global administrator or security administrator account for the Azure AD tenant.

2. In the Azure portal, click All Services. In the list of resources, type **Log Analytics**. Select Log Analytics.

3. On the Log Analytics workspace blade, click Create Log Analytics Workspace.

4. Provide a name for the new Log Analytics workspace, such as **DefaultLogAnalyticsWorkspace**.

5. Under Subscription, select a subscription.

6. For Resource Group, choose to use an existing resource group that is already set up or create a new one.

7. Under Location, select an available location nearest to you.

8. Under Pricing Tier, accept the default and click OK to initialize and validate the Log Analytics workspace deployment.

9. Stay signed in to the Log Analytics workspace.

Once the Windows Analytics workspace has been created, the next step is to route the Azure AD activity logs to your Log Analytics workspace. This can be achieved by following these steps:

1. Within the Azure portal, select Azure Active Directory, and under Monitoring, select Diagnostic Settings.

2. On the <Tenant> Diagnostic Settings blade, click Turn On Diagnostics.

3. On the Diagnostic Settings blade, provide a name for the diagnostics and then check the Send To Log Analytics check box.

4. Under Log, check the AuditLogs and SignInLogs and click Save.

5. Allow the configuration to complete, then close the Diagnostic Settings blade.

6. After about 15 minutes, you can verify that events are streamed to your Log Analytics workspace.

After you have created the workspace, you must enroll your devices. To do this, you need to know your Commercial ID. The Commercial ID is a unique reference number used to identify your tenant within the Log Analytics workspace, and it informs your devices where to send their telemetry data. The Commercial ID is obtained from Update Compliance in Azure.

If you have not already added Update Compliance to your Azure subscription, perform these steps:

1. Sign in to the Azure portal at *https://portal.azure.com* using a global administrator or security administrator account for the Azure AD tenant.

2. In the Azure portal, select +Create A Resource, and search for **Update Compliance**.

3. Select Update Compliance.

4. On the Update Compliance blade, select Create to add the solution to Azure.

5. On the Update Compliance blade, choose your existing workspace and click Create.

6. After a few minutes, click the Notification icon to confirm that the Deployment has succeeded, as shown in Figure 1-8.

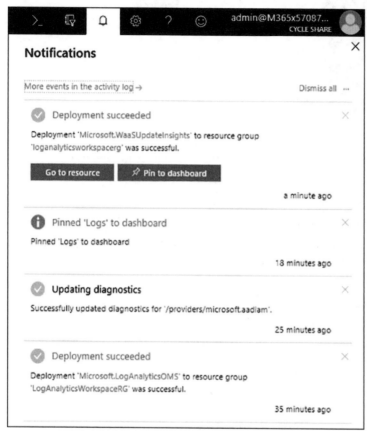

FIGURE 1-8 Update Compliance notification

7. On the Notifications page, click Go To Resource to open the Update Compliance solution.

8. Under Settings, click Update Compliance Settings to display the Commercial ID Key, as shown in Figure 1-9.

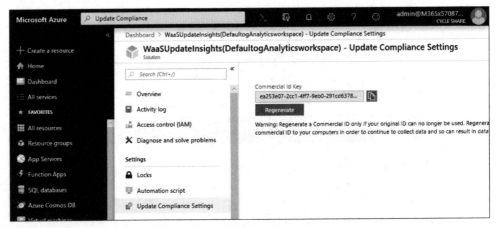

FIGURE 1-9 Commercial ID Key

9. Click the Copy icon to the left of the key and store the key for later use.

To configure Upgrade Readiness within Azure, perform these steps:

1. In the Azure portal, select Create A Resource

2. In the search box, type **Upgrade Readiness**, and then click Create.

3. In the Upgrade Readiness blade, click the Log Analytics Workspace option and choose an existing workspace or select Create New Workspace.

4. Click Create.

5. Once the deployment has completed, on the Notifications page, click Go To Resource to open the Upgrade Readiness solution.

6. Once the Upgrade Readiness solution is deployed, you then need to enroll your organization's devices.

To configure Device Health within Azure, perform these steps:

1. In the Azure portal, select Create A Resource.

2. In the search box, type **Device Health**, and then click Create.

3. In the Device Health blade, click the Log Analytics Workspace option and choose an existing workspace or select Create New Workspace.

4. Click Create.

5. After the Device Health solution has been deployed and added to a workspace in your Azure subscription, you must enroll your organization's devices.

Enroll devices in Windows Analytics

Once you've added Update Compliance to a Log Analytics workspace in your Azure subscription, you can start enrolling the devices in your organization using the Commercial ID that you obtained in the previous section.

For Update Compliance, there are three main steps relating to enrollment:

- Configure devices with the Commercial ID.
- Configure devices to send telemetry to Windows Analytics.
- Wait 48–72 hours. After enrolling your devices, it might take 48–72 hours for the first data to appear in the Update Compliance solution.

You can configure the devices using Group Policy, Mobile Device Management, or System Center Configuration Manager. This involves configuring two components:

- Enable Windows telemetry
- Configure Commercial ID

The Windows telemetry must be enabled and configured, at least to the basic level. The different levels and the corresponding values are shown in Table 1-15.

TABLE 1-15 Windows Telemetry

LEVEL	DATA GATHERED	VALUE
Security	Security data only	0
Basic	Security data, and basic system and quality data	1
Enhanced	Security data, basic system and quality, enhanced insights data, and advanced reliability	2
Full	Security data, basic system and quality data, enhanced insights data, advanced reliability data, and full diagnostics data	3

The GPO location for configuring the Commercial ID on a device is in Computer Configuration > Administrative Templates > Windows Components > Data Collection And Preview Builds. You will also find the Windows telemetry settings in this node.

If you are using Mobile Device Management, such as Microsoft Intune, you will need to create a device configuration profile that specifies the Commercial ID in a custom OMA-URI Settings field as shown in Figure 1-10.

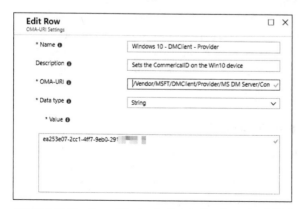

FIGURE 1-10 Configure Diagnostic Data collection using MDM

Following are the detailed steps to add the Commercial ID to your Windows 10 devices using Microsoft Intune:

1. Sign in to the Microsoft 365 Device Management portal at *https://devicemanagement .microsoft.com* using a global administrator account for the Azure AD tenant.

2. Click Device Configuration, and under Manager, click Profiles.

3. On the Profiles blade, click Create Profile.

4. On Create Profile blade, provide a name and description.

5. Under Platform, select Windows 10 And Later.

6. Under Profile Type, select Custom.

7. On the Custom OMA-URI Settings blade, click Add.

8. On the Add Row blade, configure the settings as follows:

   - **Name:** Windows 10 – DMClient – Provider

   - **Description:** (Optional: Add a description, if you like.)

   - **OMA-URI (case sensitive):** ./Vendor/MSFT/DMClient/Provider/MS DM Server/ CommercialID

   - **Data Type:** Select String from the drop-down menu.

   - **Value:** Paste your Commercial ID into the box.

9. Click OK twice.

10. On the Create Profile blade, click Create.

You will then need to enable Windows telemetry, using the same method as adding the Commercial ID; create a Device Configuration profile using these settings:

- **OMA-URI:** ./Vendor/MSFT/Policy/Config/System/AllowTelemetry

- **Date type:** Integer

- **Value:** [At least 1]

> **NOTE INSTALL AND USE THE LOG ANALYTICS VIEWS FOR AZURE ACTIVE DIRECTORY**
> You can add Log Analytics views to your Windows Analytics environment to help you analyze and search the Azure AD activity logs in your Azure AD tenant. These views include audit logs activity reports and sign-in activity reports. Review the instructions to add these views from the Microsoft website at *https://docs.microsoft.com/en-gb/azure/active-directory/ reports-monitoring/howto-install-use-log-analytics-views*.

Perform Upgrade Readiness assessment

The Upgrade Readiness section of Windows Analytics can provide insights and recommendations about computers that have been configured to send telemetry data to the Windows Analytics solution. This includes application and driver data and the status of device health, which can include service pack and Windows update information. Together, this information can be useful for analysis to identify possible issues that could affect your upgrade plan.

Upgrade Readiness supports upgrade management from Windows 7 and Windows 8.1 to Windows 10. If you already have Windows 10, you can use it to manage upgrades within the Windows as a service model.

After you have enabled Upgrade Readiness within the Azure Portal workspace (as discussed in the preceding sections) and you have configured your devices to send data to the solution, you are ready to begin using Upgrade Readiness.

> **NEED MORE REVIEW?** **GET STARTED WITH UPGRADE READINESS**
>
> If you want to know more about Upgrade Readiness, or you have not already configured your Windows Analytics environment, visit the Microsoft website at *https://docs.microsoft.com/ en-us/windows/deployment/upgrade/upgrade-readiness-get-started*.

You can now start the process of determining your organization's readiness for Windows 10 and report on the related apps and device drivers that are used in your environment. The process consists of four steps:

- **Identify important apps**   You will assign an importance level to your apps to prioritize their use in your organization.
- **Resolve issues**   Identify and resolve problems with your apps.
- **Deploy**   Start the upgrade process.
- **Monitor deployment**   Monitor important elements, such as the update progress and driver issues.

Once you begin the upgrade assessment process, you will be presented with a visual workflow, as shown in Figure 1-11, to guide you through critical high-level tasks.

Each step in the workflow is shown using blue tiles with helpful guidance, and the blue text underneath the tiles provides links to additional help. You should work through the assessment in order and complete each step.

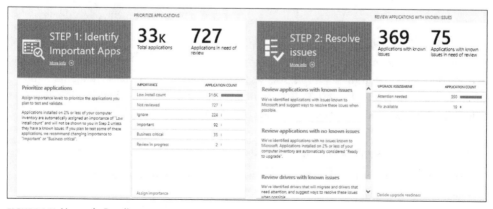

FIGURE 1-11 Upgrade Readiness process

Migrate user profiles

When you upgrade to Windows 10, unless you perform an in-place upgrade, you might overlook the migration of the user's app data and Windows settings.

Losing app data and personalized settings can have a significant effect on their productivity and even their morale. Users often invest a huge amount of time and effort configuring their Windows environment. Also, they often spend a lot of time customizing their apps, such as developing templates and toolbars. By migrating settings such as these, you are likely to reduce the number of help desk calls and avoid user downtime required to customize their desktops and find missing files.

You should aim to migrate user settings, which are often contained within their user profiles, during your Windows 10 deployment project.

Following are the two traditional methods of upgrading to Windows 10 that don't involve an in-place upgrade:

- **Side-by-side migration**   This type of migration is used when the source and destination computers for the upgrade are different machines. You install a new computer with Windows 10 and then migrate the data and user settings from the computer running the older operating system to the new computer.

- **Wipe-and-load migration**   In this scenario, the source and destination computer are the same. You back up the user data and settings to an external location and then install Windows 10 on the user's existing computer. Afterward, you restore user data and settings.

User State Migration Tool

For large-scale deployments, you can automate much of the user profile migration process by using deployment automation tools, such as System Center Configuration Manager or the Microsoft Deployment Toolkit (MDT). Both solutions use the User State Migration Tool (USMT), which is part of the Windows Assessment and Deployment Kit (Windows ADK).

For smaller migrations, you can use USMT directly from the command line to capture user accounts, user files, operating system settings, and application settings; you can then migrate the captured settings to a new Windows installation.

Although quite dated, the USMT has received several updates, which make it more secure and usable, and is available as a command line tool. The features include

- **Size estimation of the migration stores** Allows you to gauge the amount of storage you will need to perform a data capture for a targeted device running Windows.

- **Encryption of the migration stores** This protects the information stored in the user's profile, reducing the risk of data being compromised while being stored.

- **Hard links to the migration store** This is useful for PC refresh scenarios that do not involve the reformatting of the primary Windows partition. Using a hard-link migration store with USMT allows the restore process to come from the same local partition, significantly increasing transfer performance.

- **Perform offline migrations** You can run migrations from within a Windows Preinstallation Environment (WinPE). You can also perform migrations from the data stored in Windows.old directories.

You perform a user state migration in two phases as follows:

1. Settings and data are captured (collected) from the source and stored in a secure migration store using the ScanState tool.

2. Captured settings and data are restored to the destination computer using the LoadState tool.

Also, USMT can be scripted to enhance efficiency, and it can be customized with settings and rules using migration XML files:

- MigApp.xml
- MigDocs.xml
- MigUser.xml
- Custom XML files that you can create

The types of data that USMT can capture and migrate are shown in Table 1-16.

TABLE 1-16 Data Types Accessible By USMT

DATA TYPE	EXAMPLE	DESCRIPTION
User accounts, user settings, and user data	My Documents, My Video, My Music, My Pictures, Desktop files, Start menu, Quick Launch settings, and Favorites	Local and domain-based user accounts. Folders from each user profile.
Shared user data	Shared Documents, Shared Video, Shared Music, Shared Desktop files, Shared Pictures, Shared Start menu, and Shared Favorites	Folders from the Public profiles.

(Continued)

DATA TYPE	EXAMPLE	DESCRIPTION
Files, folders, and settings	Files, folders, and Registry keys	USMT searches fixed drives, collecting files that have any of the file name extensions, folders, and Registry keys that are defined in the configuration XML file.
NTFS permissions	Access control lists (ACLs)	USMT can migrate the ACL information for specified files and folders.
Operating system components	Mapped network drives, network printers, folder options, EFS files, users' personal certificates, and Internet Explorer settings.	USMT migrates most standard operating system settings.
Supported applications settings	Microsoft Office, Skype, Google Chrome, Adobe Acrobat Reader, Apple iTunes, and more	USMT will migrate settings for many applications, which can be specified in the MigApp.xml file. The version of each application must match on the source and destination computers. With Microsoft Office, USMT allows migration of the settings from an earlier version of an Office application.

As shown in Table 1-16, the list of settings that can be migrated is quite extensive. However, the following settings cannot be migrated with USMT:

- Local printers and hardware-related settings
- Device drivers
- Passwords
- Customized icons for shortcuts
- Shared folder permissions
- Files and settings if the operating systems have different languages installed

USMT is comprised of several command-line tools and configuration files, which use XML files to store customizations. The USMT components are described in Table 1-17.

TABLE 1-17 USMT Components

COMPONENT	DESCRIPTION
ScanState.exe	Scans a source computer and collects files and settings, writing them to a migration store. (The store file can be password protected and can be compressed and encrypted if required. You cannot use the **/nocompress** option with the **/encrypt** option.) You can turn off the default compression with the **/nocompress** option.
LoadState.exe	Migrates the files and settings from the migration store to the destination computer.
USMTUtils.exe	Used to compress, encrypt, and validate the migration store files.
Migration XML files	MigApp.xml, MigUser.xml, or MigDocs.xml files, and custom XML files that USMT uses to configure the process.
Config.xml	Used with the **/genconfig** option to exclude data from a migration.
Component manifests	Controls which operating system settings are to be migrated. These manifests are specific to the operating system and are not modifiable.

Use the following steps to initiate the collection of the files and settings from the source computer and back up the settings and files to a network share:

1. Ensure you have a back up of the source computer.

2. Close all applications.

3. Using an account with administrative privileges, run ScanState; use the command

   ```
   ScanState \\remotelocation\migration\mystore /config:config.xml / i:migdocs.xml
   /:migapp.xml /v:13 /l:scan.log
   ```

4. Run UsmtUtils with the **/verify** switch to ensure that the migration store is not corrupted; use the command

   ```
   UsmtUtils /verify C:\mystore\storename.img
   ```

5. On the destination computer running Windows 10, you need to install any applications that were on the source computer, and then close any open applications.

6. Run the LoadState command, specifying the same .xml files and network share location that you used when you ran ScanState; use the command

   ```
   LoadState \\remotelocation\migration\ /config:config.xml / i:migdocs.xml
   /i:migapp.xml /v:13 /l:load.log
   ```

7. Once completed, restart the device, and verify that the settings successfully migrated.

> **NOTE PCMOVER EXPRESS**
>
> In previous versions of Windows, Microsoft provided a GUI tool to help users migrate apps and settings. This is no longer available in Windows 10. For migrating the user states of a few computers, you can use PCmover Express. PCmover Express is a tool created by Microsoft partner Laplink, and it is accessed at *https://go.microsoft.com/fwlink/?linkid=620915*.

Skill 1.4: Manage updates

Windows 10 has been designed to self-update on a regular basis to remain protected from external threats, such as malware and hackers, and to add new functionality through feature updates. In earlier versions of Windows, you could decide whether the operating system was automatically updated with the latest features, security updates, and fixes through the Windows Update feature. With the vulnerabilities that could occur through disabling automatic updates, this choice has now been removed; thus, all Windows 10 devices are protected by updating them regularly.

Windows 10 changes the game with regard to updates and security because it will continually and automatically benefit from new updates rolled out by Microsoft through Windows Update.

To enhance the security protection delivered in Windows 10, the user is prevented from disabling security updates. Enterprise users will have some leeway on the timing of updates and feature upgrades, which will be delivered as defined by the IT team. Enterprise administrators can still choose to test updates and deliver them internally using Windows Server Update Service (WSUS) or other management tools to keep their devices updated. For organizations that require deployment of a static installation of Windows 10 that will not have upgrades, Microsoft ships a special build of Windows 10, Windows 10 Long Term Servicing Channel.

This skill covers how to:

- Configure Windows 10 delivery optimization
- Configure Windows Update for Business
- Deploy Windows Updates
- Implement feature updates
- Monitor Windows 10

Configure Windows 10 delivery optimization

Windows 10 introduces a feature called Delivery Optimization, which can significantly reduce the external bandwidth consumption for the organization and increase the delivery speed of updates.

Windows 10 devices can be configured to download updates from other devices that have already received the updates. You can configure this peer-to-peer method via Group Policy, or via the Settings app; this is done in the Advanced Options section of Windows Update, as shown in Figure 1-12.

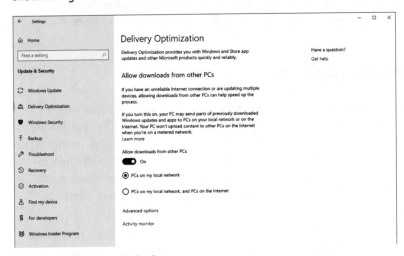

FIGURE 1-12 Delivery optimization

If bandwidth availability is a concern—for example, if devices use a metered connection or are located at a branch office or remote site—you can manually fine tune or limit the amount of bandwidth that a device can use to download and upload Windows and app updates.

Configure delivery optimization settings using Group Policy

You can also configure Delivery Optimization settings using Group Policy. The GPO settings are found at Computer Configuration > Administrative Templates > Windows Components > Delivery Optimization.

For the MD-101 exam, you should review the available GPO settings, as listed here:

- **Download Mode**   Use this setting to configure the use of Windows Update Delivery Optimization for downloads of Windows Updates, apps, and app updates. These settings offer slightly more granularity than those in the Settings app, allowing the device to receive updates from more than one place. There are six options, as follows:

  - **HTTP Only**   HTTP downloading only (no peering of updates).
  - **LAN**   HTTP downloading and Local Network/Private Peering (PCs in the same domain and NAT).
  - **Group**   HTTP downloading and peering in the same private group on a local LAN.
  - **Internet**   HTTP downloading and Internet peering only.
  - **Simple**   Download mode only using HTTP, with no peering.
  - **Bypass**   Do not use Delivery Optimization. Use BITS instead.

- **Group ID**   Set this policy to specify an arbitrary group ID to which the device belongs by using a globally unique identifier (GUID) as the group ID. This segments the devices when using the Group option in the Download Mode setting.

- **Max Cache Age**   Use this to define the maximum time (in seconds) that the Delivery Optimization cache can hold each file.

- **Max Cache Size**   This option limits the maximum cache size Delivery Optimization can use as a percentage of the internal disk size.

- **Max Upload Bandwidth**   This policy defines a limit for the upload bandwidth that a device uses for all concurrent upload activity by Delivery Optimization (kilobytes per second).

- **Minimum RAM Capacity (Inclusive) Required To Enable Use Of Peer Caching (In GB)**   This policy defines the minimum amount of RAM that a device must have to use Peer Caching. This is useful to limit the use of peer caching on small tablets.

You can also find GPO settings in this node for setting the Active Hours and limiting the amount of bandwidth that Delivery Optimization uses.

Configure Delivery Optimization settings in Microsoft Intune

You can configure delivery optimization settings for your Windows 10 devices by configuring device configuration profiles in Microsoft Intune. Once you have created a profile, you then assign or deploy that profile to your Windows 10 devices.

To create a device configuration profile that configures delivery optimization settings, use the following procedure.

1. Open the Microsoft 365 Device Management portal (at *https://devicemanagement.microsoft.com*) and sign in with a Global Administrator account.

2. Navigate to the Device Configuration, and then under Manage, click Profiles.

3. On the Device Configuration—Profiles blade, click Create Profile.

4. On the Create Profile blade, enter the following properties:

   - **Name:** Enter a descriptive name for the new profile.
   - **Description:** Enter a description for the profile.
   - **Platform:** Select the platform: Windows 10 and later.
   - **Profile Type:** Select Delivery Optimization.
   - **Settings:** Configure settings, as shown in Figure 1-13, which define how you want updates to download.

5. When you have finished entering the settings, select OK.

6. On the Create Profile page click Save.

7. You need to assign the profile to groups for the Delivery Optimization settings to take effect.

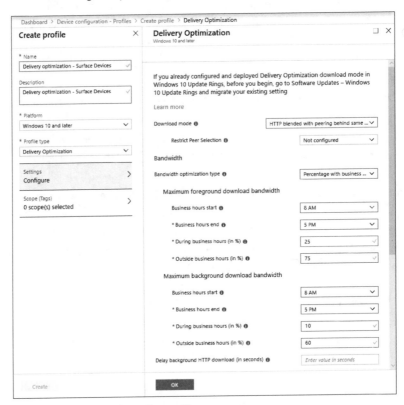

FIGURE 1-13 Device configuration profile

Once the delivery optimization settings are configured in Intune or Group Policy and have been assigned to your devices, they replace the Delivery Optimization settings in the Settings app. Users will see a notification, as shown in Figure 1-14, informing them that Some Settings Are Managed By Your Organization.

FIGURE 1-14 Settings app

Configure Windows Update for Business

Prior to Windows 10, many enterprises would use a Windows Server–based feature called Windows Server Update Service (WSUS) to keep their domain-based computers updated with monthly security fixes and periodic feature updates.

Windows 10 introduces the Windows Update for Business service for organizations to update their devices and uses the concept of update branches with different tracks that allow you to fine tune the management of updates.

The Windows Update for Business service provides the tools needed to configure Windows 10 update settings using either Group Policy or Microsoft Intune.

Traditional servicing of security updates with earlier versions of Windows is no longer appropriate today. The aim of Windows Update for Business is to allow devices to be always protected, and this requires that they receive Windows updates as quickly and efficiently as possible.

You can configure Windows Update to control the distribution and deployment of Windows updates to your devices using the following features:

- **Internal deployment groups** You allocate Windows 10 devices into groups and then specify the order in which groups will receive updates. In this way, you can create internal deployment pilot phases that can be used to stage or delay updates before allowing the update to the remaining devices.

- **Maintenance windows** Administrators can specify when updates will be applied to devices.

- **Peer-to-peer delivery** Windows 10 can be configured to receive updates from other devices or via Windows Update. Administrators can enable peer-to-peer delivery of updates and control how updates are delivered in locations that have limited bandwidth, such as branch offices and remote sites.

- **Integration with existing tools** Administrators can continue to use Windows Update for Business with traditional management tools, including WSUS, Configuration Manager, and Intune.

- **Support for Semi-Annual Channel** Windows Update for Business only supports devices configured to use the Semi-Annual Channel.

- **Upgrade testing** By employing Windows Update for Business, administrators can stage deployments and allocate time to test upgrades before rolling them out to users' Windows devices.

There are three types of updates that Windows Update for Business manages for Windows 10 devices:

- **Quality Updates** Updates for the operating system are typically released on the second Tuesday of each month. These updates include security, critical, and driver updates. If an urgent fix—perhaps in response to a zero-day vulnerability—is required, Microsoft will release the update outside of the monthly schedule. Quality Updates are cumulative in that they supersede all previous updates. Updates for Microsoft products such Microsoft Office are also classified as Quality Updates.

- **Feature Updates** These updates include all previous security and quality updates and introduce new operating system feature additions and changes. These updates accompany a change in the Windows 10 version and are released twice a year (typically around March and September).

- **Non-Deferrable Updates** The antimalware and antispyware Definition Updates that are used by Windows Security components, such as Windows Defender, are also distributed by Windows Update; often, these are offered daily and cannot be deferred.

When considering how to deploy Windows 10 in an enterprise, it is useful to break the project into at least three phases along an extended timeline:

- **Evaluate** Use the Windows Insider Program for this stage.

- **Pilot** Deploy Semi-Annual Channel (Targeted).

- **Deploy** Use the Semi-Annual Channel (Targeted) for the main deployment (this phase can be broken into multiple pilot deployment rings).

Figure 1-15 visualizes the release schedule, which is useful to overlap with your new deployment ring methodology.

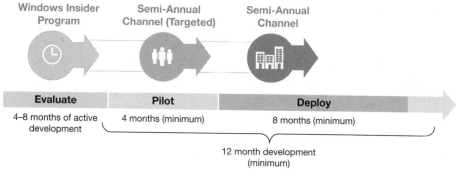

FIGURE 1-15 Deployment timeline

To use Windows Update for Business effectively, you need to adopt the following approach for how your organization manages updates:

- **Group your devices into deployment rings** Group your devices into logical or business process–related groups, or deployment rings. These allow you to manage the update process and limit the effect of any issues that you may encounter with a particular update. Each of the deployment rings should have a clearly defined audience. Suggested groups, and example audience profiles might include:

  - **Preview:** Members of the IT department and help desk
  - **Targeted:** Early adopters, team leaders, and remote workers
  - **Broad:** Mainstream workers
  - **Critical:** Kiosk devices, point of sale terminals, servers, and special purpose devices

- **Servicing Option** You need to select the appropriate servicing option or options that your organization will deploy. You will also need to define which users and device groups will receive the various types of servicing. This is typically evaluated in relation to available skilled IT resources and the operational business risk. In smaller organizations, it is expected that all user devices will use the Semi-Annual Channel because this option provides the user with the feature updates as soon as Microsoft publishes them. The three servicing options are

  - **Windows Insider Program:** This option provides organizations with the opportunity to enroll in a special early adopter program to test and provide feedback to Microsoft on features that will be shipped in the next feature update.
  - **Semi-Annual Channel:** Devices receive twice-per-year feature update release updates as soon as Microsoft publishes them.
  - **Semi-Annual Channel (targeted):** Devices typically receive feature updates 4-u6 months after the semi-annual channel.

- **Defer Updates** Administrators can define when devices receive Feature and Quality Updates, and they can defer when the updates will be applied to devices. See Table 1–18, which shows a summary of when each type of update can be deferred.

Table 1-18 highlights the deployment rings, servicing options, and update deferment choices that are available for devices supported by Windows Update for Business service. The table provides a suggestion for how these options may be applied within an organization. You can electively delay feature and quality updates into as many phases as you wish. You should periodically revisit these choices to ensure that they continue to meet the needs of your organization and its users.

TABLE 1-18 Windows Update for Business Options

DEPLOYMENT RING	CHANNEL	FEATURE UPDATE DEFERRAL	QUALITY UPDATE DEFERRAL
Preview	Windows Insider Program	None	None
Targeted	Semi-Annual Channel (Targeted)	None	None
Broad	Semi-Annual Channel	120 days	7–14 days
Critical	Semi-Annual Channel	180 days	30 days

> **NOTE UPDATE DEFERMENT**
> Windows Update for Business can be used to defer updates to devices in the Semi-Annual Channel by up to 365 days. Quality updates can be deferred up to 30 days.

Deploy Windows Updates

Windows 10 has been designed to receive updates automatically. This approach is mandatory for users of Windows 10 Home, and it is also suitable for many small- and medium-sized businesses. For larger organizations, an automated method for distributing updates is preferred. The available options that you should know are identified in Table 1-19.

TABLE 1-19 Windows Update for Business Options

SERVICING TOOL	CAN UPDATES BE DEFERRED?	ABILITY TO APPROVE UPDATES	DESCRIPTION
Windows Update	Yes (manual)	No	This option automatically updates the device and keeps it up to date and protected.
Windows Update for Business	Yes	No	This option provides enterprises some control over how updates are received and the update deployment timing.
Windows Server Update Services (WSUS)	Yes	Yes	WSUS is a Windows Server 2016 server role that downloads and distributes OS and common Microsoft app updates to Windows clients and servers.

(Continued)

SERVICING TOOL	CAN UPDATES BE DEFERRED?	ABILITY TO APPROVE UPDATES	DESCRIPTION
System Center Configuration Manager (Current Branch)	Yes	Yes	Configuration Manager performs many configuration, deployment, and update management tasks within an enterprise for Microsoft and non-Microsoft apps and across multiple operating systems.
Microsoft Intune	Yes	Yes	This MDM solution is a cloud-based management tool for managing updates on Windows and non-Microsoft platforms and apps. You can approve, deploy, pause, and uninstall updates to groups of devices configured in deployment rings.

Configure Windows Update Settings in Windows 10

By default, Windows 10 devices receive and install all updates automatically from the Windows Update service. Most updates are applied without requiring a reboot, but some updates may require a restart to complete installation. For these scenarios, Windows 10 allows the user to configure options to minimize the impact of restarting the device by scheduling the restart for a specific time.

If you have enabled the installation of app updates, these can be applied even if the application is in use. Windows 10 can save the application's data, then close the app, apply the update, and then restart the application.

To configure Windows Update settings for a single or small number of computers, follow these steps:

1. Open the Settings app and then click Update & Security. On the Update & Security page, review the last date and time Windows automatically checked for updates.

2. Click Change Active Hours. You can use this setting to ensure that Windows 10 will not restart during active hours, which are set between 8:00 AM and 5:00 PM, by default. Amend the setting and click Save or Cancel.

3. Restart Options allow you to configure a custom restart time if you want Windows 10 to restart at a certain time.

4. Click Advanced Options.

5. On the Advanced Options page, as shown in Figure 1-16, you can configure the following settings:

    -   **Give Me Updates For Other Microsoft Products When I Update Windows** Enable this option if you have Microsoft Office or other Microsoft products installed, and Windows Update will keep those products up to date as well.

    -   **Automatically Download Updates, Even Over Metered Data Connections (Charges May Apply)** This setting is set to Off by default and ensures that devices connected to mobile data services such as LTE do not consume metered data downloading updates.

- **Show A Notification When Your PC Requires A Restart To Finish Updating**
  This option will provide a visual notification to the interactive user instead of automatically restarting.
- **Pause Updates**   You can temporarily pause all updates from being installed for up to 35 days.
- **Choose When Updates Are Installed**   Choose the branch readiness level to determine when feature updates are installed on your computer. You can choose between Semi-Annual Channel (Targeted) and Semi-Annual Channel. If you are running Windows 10 Pro, Windows 10 Enterprise, or Windows 10 Education, you can defer upgrades to your computer. You can defer feature updates by up to 365 days and quality updates by up to 30 days.

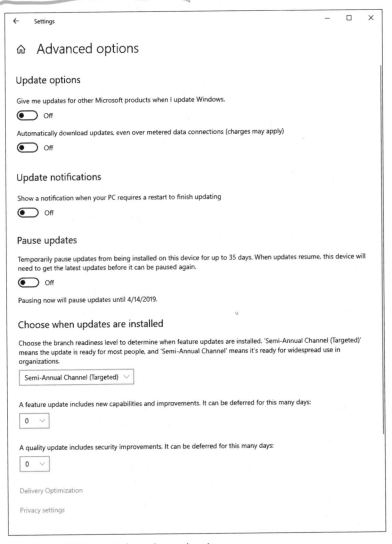

Configure Windows Update for Business using Group Policy

You can configure Windows Update for Business using Group Policy settings located at: Computer Configuration > Administrative Templates > Windows Components > Windows Update > Windows Update For Business.

There are also many GPOs for configuring Windows Update at:

Computer Configuration > Administrative Templates > Windows Components > Windows Update

For the MD-101 exam, you should review the three GPO settings for Windows Update For Business, as listed in Table 1-20.

TABLE 1-20 Windows Update for Business Group Policies

GPO	DESCRIPTION
Select When Preview Builds And Feature Updates Are Received	Administrators can choose between Fast and Slow Preview Builds, Review Preview Ring, Semi-Annual Channel (Targeted), and Semi-Annual Channel deployment rings; also, administrators can choose to defer or pause the delivery of updates.
Select When Quality Updates Are Received	Administrators can specify when to receive quality updates and optionally to defer receiving quality updates for up to 30 days. Also, you can temporarily pause quality updates up to 35 days.
Manage Preview Builds	Administrators have control over enabling or disabling Preview Build installations on a device. Stop Preview Builds once the release is public.

> **NOTE** **WINDOWS TELEMETRY DIAGNOSTIC DATA NEEDS TO BE ENABLED**
>
> For Windows Update for Business policies to be applied, the Windows telemetry diagnostic data level of the device must be set to 1 (Basic) or higher, as shown in Table 1-15 in Skill 1.3.

Configure Windows Update for Business using Intune

You can configure Windows Update for Business settings for your Windows 10 devices using Intune.

You should manage how Windows updates are deployed to your devices. This can involve rolling out the changes in phases to groups of devices. Using update or deployment rings, you allow organizations to separate machines into a deployment timeline, which defines when Windows 10 will be serviced. Each Update Ring reduces the risk of issues that could occur from the deployment of the feature updates within the organization.

You need to define the Update Rings in Intune. Update rings specify how and when Windows as a service will apply Feature Updates and Quality Updates to your Windows 10 devices. The policies will then need to be assigned to groups of devices.

Before you can use Windows updates for Windows 10 devices in Intune, you need to meet the following requirements:

- Windows 10 PCs must run at least Windows 10 Pro Version 1607 or later.
- Diagnostic and usage data must be set to
    - 1 (Basic)
    - 2 (Enhanced)
    - 3 (Full)

To create and assign update rings within Intune, perform this procedure:

1. Open the Microsoft 365 Device Management portal (at *https://devicemanagement.microsoft.com*) and sign in with a Global Administrator account.
2. Navigate to Software Updates and under Manage, select Windows 10 Update Rings.
3. On The Software Updates Windows 10 Update Rings page, click Create.
4. On the Create Update Ring page, enter a name for the Update Ring, a description (optional), and then under Settings, click Configure.
5. In the Settings blade, shown in Figure 1-17, configure settings for your business needs.
6. To confirm the settings, click OK.
7. Configure the Scope (Tags) if they have previously been created.
8. On the Create Update Ring blade, select Create.
9. To assign the Update Ring, under Manage click Assignments.
10. Use the Include and Exclude tabs to define which groups this Update Ring is assigned to, and then click Save.

Once you have created your Windows 10 Update Rings, you can manage them with Intune. Navigate to Software Updates and then under Manage select Windows 10 Update Rings; there, you can select the Update Ring that you want to manage. On the overview pane, you can view the assignment status, showing that the ring has been successfully assigned to one group, as shown in Figure 1-18, and take the following actions to manage the ring:

- **Delete**   Stops enforcing the settings of the Update Ring and removes its configuration from Intune. The settings on devices that were assigned to the Update Ring remain in place.
- **Pause**   Prevents assigned devices from receiving either Feature Updates or Quality Updates for up to 35 days from the time you pause the ring. Pause functionality automatically expires after 35 days.
- **Resum**   Used to restore an Update Ring that was paused.
- **Extend**   When an Update Ring is paused, you can select Extend to reset the pause period.
- **Uninstall**   Use Uninstall to uninstall (roll back) the latest Feature Update or Quality Update on a device running Windows 10 Version 1803 or later.

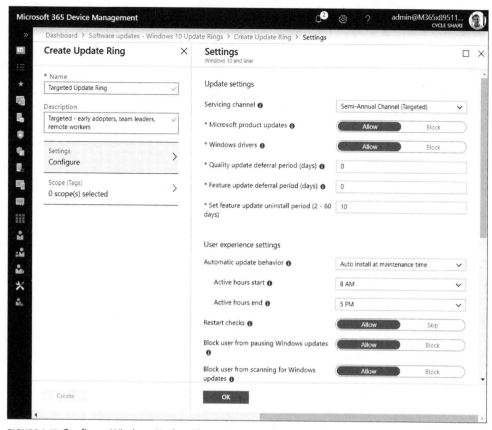

FIGURE 1-17 Configure Windows Update Rings using Intune

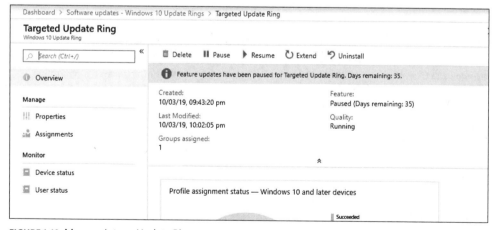

FIGURE 1-18 Manage Intune Update Rings

You can also modify the settings contained within an Update Ring by selecting Properties under the Manage heading and then amending the settings.

> **NEED MORE REVIEW?** **MANAGE SOFTWARE UPDATES IN INTUNE**
>
> If you want to know more about how to manage updates using Intune, visit the Microsoft website at *https://docs.microsoft.com/intune/windows-update-for-business-configure*.

Implement feature updates

In the preceding sections, you have learned how Windows Update for Business can be configured via Group Policy or through MDM solutions, such as Microsoft Intune. By creating deployment rings, organizations can validate new builds and deploy Windows 10 in a structured way.

Without intervention, Windows 10 will continually upgrade itself, and for some organizations, the new servicing paradigm and finite lifetime of each Windows 10 build is disconcerting. Some businesses will struggle to adopt, deploy, and support a new build of Windows on a biannual basis.

In response to this, Microsoft has extended the support for Windows 10 Enterprise and Windows 10 Education editions to 30 months from the version release date. This change also extends all past versions and future versions that are targeted for release in September (versions ending in 09, such as 1809).

Windows 10 and Office 365 Pro Plus releases that are targeted for release in March (versions ending in 03, such as 1903) will continue to be supported for 18 months from their release date. A summary of these changes is shown in Table 1-21. Windows Update for Business editions are shown in bold.

TABLE 1-21 Windows 10 Servicing and Support

PRODUCT	MARCH TARGETED RELEASES (ENDING IN 03)	SEPTEMBER TARGETED RELEASES (ENDING IN 09)
Windows 10 Enterprise	18 months	**30 months (formerly 18 months)**
Windows 10 Education		
Windows 10 Pro		18 months
Windows 10 Home		
Office 365 ProPlus		

There is no change for all releases of Windows 10 Home, Windows 10 Pro, and Office 365 ProPlus; these products will continue to be supported for 18 months.

The application of traditional and modern deployment methods using existing tools to deploy Windows 10 continue to be supported. However, the agility of the new dynamic deployment methods is the recommended approach because these enable you to transform devices efficiently and with minor disruption to user productivity. For many organizations, this adopting dynamic deployment will require a change to their current deployment and image servicing methodology.

Allowing a modern device to fall out of mainstream support is no longer an option with Windows 10. Ensuring that new feature upgrades are installed on devices ensures that Windows 10 devices using Windows Upgrade for Business continue receiving monthly security updates.

By extending the support to 30 months for all Windows 10 Enterprise and Windows 10 Education editions versions targeted for release in the September timeframe, Microsoft is providing time for organizations to evaluate new deployment methods.

Organizations can force a delay of installing feature updates by configuring Windows Update for Business and deferring updates for up to 365 days. Once an update has been installed, this version of Windows can be used for up to an additional 18 months before it needs to receive a new version of Windows 10. To remain supported, this update needs to take place prior to the end-of-service date. Table 1-22 shows the end-of-service dates for the most recent Windows 10 versions at the time of this writing.

TABLE 1-22 Windows 10 Servicing and Support

WINDOWS 10 VERSION	DATE OF AVAILABILITY	END OF SERVICE FOR HOME, PRO, AND PRO FOR WORKSTATION EDITIONS	END OF SERVICE FOR ENTERPRISE AND EDUCATION EDITIONS
Windows 10 Version 1809	November 13, 2018	May 12, 2020	May 11, 2021
Windows 10 Version 1803	April 30, 2018	November 12, 2019	November 10, 2020

> **NEED MORE REVIEW?** **WINDOWS 10 LIFE CYCLE**
>
> If you want to know more about the Windows 10 product life cycle and when it's no longer supported, see *https://support.microsoft.com/en-us/help/13853/windows-lifecycle-fact-sheet.*

Monitor Windows 10

Updates are necessary to maintain the security and reliability of Windows 10. You should ensure that devices are receiving updates, know how to review installed updates, and find more information regarding an update.

View update history

Follow these steps to view your update history and see which Windows updates failed or successfully installed on your Windows 10–based PC:

1. Open the Settings app and click Update & Security.
2. Click Windows Update and then click View Update History.

3. On the View Update History page, as shown in Figure 1-19, you can see a list of your installed Windows updates.

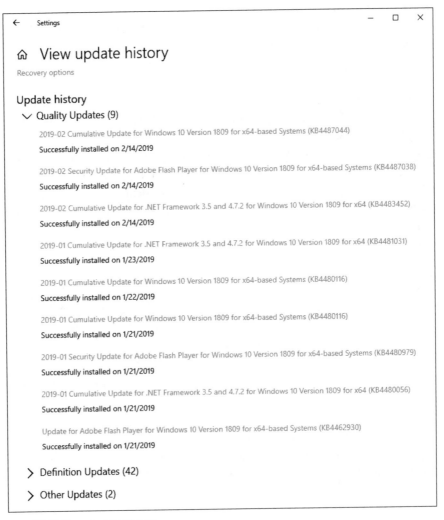

FIGURE 1-19 View Update History

4. Click one of the updates that has been successfully installed to see more details for that update.

5. In the bottom part of the screen, you can view Definition Updates, which relate to Windows Defender Antivirus and threat protection, and Other Updates.

Each update contains a summary of the payload. If you click the update link, you are directed to the detailed Knowledge Base description on the Microsoft support pages relating to the update, which allows you to review the details pertaining to the update.

There is a list of installed updates available in the Control Panel, but be aware that this list is not an exact match to the updates shown in the Settings app. If you prefer to use the Control Panel, you can see a list by following these steps:

1. Click the Start button, type **Control Panel**, and click Control Panel.

2. Select Programs > Programs And Features > View Installed Updates.

3. Select an update. The support link for the update appears in the lower part of the screen.

NEED MORE REVIEW?   **WINDOWS 10 UPDATE HISTORY**

Microsoft publishes the contents of each Windows 10 update for you to review and understand what is contained in each periodic software update. View this list at *https://support .microsoft.com/help/4464619.*

Monitor Windows Updates with Update Compliance

If you have created a Windows Analytics environment, as discussed earlier in this chapter, you can use the Update Compliance solution that enables you to

- Monitor and review detailed deployment data for Windows 10 Professional, Education, and Enterprise editions, including security, quality, and feature updates

- View a report of device and update compliance issues

- View the status of Windows Defender Antivirus signatures and threats

- Review bandwidth savings achieved by using Delivery Optimization

- Perform ad hoc queries and export data stored in Log Analytics

The Update Compliance solution is offered through the Azure portal as part of Windows Analytics, and it is available free for enterprise devices that meet the prerequisites, such as running Windows 10 Professional, Education, or Enterprise.

Update Compliance allows you to drill down into the Windows Update status of each device that has been configured to report diagnostic data to the solution. The specific services that provide data to Update Compliance include

- Windows Defender Antivirus diagnostic data

- Update deployment progress

- Windows Update for Business configuration data

- Delivery Optimization usage data

When you first configure Update Compliance, you might need to wait between 48–72 hours for data to begin being collected. Each client device is configured with the Commercial ID associated with your Log Analytics workspace, and devices report their telemetry data to the Log Analytics workspace in Azure for consumption in Update Compliance. An example of the Update Compliance workspace reporting devices that require attention is shown in Figure 1-20.

FIGURE 1-20 Update Compliance workspace

Within the Update Compliance solution, you can drill down into the diagnostic data relating to your devices. The data is split into different sections, including

Need Attention!   This is a default section in the Update Compliance workspace, which provides a summary of the different update-related issues faced by your devices, as shown in Figure 1-20.

Security Update Status   This section displays information relating to the overall status of Security Updates across all devices. Also, this section shows the percentage of devices that have been updated to the latest Security Update released for the version of Windows 10 it is running.

Feature Update Status   This section displays information relating to the overall feature update status across all devices in your environment. It shows the percentage of devices that are on the latest Feature Update that is applicable to each device.

Windows Defender AV Status   For devices that are running Windows Defender Antivirus, this section displays a summary relating to the signature and threat status across all devices. This section shows the percentage of devices running Windows Defender Antivirus that are not sufficiently protected.

Delivery Optimization Status   This section summarizes bandwidth savings incurred by using Delivery Optimization. It provides a breakdown of how Delivery Optimization has been configured in your environment and the bandwidth savings and utilization across multiple content types.

> *NOTE*   **UPDATE COMPLIANCE DIAGNOSTIC DATA LATENCY**
>
> Devices report diagnostic data gathered in the previous 12 hours to Log Analytics on a regular basis. Because of data latency and the variety of data captured, you should generally expect to see new data every 24 to 36 hours.

Skill 1.5: Manage device authentication

In a modern desktop environment, the device is as much a part of the authentication process as is the user. Traditionally, users have used passwords to gain access to corporate resources, and while this persists today, authentication is changing.

Microsoft is developing modern authentication methods that rely less on the user's ability to recall a password and place more reliance on technological advancements, such as multi-factor authentication, device-based authentication, and authentication that supports biometric attributes.

You need to understand how Windows 10 offers support for modern authentication methods and how Azure Active Directory provides a secure identity and authentication platform for your modern environment.

> **This skill covers how to:**
> - Manage authentication policies
> - Manage sign-on options
> - Perform Azure AD join

Manage authentication policies

Azure Active Directory (Active AD) allows organizations to manage their cloud-based identities and access-management requirements. Throughout this chapter, you have seen how Azure AD supports new functionality that is available for managing Windows 10, including Windows Autopilot deployment, Microsoft Intune, and Windows Update for Business.

Windows 10 security features

Many of the advancements relating to security derive from new technology becoming widely available on desktop devices, laptops, and smartphones. Windows 10 supports a variety of modern technologies that can be used by administrators to protect users' identities and resources, including

- Trusted Platform Module (TPM)
- Unified Extensible Firmware Interface (UEFI)
- Virtualization-based security
- Windows Biometric Framework
- Virtual smart cards
- Multifactor authentication (MFA)

Some of the security features built in to Windows 10 that you should have an awareness of include

- **BitLocker** A Trusted Platform Module (TPM) Version 1.2 or higher works with Bit-Locker to store encryption keys. BitLocker helps protect against data theft and offline tampering by providing for whole-drive encryption. Requirements for BitLocker include

    - A device installed with either Windows 10 Pro, Windows 10 Enterprise, or Windows 10 Education.

    - Optionally, a TPM. Using a TPM with BitLocker enables Windows to verify startup component integrity. You do not require a TPM in your computer to use BitLocker, but it does increase the security of the encryption keys.

- **Device Health Attestation (DHA)**   With the increase in use of users' personally owned devices to access corporate resources, such as email, it is important to ensure that Windows 10 devices connecting to your organization meet the security and compliance requirements of your organization. Device Health Attestation uses Measured Boot data to help perform this verification. To implement DHA, your Windows 10 devices must have TPM Version 2.0 or higher.

- **Secure Boot**   When Secure Boot is enabled, you can only start the operating system by using an operating system loader that is signed using a digital certificate stored in the UEFI Secure Boot signature database. This helps prevent malicious code from loading during the Windows 10 start process.

- **Multifactor Authentication (MFA)**   This is a process that provides for user authentication based on using at least two factors, such as

    - Something the user knows, such as a password

    - Something the user has, such as a biometric attribute (facial recognition, iris detection, or a fingerprint)

    - A device, such as a cell phone, running the Microsoft Authenticator app

- **Windows Biometric Framework**   Provides support for biometric devices, such as a fingerprint reader, a smartphone, or an illuminated infrared camera using Windows Hello. Organizations can implement secure, passwordless sign in for Azure AD and Microsoft accounts using a security key or Windows Hello when using standards-based FIDO2-compatible devices.

> **NOTE** **WINDOWS HELLO**
>
> When Windows 10 first shipped, it included Microsoft Passport and Windows Hello. These components worked together to provide multifactor authentication. To help to simplify deployment and improve supportability, these technologies are combined in Windows 10 Version 1703 into a single solution called Windows Hello. Windows Hello for Business provides enterprises the tools and policies to implement and manage multifactor authentication within their organization's infrastructure.

- **Virtual Secure Mode** This feature moves some sensitive elements of the operating system to *trustlets* that run in a Hyper-V container that parts of the Windows 10 operating system cannot access. This helps make the operating system more secure. Currently, this is only available in Windows 10 Enterprise edition.

- **Virtual Smart Card** This feature offers comparable security benefits in two-factor authentication to the protection provided by physical smart cards. Virtual smart cards require a compatible TPM (Version 1.2 or later).

Authentication methods

Now that organizations are moving toward Azure AD and cloud-based identity authentication, administrators can offer enhancements to their users, which both simplify the authentication process and offer increased security.

Traditional passwords can be forgotten, lost, stolen, and even compromised by hackers, malware, and social engineering. One policy that is quickly being adopted is to require that a user present a second authentication factor in addition to a password when they sign on.

Azure AD includes features, such as Azure Multifactor Authentication (Azure MFA) and Azure AD Self-Service Password Reset (SSPR), which allow administrators to protect their organizations and users with secure authentication methods.

Additional verification is needed before authentication is completed and may be obtained through methods shown in Table 1-23.

TABLE 1-23 Authentication Methods

AUTHENTICATION METHOD	USAGE
Password	Azure MFA and SSPR
Security questions	SSPR only
Email address	SSPR only
Microsoft Authenticator app	Azure MFA and public preview for SSPR
Open Authentication (OATH) time-based, one-time password hardware token	Public preview for Azure MFA and SSPR
SMS	Azure MFA and SSPR
Voice call	Azure MFA and SSPR
App passwords	Azure MFA

MICROSOFT AUTHENTICATOR APP

The Microsoft Authenticator app provides a quick and simple way to add additional levels of security to your Azure AD account.

Once a user has installed the Microsoft Authenticator app on his or her smartphone or tablet, the user can add multiple work or school Azure AD and Microsoft accounts. Each time the user accesses secured resources, they need to access the Microsoft Authenticator app and retrieve the verification code. Users type the verification code from the app into the resource access page and then authentication is approved.

Users can download and install the Microsoft Authenticator app from the application store for their smartphone platforms.

AZURE AD PASSWORD PROTECTION

Azure AD Password Protection offers a method to reduce the risk posed by your users choosing commonly used and compromised passwords for their access passwords. Using the password protection feature, administrators can populate a custom banned list of up to 1,000 passwords that users will be blocked from using. Also, you can choose to use the global banned password list.

Passwords that are deemed too common are stored in what is called the global banned password list. Cybercriminals also use similar strategies in their attacks. Therefore, Microsoft does not publish the contents of this list publicly. Administrators can use either a global banned password list or create a custom banned password list, which can contain lists of vulnerable passwords, such as the organization's products, variants of their brand names, and company-specific terms. These can be blocked before they become a real threat.

The Azure AD Password Protection minimum licensing requirements are shown in Table 1-24.

TABLE 1-24 Azure Ad Password Protection Licensing

DEPLOYMENT SCENARIO	AZURE AD PASSWORD PROTECTION WITH GLOBAL BANNED PASSWORD LIST	AZURE AD PASSWORD PROTECTION WITH CUSTOM BANNED PASSWORD LIST
Cloud-only users	Azure AD Free	Azure AD Basic
User accounts are synchronized from on-premises Windows Server Active Directory to Azure AD.	Azure AD Premium P1 or P2	Azure AD Premium P1 or P2

To configure Azure AD Password Protection for cloud-based accounts, perform the following procedure:

1. Open the Azure Active Directory Admin Center (at *https://aad.portal.azure.com*) and sign in with a Global Administrator account.

2. Navigate to the Security section and click Authentication Methods.

3. On the Authentication Methods page, the Password Protection blade opens.

4. Under Custom Banned Passwords, select Yes for the Enforce Custom List option.

5. In the Custom Banned Password list shown in Figure 1-21, type or paste a list of word strings. The words can have the following properties:

   - Each word should be on a separate line.

   - The list can contain up to 1000 word strings.

   - Words are case insensitive.

- Common character substitutions (such as "o" and "0" or "a" and "@") are automatically considered.

- The minimum string length is four characters, and the maximum string length is 16 characters.

6. Once you have added the word strings, click Save.

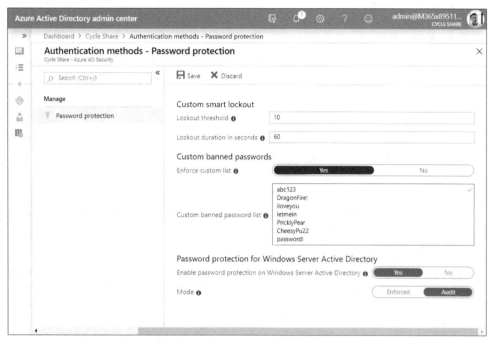

FIGURE 1-21 Azure AD Password Protection

When a user attempts to reset or update a password using a banned password, they see the following error message.

```
Choose A Password That's More Difficult For People To Guess.
```

Azure AD Password Protection is also available for hybrid scenarios. To extend the banned password lists to your on-premises users, you need to install two components—one on your Domain Controllers and another on a member server, as follows:

- **Azure AD Password Protection Proxy service** Installed on a member server. Forwards password policy requests between your domain controllers and Azure AD.

- **Azure AD Password Protection DC Agent & DLL** Installed on your domain controllers. Receives user password validation requests, processes them against the local domain password policy.

When users and administrators change, set, or reset passwords on-premises they will be forced to comply with the same password policy as cloud-only users.

SELF-SERVICE PASSWORD RESET

If you have ever worked in an IT service desk support function, you know that password-related issues are in the top three of all help desk calls. By implementing self-service password reset, you provide your users with the ability to reset their passwords, with no administrator intervention, whenever they need to.

Self-service password reset includes the following functionality:

- **Password change** Users know their passwords and want to change it to something new.
- **Password reset** A user can't sign in and wants to reset the password.
- **Account unlock** A user can't sign in because the account is locked out. If the user provides a password or passes more approved authentication methods, the account will be unlocked.

Once configured, a user can select the Can't Access Your Account link on a cloud-based resource access page, or the user can visit the Password Reset Portal at *https://aka.ms/sspr* to reset the password.

Understand Multifactor Authentication

Traditional computer authentication is based on users providing a name and password. This allows an authentication authority to validate the exchange and grant access. Although password-based authentication is acceptable in many circumstances, Windows 10 provides for several additional, more secure methods for users to authenticate their devices, including multifactor authentication (also referred to as two-factor authentication).

Multifactor authentication is based on the principle that users who wish to authenticate must have two (or more) things with which to identify themselves. Specifically, they must have knowledge of something, they must be in possession of something, or they must be something. For example, a user might know a password, possess a security token (in the form of a digital certificate), and be able to prove who they are with biometrics, such as fingerprints.

EXPLORE BIOMETRICS

Biometrics, like a fingerprint, provides a more secure (and often more convenient) method—for both the user and administrator—to be identified and verified. Windows 10 includes native support for biometrics through the Windows Biometric Framework (WBF), and when used as part of a multifactor authentication plan, biometrics is increasingly replacing passwords in modern workplaces.

Biometric information is obtained from the individual and stored as a biometric sample, which is then securely saved in a template and mapped to a specific user. To capture a person's fingerprint, you use a fingerprint reader (you "enroll" the user when configuring this). Also, you can use a person's face, retina, or even the user's voice. The Windows Biometric service can be extended to also include behavioral traits, such as the gait of a user while walking or the user's typing rhythm.

Windows includes several Group Policy settings related to biometrics, as shown in Figure 1-22, that you can use to allow or block the use of biometrics from your devices. You can find Group Policy Objects here: Computer Configuration> Administrative Templates> Windows Components> Biometrics.

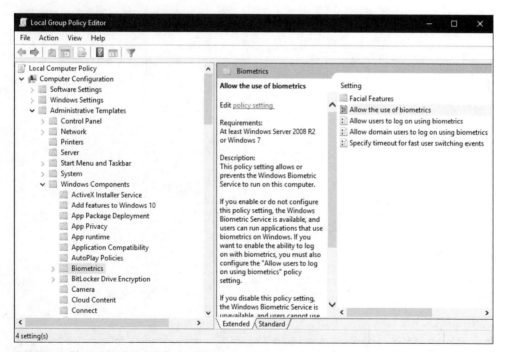

FIGURE 1-22 Biometrics Group Policy settings

Azure Multifactor Authentication

Azure Multifactor Authentication (Azure MFA) provides organizations with a highly scalable two-step verification solution, which can be used to safeguard access to data and applications and provide users with a simple sign-in process.

There are several methods you can use enable Azure MFA:

- **Enabled by conditional access policy**   Conditional access policy is available for Azure MFA in the cloud if you have Azure AD premium licensing. It requires Azure AD P1 or P2 licensing.

- **Enabled by Azure AD Identity Protection**   This method uses an Azure AD Identity Protection risk policy to enforce two-step verification for sign in to all cloud applications. It requires Azure AD P2 licensing.

- **Enabled by changing user state**   This is the traditional method for requiring two-step verification. It works with both Azure MFA in the cloud and an Azure MFA Server. An administrator can configure Azure MFA so that users must perform two-step verification every time they sign in, and it overrides conditional access policies.

When enabling Azure MFA, users are required to configure their preferred authentication methods using the registration portal at *https://aka.ms/mfasetup*, as shown in Figure 1-23.

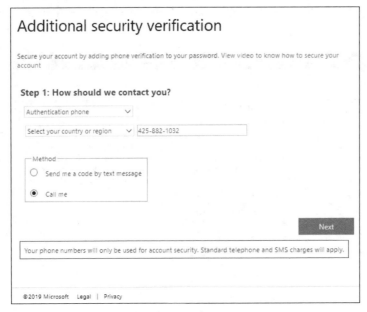

FIGURE 1-23 Azure MFA registration portal

CONFIGURE AZURE MFA

To enable Azure MFA for a single cloud-based Azure AD user, you must configure the MFA Service Settings. Then you can create a Conditional Access Policy by using this procedure:

1. Open the Azure Active Directory Admin Center (at *https://aad.portal.azure.com*) and sign in with a Global Administrator account.

2. On the Overview blade, under Manage, click Users.

3. On the menu bar, select Multi-Factor Authentication. A new browser windows opens.

4. On the Multi-Factor Authentication page, select the Service Settings tab.

5. Under Verification Options, check all the boxes for Methods Available To Contact Users (Call To Phone, Text Message To Phone, Notification Through Mobile App, Verification Code From Mobile App or Hardware Token).

6. Click Save > Close and close the browser window.

CREATE A CONDITIONAL ACCESS POLICY FOR MFA

Once MFA settings have been configured, you need to assign them to users by creating a Conditional Access Policy.

1. In the Azure Active Directory Admin Center, under favorites, select Azure Active Directory.

2. On the Overview blade, under Security, click Conditional Access.

3. Select New Policy.

4. On the Conditional Access—Policies blade, provide a name for your policy.

5. Under Assignments, click Users And Groups

6. On the Users And Groups blade, select the users for whom you want to enable Azure MFA, and then click Done.

7. Under Cloud Apps, select the All Cloud Apps radio button and click Done.

8. Under Conditions, configure the required settings and click Done.

9. Under Access Controls, select Grant, ensure the Grant access radio button is selected, and check the box for Require Multi-Factor Authentication.

10. Click Select.

11. Skip the Session section.

12. Under Enable Policy, toggle the setting to On.

13. Click Create.

14. The policy is validated, and it appears in the Conditional Access—Policy blade as Enabled.

Once you have enabled Azure MFA, you can test it to ensure that the conditional access policy works. Test logging in to a resource, such as the Office 365 portal with a user who has MFA enabled, and verify that the user is required to provide additional authentication to access the resources.

> **NOTE**   **AZURE MFA FOR ADMINISTRATORS**
>
> Microsoft offers basic Azure MFA features to Office 365 and Azure AD administrators for no extra cost. All other users require Azure AD premium licensing.

Manage sign-in options

In addition to traditional local accounts and domain user accounts, Windows 10 supports several modern methods of signing in to a device. The sign-in methods employed by an organization provide a strong first-line defense against identity theft, and you need to understand how to configure and manage sign-in options within an environment. This section teaches you how to disable PIN or picture login, and you will learn how to configure Windows Hello for Business.

Configure Microsoft accounts

A Microsoft account provides you with an identity that you can use to securely sign in on multiple devices and access cloud services. Because the identity is the same on multiple devices, your personal settings can be synchronized between your Windows-based devices.

On a device for personal use, if Windows 10 detects an Internet connection during the initial setup, you are prompted to specify your Microsoft account details. However, you can skip this step and create a local account instead. If the device is personally owned, but you want to use it for work or school, you can register your device on your work or school tenant after setup is complete.

Microsoft accounts are primarily for consumer use. Enterprise users can benefit by using their personal Microsoft accounts in the workplace though there are no centralized methods provided by Microsoft to provision Microsoft accounts to users. After you connect your Microsoft account to Windows 10, you will have the following capabilities:

- You can access and share photos, documents, and other files from sites such as One-Drive, Outlook.com, Facebook, and Flickr.

- Integrated social media services providing contact information and status for your users' friends and associates are automatically maintained from sites such as Outlook. com, Facebook, Twitter, and LinkedIn.

- You can download and install Microsoft Store apps.

- You benefit from app synchronization with Microsoft Store apps. After user sign in, when an app is installed, any user-specific settings are automatically downloaded and applied.

- You can sync your app settings between devices that are linked to your Microsoft account.

- You can use single sign in with credentials roaming across any devices running Windows 10, Windows 8.1, Windows 8, or Windows RT.

If Microsoft accounts are allowed in an enterprise environment, you should note that only the owner of the Microsoft account can change the password. A user can perform a password reset in the Microsoft account sign in portal at *https://account.microsoft.com*.

SIGNING UP FOR A MICROSOFT ACCOUNT

To sign up for a Microsoft account, use the following procedure:

1. Open a web browser and navigate to *https://signup.live.com*.

2. To use your own email address for your Microsoft account, type it into the web form; otherwise, provide a telephone number to verify that you are not a web-based robot.

3. To create a new Hotmail or Outlook.com account, click Get A New Email Address and then complete the email address line, specifying whether you want a Hotmail or Outlook suffix.

4. Press Tab to verify that the name you entered is available.

5. Complete the rest of the form and then agree to the privacy statement by clicking I Accept.

After you have created your Microsoft account, you can connect it to your device.

CONNECTING YOUR MICROSOFT ACCOUNT TO YOUR DEVICE

To connect your Microsoft account to your local or domain user account, use the following procedure.

1. Sign in with your local or domain user account.

2. Open the Settings app and click Accounts.

3. On the Your Info page, click Sign In With A Microsoft Account Instead.

4. On the Microsoft account page, enter the Microsoft account email address and then click Next.

5. On the Enter Password page, enter the password associated with your Microsoft account and click Sign In.

6. If prompted, enter your local or domain user account password to verify your local identity and click Next.

7. The device will now use your Microsoft account to log in.

8. If you want to add additional Microsoft accounts to Windows 10, you can use the Add An Account option found on the Email & Accounts tab of the Accounts page in the Settings app.

> **NEED MORE REVIEW?** **SETTING UP MICROSOFT ACCOUNTS ON DEVICES**
>
> For more information about setting up Microsoft accounts on devices, refer to the Microsoft website at *https://account.microsoft.com/account/connect-devices*.

LIMITING THE USE OF MICROSOFT ACCOUNTS

Within an enterprise, you might want to prevent users from associating their Microsoft accounts with a device and block users from accessing personal cloud resources using their Microsoft accounts.

You can configure Microsoft account restrictions using two GPOs:

- **Block All Consumer Microsoft Account User Authentication** This setting can prevent users from using Microsoft accounts for authentication for applications or services. Any application or service that has already been authenticated will not be affected by this setting until the authentication cache expires. It is recommended to enable this setting before any user signs in to a device to prevent cached tokens from being present. This GPO is located at Computer Configuration\Administrative Templates\Windows Components\Microsoft Account.

- **Accounts: Block Microsoft accounts**   This setting prevents users from adding a Microsoft account within the Settings app. There are two options: Users Can't Add Microsoft Accounts and Users Can't Add Or Log On With Microsoft Accounts. This GPO is located at Computer Configuration\Windows Settings\Security Settings\Local Policies\Security Options.

Configure Windows Hello and Windows Hello for Business

Windows Hello is a two-factor biometric authentication mechanism built in to Windows 10. The personal biometric data created and used by Windows Hello is unique to the device on which it is set up, and it is not synced with other devices. Windows Hello allows users to unlock their devices by using facial recognition, fingerprint scanning, or a PIN.

Windows Hello for Business is the enterprise implementation of Windows Hello; it allows users to authenticate to Active Directory or Azure AD, and it enables users to access network resources. Administrators can configure Windows Hello for Business using Group Policy or by using mobile device management policy; it uses asymmetric (public/private key) or certificate-based authentication.

Windows Hello provides the following benefits.

- Strong passwords can be difficult to remember, and users often reuse passwords on multiple sites, which reduces security. Windows Hello allows them to authenticate using their biometric data.
- Passwords are vulnerable to replay attacks, and server breaches can expose password-based credentials.
- Passwords offer less security because users can inadvertently expose their passwords because of phishing attacks.
- Windows Hello helps protect against credential theft. Because a malicious person must have both the device and the biometric information or PIN, it becomes more difficult to hack the authentication process.
- Windows Hello can be used in cloud-only and hybrid-cloud deployment scenarios.
- Windows Hello logs you into your devices three times faster than by using a password.

To implement Windows Hello, your devices must be equipped with the appropriate hardware. For example, facial recognition requires that you use special cameras that see in infrared (IR) light. These can be external cameras or cameras incorporated into the device. The cameras can reliably tell the difference between a photograph or scan, and a living person. For fingerprint recognition, your devices must be equipped with fingerprint readers, which can be external or integrated into laptops or USB keyboards.

If you have previously experience poor reliability from legacy fingerprint readers, you should review the current generation of sensors, which offer significantly better reliability and are less error prone.

After you have installed the necessary hardware devices, use these directions to set up Windows Hello:

1. Open the Settings app and click Accounts.

2. On the Sign-in Options page, under Windows Hello, review the options for face or fingerprint. (If you do not have Windows Hello-supported hardware, the Windows Hello section does not appear on the Sign-in Options page.)

To configure Windows Hello, follow these steps:

1. Open the Settings App and select Accounts.

2. On the Accounts page, click Sign-In Options.

3. Under the Windows Hello section, click Set Up under Face Recognition.

4. Click Get Started on the Windows Hello setup dialog page.

5. Enter your PIN or password to verify your identity.

6. Allow Windows Hello to capture your facial features, as shown in Figure 1-24.

FIGURE 1-24 Configuring Windows Hello

7. Once complete, you are presented with an All Set! message that you can close.

Users can use Windows Hello for a convenient and secure sign-in method, which is tied to the device on which it is set up.

For Enterprises who want to enable Windows Hello, they can configure and manage Windows Hello for Business. Windows Hello for Business uses key-based or certificate-based authentication for users by using Group Policy or by using a modern management approach, such as Microsoft Intune.

To manage Windows Hello for Business with Group Policy, you should review the two Windows Hello for Business GPO settings, which can be found in this node: User Configuration > Administrative Templates > Windows Components > Windows Hello for Business.

One setting is used to enable Windows Hello for Business, and the other setting is used to configure the use of certificates for on-premises authentication.

You also have additional Windows Hello for Business GPO settings available to manage your Windows Hello for Business deployment. These policies can be found in this node: Computer Configuration > Administrative Templates > Windows Components > Windows Hello for Business.

There are 10 settings that allow you to configure hardware security devices, such as TPM. These settings also allow you to configure smart cards, biometrics settings, and more.

> **NEED MORE REVIEW?   WINDOWS HELLO BIOMETRICS IN THE ENTERPRISE**
>
> To review further details about using Windows Hello in the enterprise, refer to the Microsoft website at *https://docs.microsoft.com/windows/access-protection/hello-for-business/ hello-biometrics-in-enterprise*.

Manage Windows Hello for Business with Intune

Windows Hello for Business can be deployed using a device configuration profile, which allows you to configure various settings on Windows 10.

With Intune device configuration profiles, you can permit or block the use of Windows Hello for Business, and you can configure the following settings:

- Minimum PIN Length
- Maximum PIN Length
- Lowercase Letters In PIN
- Uppercase Letters In PIN
- Special Characters In PIN
- PIN Expiration (Days)
- Remember PIN History
- Enable PIN Recovery
- Use A Trusted Platform Module
- Allow Biometric Authentication
- Use Enhanced Anti-Spoofing When Available
- Certificate For On-Premises Resources

You can also use Intune device enrollment policies to configure Windows Hello for Business settings during the initial device enrollment into management.

Configure PIN

To avoid sign in using passwords, Microsoft provides an authentication method that uses a PIN in association with Windows Hello. When you initially set up Windows Hello, you're first asked to create a PIN. This PIN enables you to sign in using the PIN as an alternative—such as when you can't use your preferred existing biometric method because of an injury, because the sensor is unavailable, or because the sensor is not working properly. The PIN provides the same level of protection as Windows Hello.

Windows Hello PIN provides secure authentication without sending a password to an authenticating authority, such as Azure AD or an AD DS domain controller. Windows Hello for Business provides enterprises compliance with the latest FIDO 2.0 (Fast Identity Online) framework for end-to-end multifactor authentication.

If the user does not use Windows Hello for Business, then the user cannot use an associated PIN. Within a domain environment, a user cannot use a PIN on its own. (This method of sign-in is known as a Convenience PIN.) You will see from the user interface shown in Figure 1-25, that the PIN settings are within the Windows Hello section of the Sign-In Options. A user must first configure Windows Hello and be already be signed in using a local account, a domain account, a Microsoft account, or an Azure AD account. The user is then able to set up PIN authentication, which is associated with the credential for the account.

After a user has completed the registration process, Windows Hello for Business performs the following operations to secure the credentials:

1. Generates a new public-private key pair on the device known as a *protector key*.

2. If installed in the device, the Trusted Platform Module (TPM) is used to generate and store this protector key.

3. If the device does not have a TPM, the Windows 10 operating system encrypts the protector key and stores it within the file system.

4. Windows Hello for Business also generates an administrative key that is used to reset credentials if necessary.

> **NOTE** **PAIRING OF CREDENTIALS AND DEVICES**
> Windows Hello for Business pairs a specific device and a user credential. Consequently, the PIN the user chooses is associated only with the signed-in account and that specific device. A user is unable to sign in on another device unless he or she initiates the Windows Hello setup on the device.

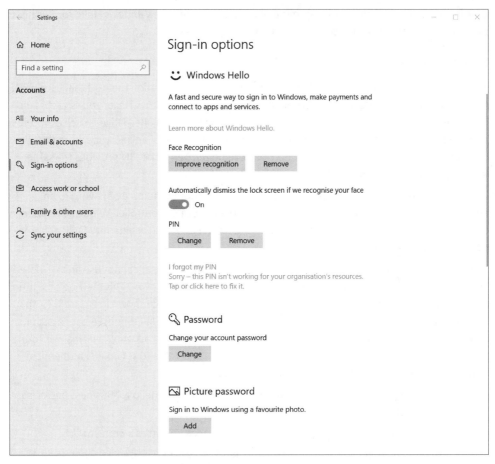

FIGURE 1-25 Configuring Windows Hello PIN

The user now has a PIN gesture defined on the device and an associated protector key for that PIN gesture. The user can now securely sign in to his or her device using the PIN; also, the user can add support for a biometric gesture as an alternative for the PIN. The *gesture* can be facial recognition, iris scanning, or fingerprint recognition, depending on available hardware in the device. When a user adds a biometric gesture, it follows the same basic sequence as mentioned earlier. The user authenticates to the system by using the PIN and then registers the new biometric. Windows generates a unique key pair and only stores this on the device. There is no Windows Hello biometric data stored in the Microsoft Cloud.

You can create and implement policies for using Windows Hello for Business in your organization. For example, you can configure a policy that enables or disables the use of biometrics on devices affected by the policy. If allowed to use Windows Hello for Business, a user can then sign in using the PIN or a biometric gesture.

You can use MDM policies or GPOs to configure settings for Windows Hello for Business.

To configure PIN complexity with Windows 10 (with and without Windows Hello for Business) you can use the eight PIN Complexity Group Policy settings that allow you to control PIN creation and management.

These policy settings can be deployed to computers or to users. If you deploy Group Policy settings to both, then the user policy settings have precedence over computer policy settings, and GPO conflict resolution is based on the last applied policy. The policy settings included are:

- Require Digits
- Require Lowercase Letters
- Maximum PIN Length
- Minimum PIN Length
- Expiration
- History
- Require Special Characters
- Require Uppercase Letters

In the Windows 10 Version 1703 and later, the PIN complexity Group Policy settings are located at Administrative Templates\System\PIN Complexity, under both the Computer and User Configuration nodes.

If an organization is not using Windows Hello for Business, they can still use the option to set a Convenience PIN. A Convenience PIN is very different from a Windows Hello for Business PIN because it is merely a wrapper for the user's domain password. This means that the user's password is cached and substituted by Windows when signing in with a Convenience PIN.

Since the Anniversary release (Windows 10 Version 1607) the option to allow a Convenience PIN is disabled by default for domain-joined clients. To modify the option to sign in with the

Convenience PIN, you can use the Turn On Convenience PIN Sign-In GPO settings at Computer Configuration\Administrative Templates\System\Logon.

Configure Picture Password

A picture password is another way to sign in to a computer. This feature does not use Windows Hello or Windows Hello for Business, and therefore, a picture password is not available to be used within a domain-based environment.

You sign in to a touch-enabled device by using a series of three movements consisting of lines, circles, and/or taps. You can pick any picture you want and provide a convenient method of signing in to touch-enabled, stand-alone devices. Picture password combinations are limitless because the pictures that can be used are limitless. Although picture passwords are considered more secure for stand-alone computers than typing a four-digit PIN, a hacker might be able guess his or her way into a device by holding the screen up to light to see where most of the gestures are (by following the smudges on the screen). This is especially true if the user touches the screen only to input the password and rarely uses touch for anything else.

To create a picture password, follow these steps:

1. Open the Settings app and click Accounts.
2. Click Sign-in Options.
3. Under Picture Password, click Add.
4. Input your current account password and click Choose Picture, which allows you to browse to and select a picture.
5. Adjust the position of the picture and click Use This Picture.
6. Draw three gestures directly on your screen. Remember that the size, position, and direction of the gestures are stored as part of the picture password.
7. You are prompted to repeat your gestures. If your repeated gestures match, click Finish.

There is only one GPO setting relating to this feature. To disable Picture Password using local group policy, you can use the Turn Off Picture Password Sign-In setting in the following location:

Computer Configuration\Administrative Templates\System\Logon.

Configure Dynamic Lock

Users with smartphones can take advantage of a feature introduced with the Creators Update for Windows 10 Version 1703, which allows users to automatically lock their devices whenever they're not using them. (At the time of this writing, iPhone devices do not support this feature.)

This feature relies on a Bluetooth link between your PC and paired smartphone.

To configure Windows 10 Dynamic Lock, use the following steps:

1. Open the Settings app and click Accounts.
2. Click Sign-in Options and scroll to Dynamic Lock.
3. Check the Allow Windows To Detect When You're Away And Automatically Lock The Device option.

4. Click the Bluetooth & Other Devices link.

5. Add your smartphone using Bluetooth and pair it.

6. Return to the Dynamic Lock page, and you should see your connected phone. as shown in Figure 1-26.

7. Your device will be automatically locked whenever Windows detects that your connected smartphone has moved away from your desk for 30 seconds.

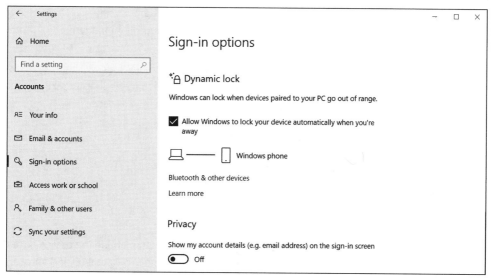

FIGURE 1-26 Configuring Dynamic Lock

You can configure dynamic lock functionality for your devices using the Configure Dynamic Lock Factors GPO setting. You can locate the policy setting at Computer Configuration\Administrative Templates\Windows Components\Windows Hello for Business.

Perform Azure AD join

In a traditional domain-based environment, the protection of user identities is a major security concern. With a username and password, a hacker can cause havoc on any system. For a cloud-enabled workplace, the device is also a key component of your infrastructure. In a similar way to the user, the device is another identity that you need to protect. Azure AD allows you to join Windows 10–based devices to the cloud-based directory, and you can provide management tools to keep the device healthy and safeguarded.

For some businesses, the traditional on-premises model serves them, and they may not want to (or need to) change. Azure AD works very well in these scenarios:

Cloud-based services and resources   When most of the applications and resources that the organization uses are in the cloud (such as Office 365 ProPlus or Dynamics 365) joining client devices to Azure AD can increase the usability and ease of access.

Bring Your Own Device (BYOD) Users can join their devices to your business environment. Azure AD can manage and protect resource access for Windows 10 and non-Microsoft devices, such as iPads or Android tablets, that cannot join an AD DS domain. Personal and business data can be kept separate, and business data can be wiped from the device when the device leaves management.

Mobility of the workforce Many organizations have employees working remotely or from home. In settings where workers infrequently visit a traditional on-premises domain environment, opting for a cloud-based management solution could be beneficial. Azure AD and Intune support the joining and remote management of mobile devices such as laptops, tablets, and smartphones.

Users can join Windows 10 devices to Azure AD during initial Windows 10 setup, or a device can be joined at a later stage by using the Settings app. Earlier in this chapter, you learned that you need to prepare Azure AD, so that devices can join the cloud service.

Windows 10 devices can connect to Azure AD in several ways, as follows:

- Join a new Windows 10 device to Azure AD
- Join an existing Windows 10 device to Azure AD
- Register a Windows 10 device to Azure AD

Join a new Windows 10 device to Azure AD

Earlier in this chapter, you learned how Windows Autopilot can manage the device once it's powered on and how it guides the user and device to be joined to Azure AD and auto-enrolled in Microsoft Intune.

If the organization does not use Windows Autopilot, the user can manually take a new Windows 10 device and join the device to Azure AD during the first-run experience.

If the device is running either Windows 10 Professional or Windows 10 Enterprise, the Out-Of-Box experience (OOBE) will present the setup process for company-owned devices, which is described below.

To join a new Windows 10 device to Azure AD during the first-run experience, use the following steps:

1. Start the new device and allow the setup process to begin.
2. On the Let's Start With Region. Is This Correct? page, select the regional setting that you need and click Yes.
3. On the Is This The Right Keyboard Layout? page, select the keyboard layout settings and click Yes.
4. On the Want To Add A Second Keyboard Layout? page, add a layout, or select Skip.
5. The computer attempts to automatically connect to the internet, but if it does not succeed, you will be presented with the Let's Connect You To A Network page where you can select a network connection.
6. On the Sign In With Microsoft page, enter your Organization or School account and password and click Next.

7. On the Do More Across Devices With Activity History page, choose whether to enable the timeline feature.

8. On the Do More With Your Voice page, choose whether to enable speech recognition and click Accept.

9. On the Let Microsoft And Apps Use Your Location page, choose whether to enable the location-based features and click Accept.

10. On the Find My Device page, choose whether to enable the feature and click Accept.

11. On the Send Diagnostic Data To Microsoft page, choose Full or Basic diagnostic data transfers and click Accept.

12. On the Improve Inking & Typing page, choose Yes or No and click Accept.

13. On the Get Tailored Experiences With Diagnostic Data page, choose Yes or No and click Accept.

14. On the Let Apps Use Advertising ID settings choose the privacy settings that you require and click Accept.

15. Depending on organizational settings, your users might be prompted to set up Windows Hello. By default, they will be prompted to set up a PIN. When prompted to set up a PIN, click Set Up PIN.

16. On the More Information Required page, click Next, provide the additional security verification information, and click Next.

You should now be automatically signed in to the device and joined to your organization or school Azure AD tenant and presented with the desktop.

Join an existing Windows 10 device to Azure AD

In this method, we will take an existing Windows 10 device and join the device to Azure AD. You can join a Windows 10 device to Azure AD at any time using the following procedure:

1. Open the Settings app and then click Accounts.

2. In Accounts, click the Access Work Or School tab.

3. Click Connect.

4. On The Set Up A Work Or Education Account page, under Alternative Actions, click Join This Device to Azure Active Directory, as shown in Figure 1-27.

5. On The Let's Get You Signed In page, enter your Work or Education username and click Next.

6. On the Enter Password page, enter your password and click Sign In.

7. On the Make Sure This Is Your Organization page, confirm that the details on screen are correct, then click Join.

8. On the You're All Set! page, click Done.

9. To verify that your device is connected to your organization or school, you should see your Azure AD email address listed under the Connect button and connected to Azure AD.

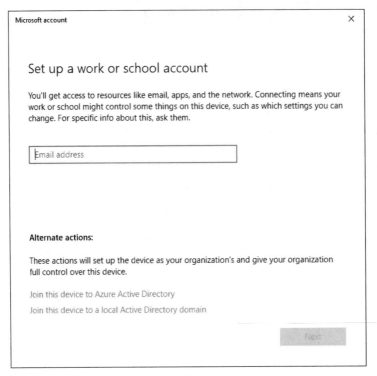

FIGURE 1-27 Joining a device to Azure AD

If you have access to the Azure Active Directory portal, then you can confirm that the device is joined to Azure AD by following these steps:

1. Sign in as an administrator to the Azure portal at *https://portal.azure.com*.

2. On the left navigation bar, click Azure Active Directory.

3. In the Manage section, click Devices > All Devices.

4. Verify that the device is listed, as shown in Figure 1-28.

FIGURE 1-28 Viewing joined devices in Azure AD

REGISTER DEVICES TO AZURE AD

You connect a Windows 10 device to Azure Active Directory using the Add Work Or School Account feature found in the Settings app. Device registration can be used to allow devices to be known by both Azure AD and MDM solutions.

Devices that are registered with Azure AD and managed by Microsoft Intune can have conditional access rules applied to them. In this way, personally owned devices can be configured so that they meet your corporate standards for security and compliance.

Use the following procedure to take an existing Windows 10 device and register it with Azure AD:

1. Open the Settings app and click Accounts.

2. In Accounts, click the Access Work Or School tab.

3. Click Connect.

4. On The Set Up A Work Or Education Account page, as shown in Figure 1-27, enter your Work or Education Account, click Next, and complete the wizard.

To verify that your device is registered to your organization or school Azure AD tenant, use these steps.

1. Open the Settings app and click Accounts.

2. In Accounts, click the Access Work Or School tab.

3. On the Access Work Or School page, verify that your organization or school Azure AD email address is listed under the Connect button.

> **NOTE** **REGISTER BYO DEVICES TO AZURE AD**
>
> You can register a personally owned device with Azure AD using the Set Up A Work Or Education Account wizard. Personal devices are then known to Azure AD but are not fully managed by the organization.

Thought experiments

In these thought experiments, demonstrate your skills and knowledge of the topics covered in this chapter. You can find the answers to these thought experiments in the next section.

Scenario 1

Contoso has 2,000 workstations currently running Windows 8.1 Pro. The company plans to perform an in-place upgrade to Windows 10 Enterprise. Most of the users work at the head office, though about 50 members of staff work remotely. Your staff already uses Office 365 Pro Plus, and you are considering purchasing a Microsoft 365 Enterprise subscription.

As a consultant for Contoso, answer the following questions:

1. Is an in-place upgrade a suitable method of deploying Window 10?

2. Your manager is concerned that moving to the cloud will be problematic and involve additional purchase costs and workload to configure Azure Active Directory for your users. How should you advise your manager?

3. Management has been given the green light to proceed with the rollout of Microsoft 365 Enterprise to all Contoso staff. You are not sure about how to manage the upgrade process from Windows 8.1 to Windows 10. What single online resource can you use to obtain a set of tools and resources to plan and manage device upgrades?

4. The devices within your research and development lab require access to a secure wireless network, which will be implemented at the same time as the upgrade rollout. You need to deploy the network WiFi settings to the R&D team devices with minimal effort. How will you deploy the settings?

Scenario 2

Contoso has 50 remote workers spread across the county. The remote workers will receive new Surface Books to replace their old laptops. You decide you will allow the vendor to ship the device directly to the user, rather than have users pick up their devices during their next visit to the head office. You have planned to deploy the devices using Windows Autopilot.

Answer the following questions for your manager:

1. How will the devices be recognized as belonging to Contoso if they have not first been configured by the IT department?

2. How will the remote users know to trust the device and that it belongs to Contoso if it is shipped direct from the vendor?

3. How will the user know that the device configuration is progressing, and can the user bypass the device configuration?

4. How will the device be secured in accordance with Contoso corporate security and compliance policies?

Scenario 3

Your organization is expanding and currently runs a mixture of operating systems on its devices, including Windows 7 and Windows 10 Pro. The company wants to have all the devices running a common operating system.

Answer the following questions for your manager:

1. Some devices were purchased with Windows 10 in S Mode. How can the company upgrade the Windows 10 in S Mode devices to Windows 10 Pro?

2. You need to recommend a tool that will provide an inventory of all devices and apps. Your choice should require the least amount of administrative effort. What will you recommend?

3. You want to reduce the impact for users during the rollout of Windows 10 Pro. What deployment approach would you recommend that retains all user and application settings wherever possible and involves the least amount of downtime for users?

Scenario 4

Adatum Corporation uses Microsoft 365 and has implemented Windows 10 Enterprise for all devices. You configure Windows Update for Business and deploy Update Rings using Microsoft Intune.

Answer the following questions for your manager:

1. Two of the remote offices are in an area with poor internet bandwidth, and the IT team is concerned that operational requirements may be difficult to maintain. What measure could you implement for the devices located at the remote locations to reduce bandwidth consumption from Windows Updates?

2. Windows Updates that are being received by the devices at the head office are consuming too much of the available bandwidth. Users are reporting that access to the internet is slow. What are several settings that you can configure within Microsoft Intune to help relieve congestion at head office?

3. Your Compliance Manager has received confirmation that Windows 10 Enterprise Version 1809 has been approved as compliant by your regulatory body. You need to ensure that all devices use only this version of Windows until the compliance manager confirms that a new version is compliant. How will you proceed?

4. You need to work with the compliance manager to ensure that future versions of Windows 10 Enterprise obtain regulatory compliance before the deployed version of Windows 10 becomes unsupported. What will you do to ensure that you can proactively evaluate the compatibility of new versions of Windows 10?

Scenario 5

Adatum Corporation uses Microsoft 365 and has implemented Windows 10 Enterprise for all devices. The Security Manager asks you to implement Azure MFA for all users.

Answer the following questions for your manager:

1. Most employees have smartphones that they can use with Azure MFA. How will a smartphone be used with Azure MFA, and what option exists for employees without a smartphone?

2. The company wants to prevent employees from using common passwords, brand names, locations, and compromised passwords. What solution will you recommend?

3. You implement the device lock screen with a short time-out, but users are frustrated because devices become locked while they are talking on the telephone. Recommend another solution to prevent users from leaving their devices unlocked whenever they step away from them.

4. An employee wants to use his or her personal device to access corporate email from home. Company security policy requires that all access to corporate email must be secure and that no copy and paste functionality is allowed between corporate and personal apps on personally owned devices. How should you proceed?

Thought experiment answers

This section provides the solutions for the tasks included in the Thought Experiments section.

Scenario 1

1. Yes, an in-place upgrade is supported and recommended by Microsoft.

2. You should advise your manager that Contoso already uses Azure Active Directory because AAD is included in Office 365 ProPlus, which is already deployed. There will be minimal additional workload and no additional cost.

3. Upgrade Readiness, which is included with Windows Analytics, provides a set of tools to plan and manage device upgrades and a visual workflow to guide you through the process.

4. By using a provisioning package, such as the built-in Provision Desktop Devices wizard, you can deploy WiFi settings to devices easily and quickly.

Scenario 2

1. The vendor will extract and register the hardware ID directly with the Windows Autopilot service, and this will be tied to the Contoso Azure AD tenant.

2. After the initial startup, the remote user will be presented with a log in screen that offers Contoso company branding. This branding has been configured within the Contoso Azure AD portal.

3. The Enrollment Status Page can be configured to be shown during the device configuration phase. This allows the user to see a visual status of how the configuration is progressing. You can prevent the device from being used by configuring the Block Device Use Until All Apps And Profiles Are Installed setting in the Enrollment Status Page settings.

4. The device will be automatically joined to Azure AD once the remote user enters his or her Azure AD credentials. It will then be auto-enrolled in Microsoft Intune, and all Contoso policies will be configured.

Scenario 3

1. The devices can be individually upgraded using the Microsoft Store or using the Settings app. If the business uses Microsoft Intune, this could also be used to configure a group of devices if they are also known to Azure AD.

2. The company could use Upgrade Readiness, which will report detailed inventory on devices and apps. Alternatively, you could have suggested the Microsoft Assessment and Planning tool, but this requires significantly more administrative effort to implement.

3. You should recommend an in-place upgrade to Windows 10 Pro. This will retain all user and application settings. USMT could back up and restore user and application settings, but it would be more time-consuming and is not necessary because the user will retain the same device, and the current operating system is capable of being upgraded directly to Windows 10 Pro.

Scenario 4

1. You should configure the Delivery Optimization option called Allow Downloads From Other PCs Option In Windows Update Section Of Settings? that allows updates to be obtained from PCs on the local network. This should be configured on all devices except for at least one device. At least one device needs to receive updates from the Microsoft update service.

2. You can implement Delivery Optimization for the head office devices, so that updates are received from other PCs on the network. You can also configure bandwidth optimization measures, which restrict the amount of bandwidth that updates consume during defined business hours.

3. You should install Windows 10 Enterprise Version 1809 (Semi-Annual Channel) and then implement policy using Windows Update for Business to defer Windows Feature Updates for the maximum allowed duration of 365 days.

4. Enroll in to the Windows Insider Program and install Windows 10 preview builds. Test these builds for compatibility issues. This should allow you to be ready to test the next Semi-Annual Channel release and obtain compliance sign off quicker.

Scenario 5

1. Users can install the Microsoft Authenticator app on their smartphones or use SMS messages or a voice call to authenticate. (Users without a smartphone can be provided with an OATH hardware token. OATH tokens generate a time-based, one-time password that can be used as a second authentication method.)

2. You can implement Azure AD Password Protection, which will allow up to 1,000 passwords to be checked whenever a user creates or modifies his or her password.

3. You should configure Dynamic Lock.

4. The device should be registered with Azure AD using the user's work account, and it should be enrolled in Microsoft Intune. MDM app protection policies can then deploy the email client app and implement corporate security requirements for when the employee accesses the corporate email app.

Chapter summary

- Dynamic provisioning methods include using Azure AD, Mobile Device Management, provisioning packages, subscription Activation, and Windows Autopilot.
- Dynamic provisioning methods seek to transform an existing Windows 10 installation, rather than replace or upgrade it.
- Provisioning packages are created using the Windows Configuration Designer, which is part of the Windows ADK or as an app from the Microsoft Store.
- Windows Analytics is a cloud-based, free solution that includes Device Health, Update Compliance, and Upgrade Readiness.
- Windows Autopilot allows you to automate the customization of the Out-Of-Box Experience and seamlessly enroll devices into MDM.
- All Windows 10 editions, Version 1703 and newer are licensed to use Windows Autopilot and require Azure AD and an MDM solution.
- The Windows Autopilot Enrollment Status Page allows users to see the progress status page during the device setup.
- Device vendors can extract and register devices with the Windows Autopilot service, or you can use the **Get-WindowsAutoPilotInfo.ps1** PowerShell cmdlet to extract the hardware ID for your existing devices.
- You cannot downgrade from any edition of Windows 10 to Windows 7, 8, or 8.1.
- Windows 10 in S Mode can be switched to another valid edition of Windows 10 at any time using the Microsoft Store.
- Upgrade Readiness, which is part of Windows Analytics, offers free tools for enterprises to plan and manage the upgrade process, end to end.
- When configuring devices to report telemetry to your Windows Analytics environment, you need to add the commercial ID to your devices so that they know where to send their telemetry data.
- You will need to wait for between 48-72 hours after configuring the Windows Analytics requirements before the first data will appear in the solution.
- Whenever possible, you should migrate user profiles and settings to reduce the impact on users.
- Enterprises can securely extract, store, and restore user state using the User State Migration Tool.
- Windows Known Folder Move for OneDrive automatically redirects users' folders and important files to their OneDrive for Business account.
- Cloud-based accounts can have their settings synced using Enterprise State Roaming.
- Windows 10 uses Delivery Optimization to increase the delivery speed of updates and reduce external bandwidth usage.

- Windows Update for Business allows you to manage three types of updates: Quality Updates, Feature Updates, and Non-Deferrable Updates.
- Businesses can defer Quality Updates for up to 30 days, and they can defer Feature Updates for up to a maximum of 365 days.
- You can implement Servicing Channels and Update Rings using Group Policy or Microsoft Intune.
- Windows 10 Enterprise and Education edition updates that are targeted for release in September are supported for up to 30 months from release.
- You can use the Settings app or Update Compliance to monitor Windows 10 updates within an enterprise.
- Windows Hello allows you to use biometrics to authenticate users.
- Azure AD Password Protection allows you to enforce a list of up to 1,000 banned passwords that cannot be used by your users.
- Multifactor authentication requires that users must have two (or more) things with which to identify themselves.
- Windows Hello for Business is the enterprise implementation of Windows Hello and allows users to authenticate to Active Directory or Azure AD, and it enables them to access network resources.
- Dynamic Lock allows users with smartphones to automatically lock their devices whenever they step away from them.

CHAPTER 2

Manage Policies and Profiles

The MD-101 Managing Modern Desktop exam focuses on how you will manage Windows 10 devices using modern management tools and services, such as Microsoft Intune. Because of the recent move toward cloud-based device management, many organizations may currently rely on traditional technologies including Group Policy and System Center Configuration Manager for their device management requirements. Microsoft supports both environments and encourages larger organizations to co-manage their infrastructure using both traditional and modern cloud-based solutions.

You need to understand how to plan and implement co-management and configure devices using both policies and profiles in Microsoft Intune. You will also understand how to use traditional user profile management and learn how Azure Active Directory enables users to roam their Windows settings from any device, even when working remotely.

Skills covered in this chapter:

- Skill 2.1: Plan and implement co-management
- Skill 2.2: Implement conditional access and compliance policies for devices
- Skill 2.3: Configure device profiles
- Skill 2.4: Manage user profiles

Skill 2.1: Plan and implement co-management

Co-management is when you manage devices using both System Center Configuration Manager (SCCM) and Microsoft Intune. Typically, an organization will use co-management if it has already deployed SCCM and have client device scenarios that are suitable for cloud management.

Microsoft Intune implements an industry standard mobile device management (MDM) mechanism for managing mobile devices, such as smart phones, tablets, laptops, and desktop computers. With an implementation such as Microsoft 365, the initial configuration of the MDM authority is enabled, which allows Windows devices to seek configuration and trust Intune. In addition to the Windows 10 operating system, Intune can manage non-Microsoft device platforms from Google and Apple.

Once you decide to manage your devices in a co-managed environment, you need to consider how devices will co-exist and become managed by Configuration Manager and

Intune at the same time. You need to understand the differences between how each management tool will affect your devices.

Some organizations may use co-management as a transition technology, allowing them to manage devices in a traditional manner while exploring how to manage Windows 10 devices using modern management features offered by Intune. There are tools available that you can use to migrate Group Policies to modern management policies within Intune. The number and scope of the features offered by Microsoft Intune has been growing constantly, and this is leading to increased enterprise use. IT administrators are embracing Azure Active Directory and implementing cloud-based functionality such as Windows Autopilot, and Enterprise State Roaming, and the adoption of cloud-management using MDM is becoming more widespread. (Windows Autopilot is discussed in more detail in Chapter 1; Enterprise State Roaming is discussed later in this chapter.)

This skill covers how to:

- Implement co-management precedence
- Migrate group policy to MDM policies
- Recommend a co-management strategy

Implement co-management precedence

Most enterprises currently use a domain-based model for authentication and identity, and this will typically use at least one Windows Server running the Active Directory Domain Services role. In these scenarios, management control will be exerted using Group Policy objects (GPOs) and Configuration Manager. There are some scenarios, such as if an organization is new or small, in which Microsoft Intune can be used to manage all devices and be fully cloud-managed.

As enterprises introduce MDM, they may strive to replicate the existing management control by using modern management functionality, such as Intune policies. In most scenarios, this is not possible because there is no parity between GPO and MDM policies. Microsoft has stated that it has no intention to re-create the many thousands of GPO settings available within traditional management for Intune. However, over the last few years, more Intune functionality has been continually added, including hundreds of extra policies that can be configured. At present, there are more than 800 policies within Intune that are the same or offer similar functionality to those available in Group Policy.

As more functionality is added to Intune, this will lead to an increase in the adoption rate of modern management, especially as IT administrators discover more scenarios that are better or only suited to use MDM. This is particularly evident for modern devices running Windows 10.

Organizations may continue using Configuration Manager for older devices, such as those running Windows 7 or Windows 8.1. In the transition period, newer operating systems can be brought into modern management, and they can even benefit from both Group Policy and MDM policies. The use of Configuration Manager and Intune is referred to as co-management.

Whenever a Windows device is managed by both Group Policy and MDM policies, a decision needs to be made relating to which policy is effective. For devices running Windows 10 Version 1709 and earlier, Group Policy would always take precedence over MDM policy where both policies are applied.

Starting with Windows 10 Version 1803 and later, Intune includes a new Configuration Service Provider (CSP) setting called **ControlPolicyConflict** that includes the **MDMWinsOverGP** policy. This policy allows administrators to configure a preference for which policy wins when both Group Policy and its equivalent MDM policy are configured to apply to the device.

To create a MDMWinsOverGP CSP policy, use these steps:

1. Log in to Intune or Microsoft 365 Device Management as a global administrator.
2. Select Device Configuration and under Manage, select Profiles.
3. Click Create Profile.
4. Enter a name and description for the profile.
5. Under Platform, select Windows 10 And Later.
6. Under Profile Type, select Custom.
7. On the Custom OMA-URI Settings dialog box, click Add.
8. Provide a name and description for the custom setting.
9. In the OMA-URI field, type this policy OMA-URI string: **./Device/Vendor/MSFT/Policy/ Config/ControlPolicyConflict/MDMWinsOverGP**.
10. In the Data Type field, select Integer.
11. In the Value field, type the number **1**, as shown in Figure 2-1. This configures the CSP as the MDM policy that is used and blocks the GP policy. To reverse this setting, enter **0**, which is the default setting.

FIGURE 2-1 MDMWinsOverGP CSP

12. Click OK twice.

13. On the Create Profile blade, click Create.

14. Under Manage, click Assignments.

15. Under Assign To, choose which devices, groups, or users the policy is assigned to and click Save.

Migrate group policy to MDM policies

It is expected that administrators will become more comfortable managing devices using modern management and features, such as remote actions that can be taken on the device. These remote actions include a selective wipe of lost or stolen devices, remote factory reset, and Autopilot reset. As organizations move more data to the cloud and shift away from traditional file server-based storage, MDM features offered by Intune, such as conditional access and mobile application management, are likely to gain more prominence. These features allow organizations to drive down the cost of supporting users and devices, while ensuring that access to their corporate resources is compliant with company security policies.

> **NEED MORE REVIEW?** **POLICIES SUPPORTED BY GROUP POLICY**
>
> If you want to review the list of Group Policies that have equivalent policies within Microsoft Intune, you can use this Microsoft website: *https://docs.microsoft.com/windows/ client-management/mdm/policy-configuration-service-provider#policies-supported-by-gp.*

One of the criticisms of Group Policy has been that as the number of GPOs targeted to a device increase, the local processing slows down the log on time for users. In some scenarios, this can increase log-on time by several minutes.

With MDM, the application of policy is more efficient and streamlined. Therefore, administrators are encouraged to use MDM policies in place of Group Policy whenever possible.

You can use a local tool to evaluate existing Group Policies to determine whether they are suitable candidates for migration to Microsoft Intune. The MDM Migration Analysis Tool (MMAT) is used to evaluate which Group Policies have been set for a target user/device and to cross-reference against its built-in list of supported Intune policies.

You can download the latest MDM Migration Analysis Tool (MMAT) at *https://github.com/ WindowsDeviceManagement/MMAT.*

Once run on a device, MMAT will generate both XML and HTML reports, which indicate the level of support for all Group Policies that have been received by the device and whether MDM provides an equivalent policy.

To run MMAT, use these steps:

1. Download and install Remote Server Administration Tools for your operating system.

2. Using the GitHub link provided earlier, download the MMAT files, and unzip the folder.

3. Open an administrative PowerShell console.

4. Change directory to the MMAT master folder, which contains the PowerShell scripts and the MdmMigrationAnalysisTool.exe.

5. Run the following scripts in PowerShell:

```
Set-ExecutionPolicy -ExecutionPolicy Unrestricted -Scope Process
$VerbosePreference="Continue"
.\Invoke-MdmMigrationAnalysisTool.ps1 -collectGPOReports -runAnalysisTool
```

6. When Invoke-MdmMigrationAnalysisTool.ps1 is completed, review the generated files:

- **MDMMigrationAnalysis.xml** This is an XML report containing information about policies for the target user and computer and how they map, if at all, to MDM.

- **MDMMigrationAnalysis.html** This is an HTML representation of the XML report as shown in Figure 2-2.

- **MdmMigrationAnalysisTool.log** This is a log file with details relating to the last operation of MMAT.

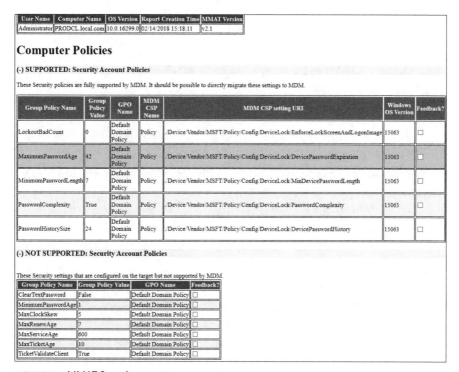

FIGURE 2-2 MMAT Sample output

Microsoft welcomes feedback from customers relating to policies that are not supported by MDM and that are critical to the migration plans of an organization. Microsoft uses the feedback to create the policies that enterprises require, and this will speed up the adoption of MDM. Feedback relating to MMAT can be sent to *mmathelp@microsoft.com*.

> **NOTE**   **MMAT SUPPORTS GROUP POLICY ONLY**
>
> The MDM Migration Analysis Tool Version 2.0 only queries Group Policies. In future iterations of the MMAT tool, other technologies may be supported, such as SCCM, MDM, WMI, and PowerShell. Before taking the MD-101 exam, you should review the current version of the MMAT tool and review any changes.

Recommend a co-management strategy

You have learned that co-management offers many benefits, especially if you have a mixed environment of Windows versions, existing Configuration Manager clients, and new Internet-based devices.

Some of the benefits that can be obtained with devices in a co-management state include

- Conditional access with device-compliance policies.
- Intune-based remote actions, such as Restart, Remote Control, or Factory Reset.
- Centralized visibility of device health status.
- Hybrid Azure Active Directory using Azure AD Connect.
- Users, devices, and apps can be cloud-managed.
- Modern provisioning with Windows Autopilot.

To use co-management, the device needs to be managed by both Configuration Manager and Intune. You choose one of the two options available for your clients:

- **Existing Configuration Manager clients**   Windows 10 devices managed by Configuration Manager already have the Configuration Manager client installed. Once you have set up hybrid Azure AD (using Azure AD Connect), you can enroll the device into Intune.
- **New Internet-based devices**   New Windows 10 devices will join Azure AD and will be enrolled into Intune automatically. You need to install the Configuration Manager client to allow the device to be co-managed.

> **NEED MORE REVIEW?**   **SET UP HYBRID AZURE AD FOR CO-MANAGEMENT**
>
> If you want to learn more about how to join your on-premises domain-joined Windows 10 devices to Azure AD using hybrid Azure AD Join, you can view this Microsoft website: *https://docs.microsoft.com/sccm/comanage/quickstart-setup-hybrid-aad*.

Before you can achieve co-management, you should ensure your organization has implemented the prerequisites shown in Table 2-1.

TABLE 2-1 Co-management prerequisites

CO-MANAGEMENT SCENARIO	PREREQUISITES
Co-management for existing Configuration Manager clients	■ Azure Subscription (or free trial). ■ Azure Active Directory Premium P1 or P2. ■ Microsoft Intune subscription. ■ Users must be assigned licenses for Intune and Azure AD Premium. ■ Azure AD Connect. ■ System Center Configuration Manager Current Branch. ■ MDM Authority must be set to Intune.
Co-management for new Internet-based devices	■ Azure Subscription (or free trial). ■ Azure Active Directory Premium P1 or P2. ■ Microsoft Intune subscription. ■ Users must be assigned licenses for Intune and Azure AD Premium. ■ Intune is configured to auto-enroll devices. ■ System Center Configuration Manager Current Branch Version 1810 or later. ■ MDM Authority must be set to Intune. ■ SSL certificate from a public and globally trusted certificate provider.

When implementing a transition to co-management, organizations are encouraged to deploy a phased approach, which allows administrators to roll out features and functionality to increasing numbers of devices over a defined period. With a staged rollout, support issues and feedback can be obtained and used to improve the process for future groups of users and devices.

You could configure rollout groups based on a number of criteria including

- **Pilot Group** Internal IT groups running Windows 10 Version 1709 or later should be selected for inclusion in the pilot group for co-management. Users should have sufficient technical abilities to provide valuable feedback to the rollout coordinating team.

- **Extended Pilot Group** After a successful pilot rollout, you can choose to roll out co-managing to an extended pilot group. This rollout will incorporate the devices, findings, and feedback from the initial pilot group, and it applies to a larger number of devices and users.

- **Production Group** Once the pilot rollout is completed, you should proceed to configure co-management for your production devices.

- **Exclusion Groups** When configuring a production rollout group, you may select a group of devices that will be excluded from co-management in your production environment, such as computers that run mission-critical applications.

A graphical representation of the rollout groups for staging co-management is shown in Figure 2-3.

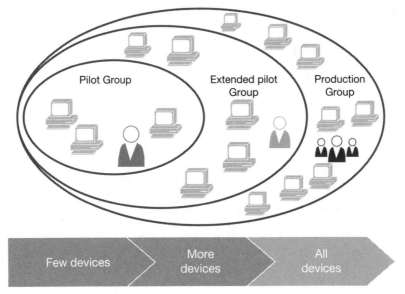

FIGURE 2-3 Co-Management Staging Groups

System Center Configuration Manager (SCCM) and Intune consoles can be used simultaneously to manage different workloads (or device and user scenarios) for the same devices. Some devices may be on-premises; others can be remote, which favors cloud-based management.

> **NOTE HYBRID MOBILE DEVICE MANAGEMENT DEPRECATED**
>
> A previous feature called hybrid mobile device management is now deprecated. Hybrid MDM is not the same as co-management. Support for Hybrid MDM ends September 1, 2019, and new customers can no longer create a new hybrid connection. To determine whether your organization is using Hybrid MDM, launch the Administration workspace of the Configuration Manager console, expand Cloud Services, and click Microsoft Intune Subscriptions. If you have a Microsoft Intune subscription set up, your tenant is configured for Hybrid MDM.

Skill 2.2: Implement conditional access and compliance policies for devices

Once you begin to manage Windows 10 devices using Intune, you will want to implement conditional access to provide granular access control for your corporate resources, such as controlled applications containing your data. Intune works together with Azure Active Directory (Azure AD) to actively check the status of enrolled devices against your conditional access policies each time a resource such as corporate email is accessed.

You need to understand how conditional access policies work, how they are implemented, and how to manage them within your environment.

With Microsoft Intune, you can stipulate the necessary compliance checks that Azure AD will perform on enrolled devices. By deploying compliance policies, devices can be allowed or denied access to your corporate resources, and you need to understand how to plan, implement, and manage them to meet organizational security requirements.

This skill covers how to:

- Plan conditional access policies
- Implement conditional access policies
- Manage conditional access policies
- Plan device compliance policies
- Implement device compliance policies
- Manage device compliance policies

Plan conditional access policies

Intune and Azure AD work together to provide new functionality that is useful for users who access resources while away from the traditional office environment. Modern management offers administrators control over any device that has been enrolled in Intune. Once enrolled, you can control how users and devices can access your corporate data and apps. You can also implement controls to apply depending on the physical location of the device. For example, controls can be implemented for when users are connecting to corporate resources from a trusted network, such as at work or the user's home, or when users are connecting to corporate resources from an untrusted location, such as a café or airport lounge.

When a client device requests access to corporate resources such as data contained in a controlled application, Azure AD will first check whether any conditional access policies are in place with Intune, and if a conditional access policy defines a condition that has not been met. For example, if the device needs to be encrypted, then the device can be denied access to the resource. If the device is brought into compliance, then the access will be granted.

Conditional access provides administrators with a tool that allows complex scenarios to be easily managed, such as in the following examples:

- **Support apps that require multifactor authentication (MFA)** MFA is easy to configure within Azure AD and provides enhanced protection. When conditional access requires MFA to access specified apps, you add an additional layer of protection to your data.

- **Require MFA for untrusted networks** When a user accesses your corporate resources from an untrusted location, such as an airport lounge or coffee shop, you can require extra security measures to be in place. Using conditional access, you can require users to use MFA only when connecting from untrusted locations.

- **Allow Office 365 access only to trusted devices.** If you store all your data in Office 365 services such as Exchange Online, OneDrive for Business, or SharePoint Online, you may require that this data can be accessed only from trusted devices. Using conditional access, only devices enrolled in Intune and PCs that are members of the on-premises domain can be granted access to the Office 365 apps and services.

Conditional access policies use conditions and controls that can be used to build the rules that will be evaluated by Azure AD when determining access to corporate resources. These are defined as shown in Table 2-2.

TABLE 2-2 Conditions and Controls

ELEMENT	DESCRIPTION
Controls	Defines the actions that are allowed or disallowed when a condition is met. Controls include <ul><li>Allowing access</li><li>Blocking access</li><li>Granting access if additional requirements are met</li></ul>
Conditions	Relates to rules that are checked in accordance with conditional access requirements, such as device encryption or password requirements. Conditions can be based on the <ul><li>Device platform being used</li><li>Location from where the data is being accessed</li><li>Client apps that are used to access the data</li></ul>

You can see from Table 2-2 that to evaluate conditional access requirements, Intune needs to obtain the relevant information relating to the status of the device. As part of the MDM framework, extensive information from enrolled devices is exchanged by the built-in device MDM agent and Intune during each sync.

Conditional access policies are enforced after authentication has been completed on the user's device. A visual conceptual overview of conditional access is shown in Figure 2-4.

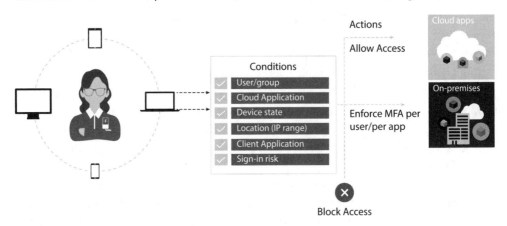

FIGURE 2-4 Conditional Access overview

The device data can be used when generating reports within Intune. Also, the device data can be used when creating membership rules for dynamic groups, which can be used for deploying profiles, policies, and apps to users and devices.

In addition to the detailed list of device details shown in Table 2-3, Intune can obtain a list of installed apps and their versions. This is only available from corporate-owned devices, and the list is updated every 7 days. For corporate-owned Windows 10 devices, only modern apps are retrieved.

TABLE 2-3 Device data available in Intune

DETAIL	DESCRIPTION	PLATFORM
Name	The name of the device.	Windows, iOS
Management Name	The device name used only in the console. Changing this name won't change the name on the device.	Windows, iOS
UDID	The device's Unique Device identifier.	Windows, iOS
Intune Device ID	A GUID that uniquely identifies the device.	Windows, iOS
Serial Number	The device's serial number from the manufacturer.	Windows, iOS
Shared Device	If Yes, the device is shared by more than one user.	Windows, iOS
User Approved Enrollment	If Yes, then the device has user approved enrollment, which lets admins manage certain security settings on the device.	Windows, iOS
Operating System	The operating system used on the device.	Windows, iOS
Operating System Version	The version of the operating system on the device.	Windows, iOS
Operating System Language	The language set for the operating system on the device.	Windows, iOS
Total Storage Space	The total storage space on the device (in gigabytes).	Windows, iOS
Free Storage Space	The unused storage space on the device (in gigabytes).	Windows, iOS
IMEI	The device's International Mobile Equipment Identity.	Windows, iOS, Android
MEID	The device's mobile equipment identifier.	Windows, iOS, Android
Manufacturer	The manufacturer of the device.	Windows, iOS, Android
Model	The model of the device.	Windows, iOS, Android
Phone Number	The phone number assigned to the device.	Windows, iOS, Android
Subscribe Carrier	The device's wireless carrier.	Windows, iOS, Android
Cellular Technology	The radio system used by the device.	Windows, iOS, Android

(Continued)

DETAIL	DESCRIPTION	PLATFORM
WiFi MAC	The device's Media Access Control address.	Windows, iOS, Android
ICCID	The Integrated Circuit Card Identifier, which is a SIM card's unique identification number.	Windows, iOS, Android
Enrolled Date	The date and time the device was enrolled in Intune.	Windows, iOS, Android
Last Contact	The date and time the device last connected to Intune.	Windows, iOS, Android
Activation Lock Bypass Code	The code that can be used to bypass the activation lock.	Windows, iOS, Android
Azure AD Registered	If Yes, the device is registered with Azure Directory.	Windows, iOS, Android
Compliance	The device's compliance state.	Windows, iOS, Android
EAS Activated	If Yes, then the device is synchronized with an Exchange mailbox.	Windows, iOS, Android
EAS Activation ID	The device's Exchange ActiveSync identifier.	Windows, iOS, Android
Supervised	If Yes, administrators have enhanced control over the device.	Windows, iOS, Android
Encrypted	If Yes, the data stored on the device is encrypted.	Windows, iOS, Android

Implement conditional access policies

You can implement conditional access policies either from Azure AD, Intune, or the Microsoft 365 Device Management console. Conditional access policies allow you to automatically control access to your cloud apps and corporate data based on conditions that you define.

You can assign conditional access policies to the following types of objects:

- Users and groups
- Cloud apps
- Devices

You can set conditional access within the Azure AD admin center if you have an Azure AD premium subscription, or you can also set up these same policies from within the Intune portal or the Microsoft 365 Device Management console.

Conditional access policies work alongside compliance policies. A condition is used to check whether a device is compliant with something, such as whether the device is encrypted. If the device passes the compliance check, then the action within the conditional access policy, such as accessing a particular app, will be allowed.

A simplified view of how a conditional access policy is defined is shown in the flow diagram in Figure 2-5.

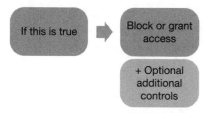

FIGURE 2-5 Devices—conditional access flow

Following is a detailed description of each box in Figure 2-5:

- **If this is true** This defines the reason for triggering the conditional access policy, such as a set of conditions that must be satisfied. You can assign conditional access to Users (Who), or the targeted Cloud apps (What), and then set additional conditions such as location. An example could be: Are members of the Sales Team accessing Microsoft Teams from a Windows device that is being used in a trusted location?

- **Block or grant access** This defines what the policy should do. This could be to block or grant access to the cloud app.

- **Optional additional controls** Once the policy has reached an outcome—to block or grant access—you can then enforce additional requirements, such as require multifactor authentication or require that the device is a Hybrid Azure AD–joined device.

Conditional access policies can be created and not used. They will appear in the Conditional Access–Policies blade. To enforce a conditional access policy, first, you need to enable it.

To create conditional access policy, use these steps.

1. Sign in to the Intune portal at *https://devicemanagement.microsoft.com* as a global administrator.

2. Select Conditional Access, and then on the Policies page, click New Policy.

3. Give the policy a name.

4. Under Assignments, select Users And Groups.

5. On the Include tab, identify the users or groups to whom you want this policy to apply. You can also use the Exclude tab if there are any users, roles, or groups you want to exclude from this policy. Click Done.

6. Under Assignments, select Cloud Apps.

7. On the Include tab, identify the apps and services you want to protect with this policy. You can also use the Exclude tab if there are any apps or services you want to exclude from this policy. Click Done.

8. Under Assignments, select Conditions.

9. Review the following options:

   - **Sign-In Risk** Enables Azure AD Identity Protection sign-in risk detection.
   - **Device Platforms** Specifies the device platforms you want this policy to apply to.
   - **Locations** Specify whether the policy applies to any location, trusted network locations that are under the control of your IT department, or specific network locations.

- **Client Apps** Specify whether the policy should apply to browser apps, mobile apps, and desktop clients. You can also select Modern Authentication Clients (such as Outlook for iOS or Outlook for Android) and Exchange ActiveSync clients.
- **Device State** Choose to apply or exclude specific device states.

10. Select Done.

11. Under Access Controls, select Grant Access or Block Access to enforce the controls as shown in Figure 2-6. If you select Grant Access, you must choose one or many of the following further actions:

- Require Multi-Factor Authentication
- Require Device To Be Marked As Compliant
- Require Hybrid Azure AD Joined Device
- Require Approved Client App
- Require App Protection Policy (Preview)

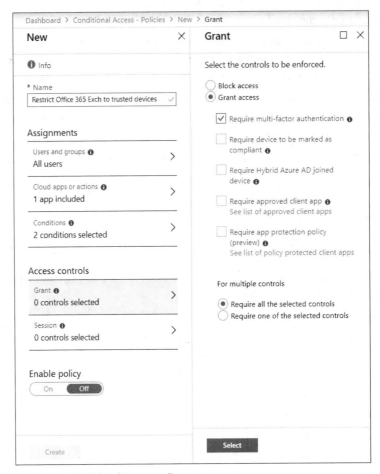

FIGURE 2-6 Conditional Access policy

12. Under For Multiple Controls, select Require All The Selected Controls or select Require One Of The Selected Controls. Click Select.

13. Under Enable Policy, to turn the policy on, select **On**.

14. Select Create.

> **NOTE   CONDITIONAL ACCESS POLICIES**
>
> All conditional access policies are disabled by default. Once you have configured the desired settings, you must enable the policy for it to be processed by Azure AD.

Manage conditional access policies

When you create and use conditional access, you should test each policy on a test user, group, or device to verify that it behaves as expected.

When testing, you can create a set of users within your non-production environment that is similar to the users in your organization. This allows you to verify that your policies work as expected. This minimizes the potential disruption to your real users and their existing access to apps and resources.

As with all testing, you should draw up a test plan, which will record the comparison between the expected results and the actual results. Table 2-4 provides some example test-case scenarios for conditional access. The Actual Result column is blank because this is where you would record what happens in each scenario.

TABLE 2-4 Conditional access test plan

POLICY	SCENARIO	EXPECTED RESULT	ACTUAL RESULT
Require MFA when remote working	Authorized user signs into app from a trusted location, such as work	User isn't prompted to MFA	
Require MFA when remote working	Authorized user signs in to app from an untrusted location, such as a café	User is prompted to MFA and can sign in successfully	
Device management	Authorized user attempts to sign in from an authorized device	Access granted	
Device management	Authorized user attempts to sign in from an unauthorized device	Access blocked	

Once you have verified that your conditional access policies work as expected, you can roll out a policy into a production environment and then continue to monitor the policy and refine it as necessary based on operational feedback.

To manage conditional access capabilities within your enterprise, you should allocate the Conditional Access Administrator role. The Conditional Access Administrator can perform the tasks shown in Table 2-5. Users with the Conditional Access Administrator role only have permissions to view, create, modify, and delete conditional access policies.

TABLE 2-5 Conditional Access Administrator role permissions

ACTIONS	DESCRIPTION
Read	Read conditional access policies in Azure Active Directory
Update	Update conditional access policies in Azure Active Directory
Create	Create conditional access policies in Azure Active Directory
Delete	Delete conditional access policies in Azure Active Directory

> **NOTE EXCHANGE ACTIVESYNC**
>
> To deploy Exchange ActiveSync conditional access policy in Azure AD, the user must also be a Global Administrator.

Plan device compliance policies

Many organizations are regulated and must comply with laws and regulations, such as those shown in Table 2-6. To remain in compliance, administrators need to configure and manage devices and any data contained on them, in accordance with the corporate security and compliance requirements. Modern management allows administrators to control devices and restrict their usage when accessing corporate data.

TABLE 2-6 Regulations and compliance

REGULATION	REGION	REQUIREMENT
HIPAA (Health Insurance Portability and Accountability Act of 1996)	USA	User isn't prompted to MFA.
Sarbanes–Oxley Act	USA	The Chief Financial Officer (CFO) and Chief Executive Officer (CEO) have joint responsibility for the financial data. Administrators will need to keep financial data secure and free from tampering, theft, and deletion.
Gramm–Leach–Bliley Act	USA	Responsibility for security lies within the entire board of directors. IT administrators, while not legally bound, will be delegated the implementation and management of IT security.
GDPR (General Data Protection Regulation)	EU	Requires all enterprises to adhere to EU privacy laws relating to any individual living in the EU.

Using Microsoft Intune, you can define compliance policies. Once compliance policies have been created, they can be assigned to enrolled devices and device groups. Devices will be configured using the compliance policy and become compliant.

Each time that a device attempts to access corporate resources, such as a SharePoint TeamSite or corporate email client, the policy on the device will be evaluated and its compliance status determined. Only compliant devices will be granted access to the resources.

Organizations must have Azure AD Premium P1 or P2 licenses, and each device requires an Intune license to use compliance policies.

The following device platforms can be managed using compliance policies once they have been enrolled into Intune:

- Android and Android Enterprise
- iOS and macOS
- Windows 10, Windows 8.1, and Windows Phone 8.1

When considering how your organization will achieve compliance, you may need to review the features available and support for compliance policies. Each compliance policy within Intune is platform specific, and the actual compliance policy settings available will vary depending on the settings that are exposed to the MDM framework by the platform vendor. For example, BitLocker encryption is only available on Windows devices and Google Play Protect is available only on the Android platform.

Some of the more commonly used device compliance settings that you can implement include:

- **Require A Password To Access Devices**   For example, a PIN or password.
- **Local Data Encryption**   BitLocker encryption or other boot protection such as Secure Boot.
- **Is The Device JailBroken Or Rooted**   Often, a device that has been jailbroken or rooted will be more vulnerable to malware attack.
- **Minimum Operating System Version Required**   Prevents outdated software being used, which may be more vulnerable to malware attack.
- **Maximum Operating System Version Allowed**   Prevents software that has not been tested or approved for corporate use from being used.
- **Protected Against Malware Threats**   Requires the device to have an antimalware solution enabled, signatures are up to date, or real-time protection is enabled.
- **Network Location-Based**   Blocks access to a corporate network if a device leaves a defined location.

Noncompliant devices

An unenrolled device that attempts to access corporate resources will be deemed to be noncompliant and access will be blocked. If a user subsequently enrolls the device in Intune and re-attempts to access corporate resources, the Intune compliance policies will be evaluated again, and the device may or may not be granted access based on the current policies in place.

The outcome for noncompliant, but enrolled devices will typically be to block access to company resources. However, you can configure actions for noncompliance as follows:

- **Send Email To End User**   You can customize an email notification that is sent to the end user. You can customize the recipients, subject, and message body. Also, you can add a company logo and contact information. Lastly, you can add any instructions on how the user can bring the device into a compliant state.

- **Remotely Lock The Noncompliant Device**   Devices that are noncompliant can be remotely locked. The user will need to enter a PIN or password to unlock the device.

- **Mark Device Non-Compliant**   The non-compliant device can be allowed access to company resources as long as the device is made compliant within a specified grace period. After the grace period has expired, non-compliant devices will be blocked. Alternatively, the grace period can be set to zero, and the action will take effect immediately.

To configure a notification email message template, use these steps:

1. Sign into the Intune portal at *https://devicemanagement.microsoft.com* as a global administrator.

2. Select Device Compliance and then under Manage, click Notifications.

3. Select Create Notification.

4. On the Create Notification blade, as shown on Figure 2-7, enter information for the email Name, Subject, and Message.

5. On the Email Header–Include Company Logo, select Enable or Disable.

6. On the Email Footer–Include Company Name, select Enable or Disable.

7. On the Email Footer–Include Contact Information, select Enable or Disable.

8. Click Create.

> *NOTE* **CORPORATE LOGO AND BRANDING WITHIN INTUNE**
>
> You can add your corporate logo, branding, and support information to the notification email, which will provide a familiar and helpful experience for your users. From the Intune Dashboard, select Client Apps. Under Setup, choose Branding And Customization, and then configure the required settings.

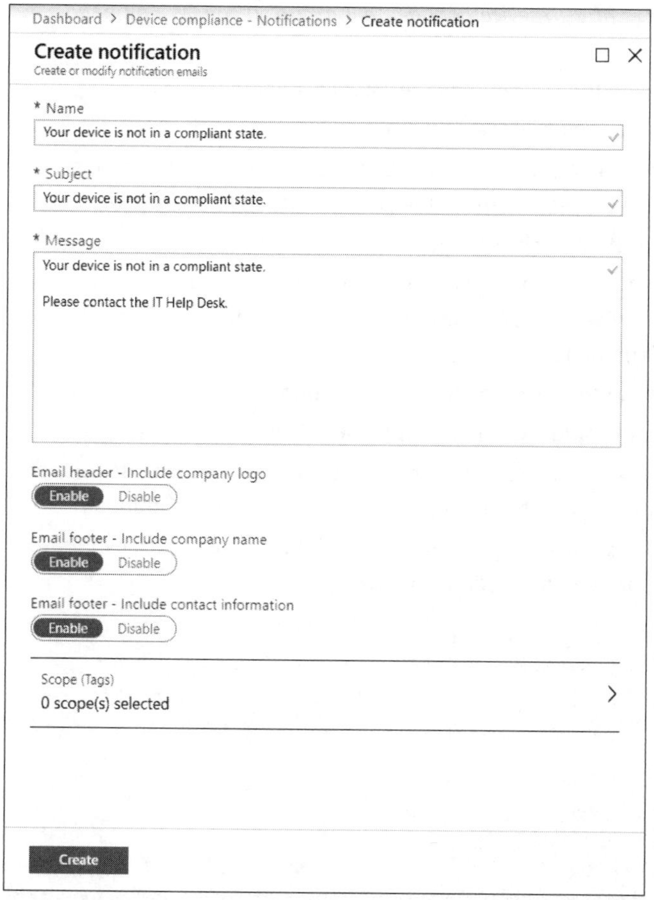

Create notification
Create or modify notification emails

☐ ✕

* Name

Your device is not in a compliant state.   ✓

* Subject

Your device is not in a compliant state.   ✓

* Message

Your device is not in a compliant state.   ✓

Please contact the IT Help Desk.

Email header - Include company logo
Enable Disable

Email footer - Include company name
Enable Disable

Email footer - Include contact information
Enable Disable

Scope (Tags)
0 scope(s) selected   >

Create

FIGURE 2-7 Configure notification email

Network location–based compliance policy

Managing devices is easy when they are confined within a traditional office setting. Administrators often find that once mobile devices are permanently away from the office and require access to corporate resources, the challenge of managing them can become more difficult.

Within the office, devices are provided with network access, such as wired ethernet and secured WiFi connections. Access to corporate resources via office-based devices is strictly controlled and monitored, with all user activity to cloud apps and web traffic subject to firewall constraints and corporate security and compliance scrutiny.

Using MDM, administrators can block access to a corporate network, app, or resource even when a device leaves a location. You must first define a location within Intune to provide this functionality.

To create a network location–based compliance policy (also known as network fencing), use these steps.

1. Sign into the Intune portal at *https://devicemanagement.microsoft.com* as a global administrator.
2. Select Device Compliance and then under Manage, click Locations.
3. On the Device Compliance–Locations page, click Create.
4. On the Create Location page, as shown in Figure 2-8, complete the following properties. Note that some properties are required, and some are optional, as noted below.
   - Enter a Name for the location, such as Head Office. (Required)
   - Enter an IPv4 Range with CIDR (Classless Interdomain Routing) notation, such as **10.0.1.0/22**. If the device uses one of these IPv4 addresses, then the device will be deemed compliant. (Optional)
   - Enter the IPv4 Gateway address, such as **10.0.1.254**. (Optional)
   - Enter the IPv4 DHCP Server address, such as **10.0.1.10**. (Optional)
   - Enter a list of IPv4 DNS Server addresses, such as: **10.0.10.1**. If the device uses one of these IPv4 DNS Server addresses, then the device will be compliant. (Optional)
   - Enter a list of DNS Suffixes, such as: **cycleshare.com**. If the device uses one of these DNS Suffixes, then the device will be compliant. (Optional)
5. Click Save.

FIGURE 2-8 Create location

Once you have created one or more locations, you can create a policy to ensure devices must be connected to a trusted work network to be compliant. The policy can be used with conditional access policies to provide access to corporate resources only when the device is connected to the work network as defined in the location. Whenever the device moves away from the work network, the device becomes not compliant and loses access to corporate resources.

You can create a standalone compliance policy that requires devices to be connected to your corporate network, which is assigned to the device or device group. This is then evaluated independently, or you can use an existing compliance policy and select a pre-defined location within the policy properties.

To add a location to an existing compliance policy, use these steps.

1. Sign into the Intune portal at *https://devicemanagement.microsoft.com* as a global administrator.
2. Select Device Compliance and then under Manage, click Policies.
3. On the Device Compliance blade, select an existing compliance policy.
4. Under Manage, click Properties.
5. On the Properties blade, choose Locations.
6. On the Locations blade, click Select Locations.
7. From the list on the Select Locations blade, check your location and choose Select.
8. Click Save, and then on the Policy Properties page, click Save.

Once you have added a location in a compliance policy, if the device isn't connected to the selected locations, then it's immediately considered not compliant.

Implement device compliance policies

Device compliance policies can be used with or without conditional access policies and achieve the following outcomes:

- **With conditional access.** Devices in compliance can access corporate resources. Devices that are not compliant will be blocked from accessing corporate resources.
- **Without conditional access.** Effectively, these policies evaluate the compliance status of a device only. Used alone, there are no access restrictions to corporate resources because of a compliance policy.

You can use compliance policies without conditional access policies to evaluate the status of your devices. You can report information relating to device platform characteristics, such as

- The number of devices that do not have compliance policies
- The number of devices that are not encrypted

- Whether devices are jailbroken or rooted
- Threat agent status

A list of the device attributes that can be reported is shown earlier in Table 2-3.

Create a device compliance policy

Before creating a device compliance policy, you should create a compliance notification so that Intune understands how to respond to both compliant and non-compliant devices. You created a compliance notification in the previous section. With the notification in place, it serves as a backstop should the device be non-compliant.

Perform these steps to create an Intune compliance policy that requires enrolled Android devices to enter a password of a specific length before access is granted to corporate resources:

1. Sign into the Intune portal at *https://devicemanagement.microsoft.com* as a global administrator.
2. Select Device Compliance and then under Manage, click Policies.
3. On the Device Compliance blade, click Create Policy.
4. In the Name field, type **Android Password Compliance** and add a Description.
5. Under Platform, select Android.
6. Select Settings and then on the Android Compliance Policy blade, click System Security.
7. On the System Security blade, click Require for the Require A Password To Unlock Mobile Devices option.
8. Select At Least Numeric for the Required Password Type option, as shown in Figure 2-9.
9. Type **6** in the Minimum Password Length dialog box.
10. Review the remaining security settings.
11. Click OK twice, and then click Create to create the policy.
12. Under Manage, click Assignments.
13. Under Assign To, choose the Android device or device group to assign the policy to, click Select, and then click Save.

When you've successfully created the compliance policy and assigned it, the policy will appear in your list of device-compliance policies.

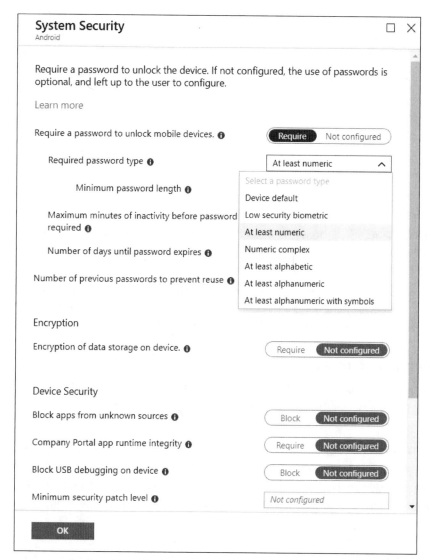

FIGURE 2-9 Configure Compliance Policy

Manage device compliance policies

Once you have created compliance policies within MDM, you can enforce the protection of your organizational data by requiring users and devices to meet business requirements. You have seen that the rules and settings available are extensive; when combined with conditional access, these rules and settings allow administrators to block users and devices that don't meet the rules.

Whenever a device has a compliance policy assigned, a compliance status will be determined, as shown in Table 2-7.

TABLE 2-7 Compliance policy status

STATUS	SEVERITY
Unknown	1
NotApplicable	2
Compliant	3
InGracePeriod	4
NonCompliant	5
Error	6

You can see that the severity increases where the device is in an error state or is non-compliant. The severity is reported to Microsoft Intune and is used when determining access to your organizational data.

When a device has multiple policies assigned, the device may have different compliance statuses. In these situations, Intune assigns a single resulting compliance status, which is based on the highest severity level of all the policies that are assigned to that device.

> **NOTE   WHEN POLICIES CONFLICT**
>
> If a device has two policies applied and one is compliant and the other non-compliant, the resulting status for the device will be non-compliant.

Policy refresh cycle times

Devices connect to Intune on a periodic basis and the compliance status is checked. The refresh cycle is the same as configuration profiles and can be found in Table 2-8. You will notice that if a device has been recently enrolled, the compliance check-in runs more frequently during this initial period.

TABLE 2-8 Compliance policy refresh cycle

PLATFORM	INITIAL CHECK-IN FREQUENCY	ONGOING REFRESH CYCLE
iOS	Every 15 minutes for 6 hours, and then every 6 hours	6 hours
macOS	Every 15 minutes for 6 hours, and then every 6 hours	6 hours
Android	Every 3 minutes for 15 minutes; then every 15 minutes for 2 hours; and then every 8 hours	8 hours
Windows 10 (enrolled as a device)	Every 3 minutes for 30 minutes, and then every 8 hours	8 hours
Windows 8.1	Every 5 minutes for 15 minutes; then every 15 minutes for 2 hours; and then every 8 hours	8 hours

If a user opens the Company Portal app on his or her device, the user can sync the device to immediately check for new or updated policies. The Company Portal app also shows the compliance status of the managed device. For scenarios that include urgent compliance actions, such as Wipe, Lock, Passcode Reset, New App Deployment, New Profile Deployment, Or New Policy Deployment, Intune will immediately notify the devices to perform a sync.

Skill 2.3: Configure device profiles

Administrators can implement Mobile Device Management (MDM) functionality using Microsoft Intune or to a more limited extent, with MDM for Office 365. In addition to managing settings on iOS and Android mobile devices, MDM allows you to configure policies that control settings on any Windows 10 device, such as desktop PCs and laptops.

Administrators can now manage devices from the cloud using an MDM solution such as Intune. By removing the traditional domain-based constraints that are often imposed on devices, MDM allows new management and device functionality to be used. You need to understand how devices enrolled into Azure Active Directory and Intune can be cloud-managed. Also, you need to understand how you can plan and use profiles and policies to configure devices, control user access, and set device settings to comply with company security and compliance policy.

> **This skill covers how to:**
> - Plan device profiles
> - Implement device profiles
> - Manage device profiles

Plan device profiles

When planning how your organization will use MDM to manage your devices, there are several areas that you should include in your scope.

Intune uses Azure Active Directory (Azure AD) for authentication, and if you already have a local Active Directory Domain Services (AD DS) environment, you can connect the two identity services using a tool called Azure AD Connect. You have seen in the "Skill 2.1: Plan and implement co-management" section of this chapter that you can also co-manage devices using both System Center Configuration Manager (SCCM) and Intune.

The two common elements to modern management are your users, and the devices they use. In a traditional environment, an administrator will retain full control of a user's computing environment, including the user's desktop, by using SCCM or Group Policy. This can be restrictive for the user, but it can also provide the strictest level of control for the administrator. Using Intune, a similar level of control is possible. Also, the cloud-based nature of Intune can be especially useful for devices that are beyond the management scope of Group Policy, such as in the following scenarios:

- Devices that are not domain members
- Mobile phones
- Windows 10 devices that are joined to Azure AD only
- Devices that are used entirely remotely and without access to VPN solutions

Intune provides excellent features for managing devices that connect to your corporate data, allowing you to remain compliant with your corporate security and compliance requirements. All enrolled devices can be forced to comply with the device configuration policies you have defined.

MDM is a platform-independent device management protocol that is supported by mobile phones, tablets, and PCs. Intune includes settings and features that you can enable or disable on a variety of mobile devices. Microsoft has built the MDM functionality into PCs running Windows 10. Because of the built-in MDM client within Windows 10, Intune is capable of fully managing Windows 10 as though it is a mobile device. The full list of platforms supported by Intune through device enrollment is as follows:

- Apple iOS 9.0 and later
- Mac OS X 10.9 and later
- Android 4.4 and later, including Samsung Knox 4.4 and later and Android for Work
- Windows Phone 8.1, Windows RT 8.1, and Windows 8.1 (sustaining mode)
- Windows 10 and Windows 10 Mobile
- Windows 10 IoT Enterprise and Windows 10 IoT Mobile Enterprise

Because of the variety of platforms and devices, not all settings and features are available to be configured on every device platform. You should review the settings and features that you can add to a configuration profile for the different devices and different platforms that you use—or plan to use—in your organization.

You can view the most common device profiles in Table 2-9. Profile features are available on supported devices, indicated with an X.

The number and scope of the built-in device settings that are supported by Intune continues to grow as more organizations provide feedback to Microsoft requesting additional support for new scenarios. For each new Windows 10 version, there will be new MDM functionality added to the built-in MDM client to reflect new features that ship with that version of Windows 10.

In Table 2-9, the last item relates to creating custom Open Mobile Alliance Uniform Resource Identifier (OMA-URI) profiles. Custom profiles allow you to create and use device settings and features that aren't natively built in to Intune. If a setting or feature is supported on devices in your organization, you should be able to create a custom profile that sets the same feature for every device by using OMA-URI settings.

TABLE 2-9 Common Intune device-configuration profiles

PROFILE	DESCRIPTION	ANDROID	ANDROID ENTERPRISE	IOS	MAC OS	WINDOWS 10
Email	Manages Exchange ActiveSync settings on devices.	X	X	X		X
Device restrictions	Prevent device usage, such as disabling the built-in camera, connecting to Bluetooth devices, or using cellular data.	X	X	X	X	X
WiFi	Allows you to manage wireless network settings for users and devices. In Windows 10, managing settings for users allows them to connect to corporate WiFi without having to configure the connection manually. Instead, users can import a configuration that was previously exported from another device.	X	X	X	X	X
Administrative templates (Preview)	Allows you to manage hundreds of settings for Internet Explorer, OneDrive, Remote Desktop, Word, Excel, and other Office programs for Windows 10 devices. Administrative templates (Preview) provide a simplified view of settings similar to group-policy. Windows 10 Version 1703 and later.					X
Kiosk	Allows you to configure a device to run one or multiple apps, such as a web browser. This feature supports Windows 10, and kiosk settings are also available as device restrictions for Android, Android Enterprise, and iOS devices.	X	X	X		X
VPN	Configures VPN settings for devices. This feature supports: ■ Android ■ Android Enterprise ■ iOS ■ macOS ■ Windows Phone 8.1 ■ Windows 8.1 ■ Windows 10 and later	X	X	X	X	X
Education	Configures options for the Take a Test app in Windows 10. iOS uses the iOS Classroom app.			X		X
Certificates	Allows you to configure trust and other certificates used for WiFi, VPN, and email profiles.	X	X	X		X
Edition upgrade	Allows you to permit users to upgrade some versions of Windows 10.					X
Endpoint protection	Configures settings for BitLocker and Windows Defender.					X
Windows Information Protection	Allows you to configure Windows Information Protection for data loss prevention.					X
Custom profile	Custom settings allow administrators to assign device settings that aren't built in to Intune. These use the Open Mobile Alliance Uniform Resource Identifier (OMA-URI) values for Android and Windows devices. For iOS devices, you can import a configuration file you created in the Apple Configurator or Apple Profile Manager.	X	X	X	X	X

Implement device profiles

A device profile allows you to add and configure settings which can then be deployed to devices enrolled in management within your organization. Once the device receives the device profile, the features and settings are applied automatically.

To create a device profile for Windows 10 devices that will configure BitLocker Drive Encryption for enrolled devices, use these steps:

1. Sign in to the Intune portal at *https://devicemanagement.microsoft.com* as a global administrator.

2. Select Device Configuration.

3. Under Manage, select Profiles, and then click Create Profile.

4. On the Create Profile blade, enter the following properties:

   - **Name**   Enter a descriptive name for the profile.

   - **Description**   Enter a description for the profile.

   - **Platform**   Choose the device platform.

   - **Profile Type**   Select the type of settings you want to create. You can find the list of the common configuration types in Table 2-9. (The list shown depends on the platform you choose.) Choose Endpoint Protection.

5. Under Settings, click Configure.

6. Under Endpoint Protection, click Windows Encryption.

7. The Windows Encryption dialog box appears. Under Windows Settings, to the right of Encrypt Devices, click Require, as shown in Figure 2-10.

8. Review the other settings within this blade and then click OK.

9. On the Endpoint Protection blade, review the other settings available and then click OK.

10. On the Create Profile blade, click Create.

To assign the policy to users, devices, or groups, click Assignments under Manage on the Device Configuration Profile blade.

Deploy Administrative Template Profiles

In addition to using built-in configuration profiles and custom profiles, Windows 10 Version 1703 and later allows you to expand the current set of built-in policies by using Group Policy administrative templates (ADMX-backed policies). The ADMX-backed policies offer administrators the ability to implement GPO settings via Intune for both user and device targets. The current functionality is in Preview release at the time of writing and adds more than 250 popular settings to Intune.

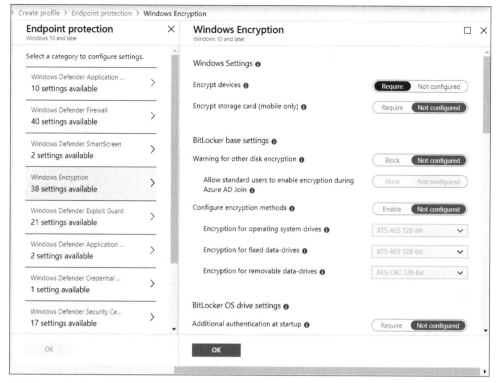

FIGURE 2-10 Configure device configuration policy

To create a template for a Windows 10 device using an administrative template, use these steps:

1. Sign into the Intune portal at *https://devicemanagement.microsoft.com* as a global administrator.
2. Select Device Configuration.
3. Under Manage, select Profiles, and then click Create Profile.
4. On the Create Profile page, enter the following properties:
   - **Name** Enter a name for the profile.
   - **Description** Enter a description for the profile.
   - **Platform** Select Windows 10 and later.
   - **Profile Type** Select Administrative Templates (Preview).
5. Select Create.
6. On the Administrative Template Profile (Preview) blade, under Manage, select Settings.
7. Use the Search bar at the top to search for a setting or scroll through the pages of settings.

8. Select a setting, for example, select Allow Users To Connect Remotely By Using Remote Desktop Services (see Figure 2-11). Choose Enabled, Disabled, or leave the setting as Not Configured (default).

9. Select OK to save your changes.

10. Close the Administrative Template Profile (Preview) blade.

11. The profile appears in the Profiles list.

For the Administrative Template Profile (Preview) to be applied to an enrolled device, you need to assign the profile to users or devices using Azure (Azure AD) groups. This is covered in the "Manage device profiles" section of this chapter.

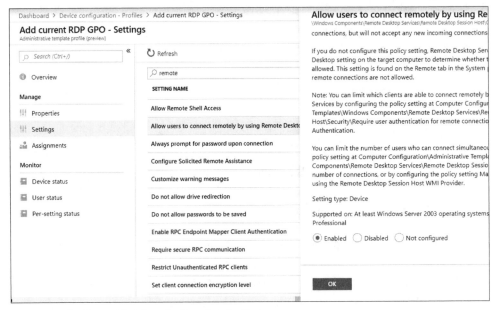

FIGURE 2-11 Configure Administrative Template Profiles

> **NEED MORE REVIEW?** **UNDERSTANDING ADMX-BACKED POLICIES**
>
> If you want to know how to use ADMX-backed policies, use this Microsoft website: *https://docs.microsoft.com/en-us/windows/client-management/mdm/understanding-admx-backed-policies*.

Deploy PowerShell scripts in Intune

For Windows 10 devices running Version 1607 or later, you can upload PowerShell scripts in Intune, which can then be run on Windows 10 devices. Intune includes a management extension, which facilitates adding PowerShell scripts. In addition to the Windows 10 version, you must also enable automatic MDM enrollment in Azure AD, and devices must be auto-enrolled to Intune. Deployment of PowerShell scripts using Intune is supported for all enrolled Windows 10 devices that are Azure AD–joined, Hybrid Azure AD domain–joined, or co-managed.

When you choose to run a PowerShell script using Intune, there are three script settings, as shown in Table 2-10.

TABLE 2-10 PowerShell script runtime settings

SETTING	DESCRIPTION
Run This Script Using The Logged-On Credentials	By default, the script will run in the system context. Optionally, this can be modified to run the script with the user's credentials on the device.
Enforce Script Signature Check	By default, the signature check is not enforced. If there is a requirement for the script to be signed, you can choose to enforce the signature check, and the script must be signed by a trusted publisher.
Run Script In 64-Bit PowerShell Host	By default, the script is run in a 32-bit PowerShell host. Optionally, you can choose to run the script in a 64-bit PowerShell host on a 64-bit client.

For example, you can create a PowerShell script that installs a Win32 app to your Windows 10 device. This scenario involves these stages:

- Write a PowerShell script to install Win32 app.
- Upload the script to Intune as a Device Configuration profile.
- Configure the script runtime settings.
- Assign the script to an Azure AD group of users or devices.
- The script runs on the assigned group.
- You can then use Intune to monitor the run status of the script.

To create a PowerShell script policy, use these steps.

1. Sign in to the Intune portal at *https://devicemanagement.microsoft.com* as a global administrator.
2. Select Device Configuration.
3. Under Manage, select PowerShell Scripts.
4. On the Device Configuration PowerShell Scripts blade, click Add.
5. Enter a Name and Description for the PowerShell script.
6. Next to Script Location, browse to the PowerShell script file. (The script must be less than 200KB [ASCII] or 100KB [Unicode] in size.)
7. Under Settings, click Configure.
8. On the Script Setting blade, choose the appropriate script runtime settings for the PowerShell script, as shown in Figure 2-12.
9. Select OK.
10. On the Add PowerShell Script blade, click Create.

To assign the policy to users, devices, or groups, click Assignments under Manage on the Device Configuration Profile blade.

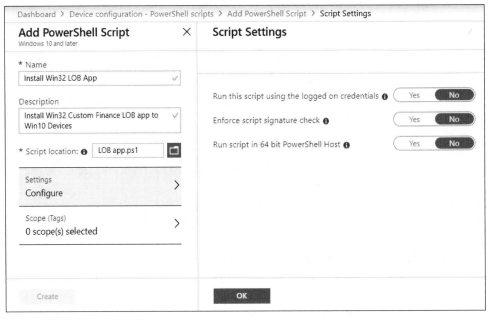

FIGURE 2-12 Add PowerShell Script

Once you have uploaded a PowerShell script to Intune, the management extension client checks with Intune for any new PowerShell scripts or changes; this check is done once every hour and after every reboot. After the PowerShell script has been executed on a targeted device, the PowerShell script is not executed again unless there's a change in the script or policy.

> **NOTE POWERSHELL PERMISSIONS**
> When you deploy PowerShell scripts using Intune, the script can be executed with or without a user signed in to the device. PowerShell scripts can be targeted to Azure AD device security groups and Azure AD user security groups.

Manage device profiles

For a device profile to be applied to an enrolled device, you need to assign the profile to users or devices using Azure (Azure AD) groups.

To assign a device profile using Azure (Azure AD) groups, follow these steps.

1. Sign in to the Intune portal at *https://devicemanagement.microsoft.com* as a global administrator.

2. Select Device Configuration.

3. Under Manage, select Profiles. If a profile has been assigned, there will be a Yes status under the Assigned column in the list of profiles.

4. On the Device Configuration\Profiles blade, select the profile that you want to assign.

5. On the Device Configuration Profile page for your profile, under Manage, select Assignments.

6. Choose either the Include or Exclude tab, select the Selected Groups item from the Assign To drop-down menu, and then select the Azure AD groups, as shown in Figure 2-13. You can select multiple groups by selecting them one at a time. Alternatively, you can also choose from three pre-defined groups:

   - All Users & All Devices
   - All Devices
   - All Users

7. Click Select.

8. On the menu, click Save.

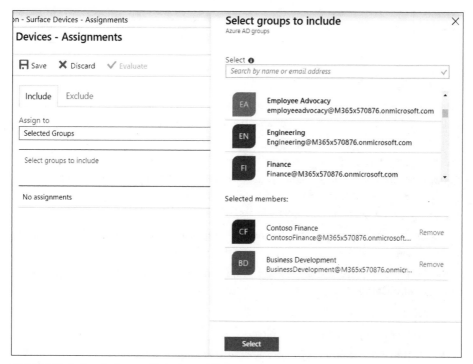

FIGURE 2-13 Assign device profile to Azure AD groups

You can also exclude groups from policy assignment by using the Exclude tab, as shown in Figure 2-13. Care should be taken to ensure that the assignment outcome is as desired. You can use the Evaluate option on the menu bar, which will evaluate the number of users who will be affected by the selection.

Policy refresh cycle times

The refresh cycle for device configuration policies is the same as the compliance profiles, which can be found in Table 2-11.

TABLE 2-11 Compliance policy refresh cycle

PLATFORM	INITIAL CHECK-IN FREQUENCY	ONGOING REFRESH CYCLE
iOS	Every 15 minutes for 6 hours, and then every 6 hours	6 hours
macOS	Every 15 minutes for 6 hours, and then every 6 hours	6 hours
Android	Every 3 minutes for 15 minutes; then every 15 minutes for 2 hours; and then every 8 hours	8 hours
Windows 10 (enrolled as a device)	Every 3 minutes for 30 minutes, and then every 8 hours	8 hours
Windows Phone	Every 5 minutes for 15 minutes; then every 15 minutes for 2 hours; and then every 8 hours	8 hours
Windows 8.1	Every 5 minutes for 15 minutes; then every 15 minutes for 2 hours; and then every 8 hours	8 hours

Scope tags

When you create Intune policies and after you add the settings, you can also add a scope tag to the profile. Scope tags are used to assign and filter policies to specific groups, such as your marketing team or sales employees.

You can also use scope tags to provide admins with the right level of access and visibility to objects in Intune. In this scenario, you would combine Azure AD role-based access control (RBAC) and scope tags. The role determines what access admins have to which objects, and the scope tags determine which objects admins can see.

To add a scope tag to a policy, you must have already created the tag. To add a scope tag, use these steps:

1. Sign in to the Intune portal at *https://devicemanagement.microsoft.com* as a global administrator.
2. Select Roles.
3. Under Manage, select Scope (Tags).
4. On the Intune Roles–Scope (Tags) blade, click Create.
5. On the Create Scope Tag blade, enter a Name for your Tag and an optional description.
6. Click Create.
7. The Scope Tag is created and appears in the list.

TO ADD A SCOPE TAG TO A CONFIGURATION PROFILE

Once you have created one or more scope tags, you can add them to your device configuration profile using these steps:

1. Sign in to the Intune portal at *https://devicemanagement.microsoft.com* as a global administrator.

2. Select Device Configuration.

3. Under Manage, select Profiles.

4. On the Device Configuration–Profiles page, choose a profile.

5. On the Device Configuration Profile page, select Properties.

6. Click Scope (Tags), and on the Tags blade, click Add.

7. On the Select Tags blade, choose the tag(s) that you want to add to the profile, as shown in Figure 2-14.

8. Choose Select, and then click OK.

9. On the Device Configuration Profile page, click Save.

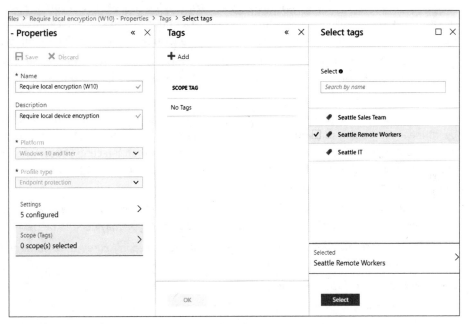

FIGURE 2-14 Add Scope Tags

The Intune Service Admins and Global Admins roles have full admin access to all the Intune features, regardless of what scope tags have been configured.

Common issues and troubleshooting

Some of the common issues and resolutions that you may encounter with policies and profiles with Intune relate to profile conflicts and Azure AD enrollment.

When two profile settings are applied to the same device, the most restrictive value will be applied. Any settings that are the same in each policy are applied as configured.

If a policy is deployed to a device and is active when a second policy is deployed, then the first policy takes precedence, and it will stay applied. Any conflicting settings are set to the most restrictive values.

You may also consider how different types of policy interact with each other.

- Compliance policy settings have precedence over configuration profile settings.
- If a compliance policy includes the same setting found in another compliance policy, then the most restrictive compliance policy setting will be applied.
- If a configuration policy setting conflicts with a setting in another configuration policy, the conflict will be displayed in Intune. You will need to manually resolve the conflict.

If you configure custom policies, you should know that Intune doesn't evaluate the payload of a custom Open Mobile Alliance Uniform Resource Identifier (OMA-URI) policy. Intune will deliver the policy without reference to other policies, and this can cause potential conflicts.

You should confirm that the configured settings within a custom policy don't conflict with compliance, configuration, or other custom policies. For example, if iOS custom policy settings conflict, then the settings are applied randomly.

If Intune policies are not being applied to a specific device, or PowerShell scripts deployed by Intune are not being run, you may need to troubleshoot the client. You should first perform a full reboot of the device by holding down the Shift key and then selecting Shutdown from Start. After powering on the device, the Intune client built into Windows 10 should check whether any changes or new policies are available.

You should allow devices time after rebooting to sync to Intune and receive any changes. Sometimes, the sync can take several minutes to complete, so you may need to be patient.

Devices won't receive policy if the device is not auto-enrolled in Azure AD. To confirm that a device is auto-enrolled, perform these steps:

1. On the client device, open the Settings app.
2. Click Accounts.
3. Under Accounts, click Access Work Or School.
4. Select the joined account and click Info.
5. Under Advanced Diagnostic Report, select Create Report.
6. Open the MDMDiagReport in a web browser and locate the Enrolled Configuration Sources section.
7. If you cannot find the MDMDeviceWithAAD property, then the device is not auto enrolled and will need to be enrolled to receive policies.

Skill 2.4: Manage user profiles

Unless you intend to use a device solely in a kiosk role or as an interactive display without a user, you need to understand the various types of user profiles that can exist on Windows 10 devices. Device profiles hold information and settings relating to the device user and provide the user with a consistent and personalized experience while using the device.

There are several profile types that can be configured, and you need to understand when each type should be used; also, you need to understand how data is stored within the profile. Modern devices are increasingly connected to Microsoft cloud services and enrolled in Azure Active Directory. Being cloud-enabled allows devices to roam their profile data between multiple devices, which allows user and app settings to sync between devices, wherever the user is located. This is known as Enterprise State Roaming. You need to know how to configure Enterprise State Roaming and understand when this feature is beneficial to use within an organization.

With internet connectivity becoming ubiquitous in the modern workplace, more enterprises are seeking to reduce or restrict data that can be stored locally on devices. You need to understand how to move data off devices and redirect it to cloud-based storage, such as OneDrive for Business.

This skill covers how to:

- Configure user profiles
- Configure sync settings
- Implement Folder Redirection
- Implement OneDrive Known Folder Move
- Configure Enterprise State Roaming in Azure AD

Configure user profiles

The types of user profiles that were available with earlier versions of Windows continue to exist with Windows 10. When a user first signs into a device, a user profile is created, and this is based on the Default profile in the Users folder.

This user profile is then loaded by the system at subsequent logons, and the user's environment and system components are configured according to the information in the profile.

A user profile consists of two elements.

- **A registry hive** Each user profile contains a Ntuser.dat file. When a user signs in to Windows, the system loads this file into the registry and maps it to the HKEY_CURRENT_USER registry subtree. The user part of the registry contains user settings, such as desktop background and screen saver.
- **A set of profile folders stored in the file system** Each user profile created by Windows has a separate subfolder with his or her name. The Users folder contains a

set of folders that contain user settings, application settings, and user data in various subfolders, such as AppData, Desktop, Downloads, and Documents.

There are multiple types of user profiles: Local, Roaming, Mandatory, Super Mandatory, and Temporary User Profiles.

- **Local User Profiles** A local user profile is stored on the computer's local hard disk. Any changes made to the local user profile belong to the user and to the computer on which the changes are made.

- **Roaming User Profiles** A roaming user profile is a copy of the local profile that has been copied to and stored on the network, such as a server share. Each time the user logs on to a device on the network, this profile is used. If the profile has been modified since the last logon on the current device, Windows will download the latest profile from the network location. Changes made to a roaming user profile are synchronized with the network copy of the profile each time the user logs off. Roaming user profiles allow the user to use his or her personalized environment and system settings on each computer he or she uses on a network. One of the downsides to using this type of profile is that if a user has a large profile—for example, the user stores and works with many large files on the desktop—then signing in to the user's computer might take a long time. When using roaming user profiles, folders such as Temporary Internet Files or AppData\Local are not synchronized.

- **Mandatory User Profiles** A mandatory user profile is a fixed profile. Any user changes to the desktop settings are lost when the user logs off. An administrator can make changes to mandatory user profiles. This type of profile is usually quick to load and allows administrators to deploy a consistent, if inflexible, environment to users. Another scenario when mandatory user profiles are used is for kiosk devices or in educational environments. Only system administrators can make changes to mandatory user profiles. To create a mandatory user profile, an administrator should first configure a roaming user profile, modify the profile settings as required, and then rename the NTuser.dat file (the registry hive) to Ntuser.man. The .man extension creates the read-only mandatory profile, and all user modifications to the profile will not be saved.

- **Super-Mandatory User Profiles** A super-mandatory profile is when an administrator adds the .man extension to a user's roaming user profile folder name. Mandatory and super-mandatory user profiles behave similarly and do not preserve user modifications. The benefit of using a super-mandatory profile is to prevent a user from obtaining a temporary profile. Normally, if the network copy of a roaming mandatory profile is not available, a user will be provided with a temporary profile. A user able to access a device using a temporary profile may breach organizational security policy. To create a super-mandatory user profile, for User 1, an administrator should first configure a mandatory user profile, which is stored in the \\Server\Profiles \User1.V6 folder, add the .man extension to the folder, and store the profile at \\Server\Profiles\User1.man.V6.

- **Temporary User Profiles** When an error condition prevents the user's normal profile from loading, a temporary profile is created. This profile is deleted at the end of each session, and all changes made by the user are lost when the user logs off.

NEED MORE REVIEW?   **MANDATORY USER PROFILES**

If you want to know how to create mandatory user profiles, use this Microsoft website:
https://docs.microsoft.com/en-us/windows/client-management/mandatory-user-profile.

Windows 10 profiles are stored within the shared folder on the network server, on a folder per-user basis. The user profile folder contains application settings and other system components settings. Unless redirected elsewhere, the profile will also contain per-user data, such as the user's Desktop, Start menu, and Documents folder.

Settings in the user profile are unique to each user and to the version of Windows. When you create a roaming or mandatory profile, this file must be stored in a shared folder that matches the correct extension for the operating system it will be applied to. An example profile for User1 running Windows 10 Version 1809 would require a folder named \\Server\Profiles\ User1.v6. Table 2-12 lists the extensions for the most recent operating system versions.

TABLE 2-12 Mandatory profile extension

OPERATING SYSTEM VERSION	PROFILE EXTENSION
Windows 7	v2
Windows 8.1	v4
Windows 10, versions 1507 and 1511	v5
Windows 10, versions 1607, 1703, 1709, 1803, and 1809	v6

In some scenarios, mandatory profiles can be useful. However, many organizations use roaming profiles for all users. User profiles allow users to access the same settings that were in use when they last logged off. In a shared computer environment, each user receives his or her customized desktop after logging on.

Data and settings stored in the user's profile folders are private to that user and cannot be accessed or modified by other users. Changes made on a shared computer are stored in the user's profile and do not affect the computer settings for another user. For example, modifying the default font size in Word or Notepad for one user will not affect other users when they log onto the same computer.

Minimizing user profile size

One of the drawbacks to using roaming profiles to contain the user state (their folders, application settings, and other system components settings) is that profiles can grow large, which can slow down the log on process for users.

Users have Write permissions to the user profile files and folders. Therefore, by default, the profile can grow large, especially if users store large CAD or multimedia files in their profile folders. You have seen that administrators can implement mandatory user profiles, which do not allow users to modify their user profiles. This option, however, is not ideal for most environments.

The following methods are available for administrators to restrict how large a profile can grow; this is done by limiting the physical space where user profiles are stored.

- **Quotas** You can apply file quotas to limit the space that is available to a user on a volume or on a shared folder where the roaming user profile is stored. A local computer can use the disk quota option within the volume properties. Where profiles are stored on a file server, you can use the Quota Management node of the File Server Resource Manager in Windows Server 2019 to create quotas limiting the space allowed for folders that contain roaming user profiles or redirected folders. File Server Resource Manager enables you to manage and classify data stored on file servers, including set quotas on folders; File Server Resource Manager also allows you to create reports that monitor storage usage.

- **Redirect the profile folders** You can redirect specific folders, such as the Documents folder, to be stored outside the user profile. These can be stored on a shared folder on a file server or redirected to OneDrive for Business. For domain users, you can configure Folder Redirection and the various settings, including setting quotas, to limit the size of redirected folders by using Group Policy.

- **Limit user profile size using Group Policy** You can limit the size of local or roaming user profiles by configuring the Limit Profile Size Group Policy, as shown in Figure 2-15. This policy allows you to define the maximum profile size and a custom message that users see when their profile exceeds the quota.

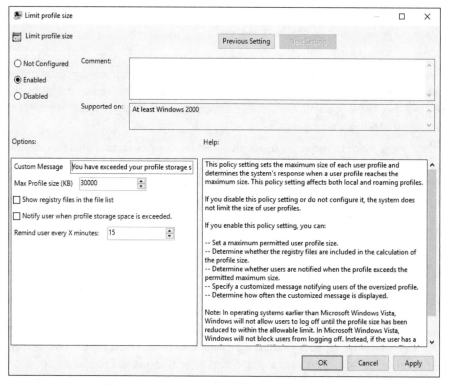

FIGURE 2-15 Limit profile size

Configure sync settings

Windows 10 includes a feature that allows a copy of your device settings to be securely stored in your Microsoft account. This feature was first introduced in Windows 8. When a user signs in to a device using the user's Microsoft account, the settings are pulled down from the cloud-based account and applied to the device. Settings are kept synchronized, and any new profile changes, such as a new theme or change of wallpaper, will take effect on other devices following the user log-on process completion.

Users appreciate the unified experience across their Windows devices and that they do not need to configure settings on all their devices. This saves users time and effort and increases their productivity with minimal administrative effort.

On a newly installed device—or after the first time you add your Microsoft account to the device—you may be presented the following warning within the Settings app when you try to enable Sync settings:

```
Your passwords won't sync until you verify your identity on this device.
```

To sync passwords, you are required to verify your identity using an alternative email account that you have previously set up; doing so helps protect your Microsoft account.

When you've enabled the Sync setting, Windows syncs the settings you choose across all your Windows 10 devices that you've signed in to with your Microsoft account.

To enable device Sync settings, perform these steps.

1. Open the Settings app.
2. Select Accounts.
3. In the Your Info section, ensure that you have signed in using a Microsoft account. If you have not, you can click the link on screen to sign in using a Microsoft account.
4. Under Accounts, select the Sync Your Settings section.

5. Under Sync Settings, toggle the setting to On, as shown in Figure 2-16.

6. Under Individual Sync Settings, you can turn on or off the following settings:

- Theme
- Passwords
- Language Preferences
- Ease of Access
- Other Windows Settings

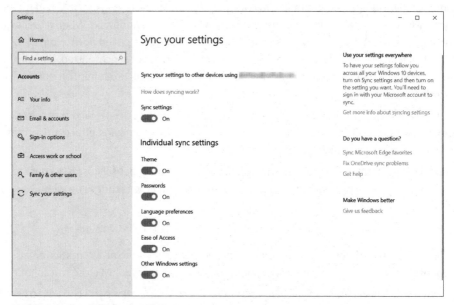

FIGURE 2-16 Sync Windows settings

The settings that are synchronized are extensive and can certainly reduce the user effort when configuring additional devices for use. Table 2-13 displays some of the categories and common settings that are included on a Windows 10 desktop device.

TABLE 2-13 Windows Sync settings

GROUP OF SETTINGS	SETTING
Other Windows settings	**Mouse:** ■ Change the size of mouse cursor ■ Change the color of mouse cursor
Theme	**Accounts:** Account Picture **Desktop Personalization:** ■ Desktop Theme (background, system color, default system sounds, and screen saver) ■ Slideshow Wallpaper ■ Taskbar Settings (position, auto-hide, and so on)

(Continued)

GROUP OF SETTINGS	SETTING
Passwords	**Credentials:** Credential Locker **WiFi:** WiFi profiles (only WPA)
App-Specific	**App data:** Individual Apps Can Sync Data **Command prompt:** Command prompt "Defaults" settings
Microsoft Edge browser	■ Reading List ■ Favorites ■ Top Sites ■ Typed URLs ■ Favorites Bar Settings ■ Show The Home Button ■ Block Pop-Ups ■ Ask Me What To Do With Each Download ■ Offer To Save Passwords ■ Send Do Not Track Requests ■ Save Form Entries ■ Show Search And Site Suggestions As I Type ■ Cookies Preference ■ Let Sites Save Protected Media Licenses On My Device ■ Screen Reader Setting
Internet Explorer browser	■ Open tabs (URL and title) ■ Reading List ■ Typed URLs ■ Browsing History ■ Favorites ■ Excluded URLs ■ Home Pages ■ Domain Suggestions
Ease Of Access	**High Contrast:** On or Off, Theme settings **Keyboard**: Users can ■ Turn on/off on-screen keyboard ■ Turn on sticky keys (off by default) ■ Turn on filter keys (off by default) ■ Turn on toggle keys (off by default) **Magnifier:** ■ Turn inversion color on or off (off by default) ■ Tracking (follow the keyboard focus) ■ Tracking (follow the mouse cursor) ■ Start when users sign in (off by default)

(Continued)

GROUP OF SETTINGS	SETTING
	Narrator: Quick launch
	■ Change Narrator speaking pitch
	■ Turn on or off Narrator reading hints for common items (on by default)
	■ Turn on or off whether they can hear typed characters (on by default)
	■ Turn on or off whether they can hear typed words (on by default)
	■ Make insert cursor follow Narrator (on by default)
	■ Enable visual highlighting of Narrator cursor (on by default)
	■ Play audio cues (on by default)
	■ Activate keys on the touch keyboard when you lift your finger (off by default)
	Ease Of Access:
	■ Set the thickness of the blinking cursor
	■ Remove background images (off by default)
Language	**Date, Time, and Region:**
	■ Automatic Time (Internet Time Sync)
	■ 24-Hour Clock
	■ Date And Time
	■ Daylight Savings Time
	■ Country/Region
	■ First Day Of Week
	■ Region Format (Locale)
	■ Short Date
	■ Long Date
	■ Short Time
	■ Long Time
	Language:
	■ Language Profile
	■ Spellcheck (autocorrect and highlight misspellings)
	■ List Of Keyboards
	Typing: Spelling Dictionary
	■ Autocorrect Misspelled Word
	■ Highlight Misspelled Words
	■ Show Text Suggestions As I Type
	■ Add A Space After I Choose A Text Suggestion
	■ Add A Period After I Double-Tap The Spacebar
	■ Capitalize The First Letter Of Each Sentence
	■ Use All Uppercase Letters When I Double-Tap Shift Key
	■ Play Key Sounds As I Type
	■ Personalization Data For Touch Keyboard

The following device settings are not able to be synchronized across devices:

- Accounts: Other account settings.
- All Bluetooth settings.
- Desktop personalization: Start screen layout.
- All lock screen settings.
- Mouse: All other settings.
- All Power and Sleep settings.

The Microsoft Edge browser allows users to customize the sync settings within the app. Users can enable or disable the Microsoft Edge browser sync settings by using these steps:

1. Click the Microsoft Edge Settings menu (represented by three ellipses).
2. Select the Settings (represented by a cog or gear icon).
3. On the General tab, under Account, toggle the Sync Your Microsoft Edge Favorites, Reading List, Top Sites, And Other Settings Across Your Devices settings on or off.
4. Click anywhere on the web page to hide the settings flyout menu.

Windows 10 Version 1803 and later users can enable or disable Internet Explorer sync settings through Internet Explorer by using these steps:

1. Click the Internet Explorer Tools (cog icon) menu.
2. Click Internet Options.
3. Choose the Advanced tab.
4. Under Settings, clear the Enable Syncing Internet Explorer Settings And Data check box under the Browser section.
5. Click OK.

To stop syncing your settings between all your devices and remove the cloud backup of your personal settings, you should perform these high-level steps.

1. On all the devices connected to your Microsoft account, turn off synced settings in the Settings app.
2. Open a web browser and sign in to your Microsoft account at *https://account.microsoft.com/devices*.
3. Select the device that you want to manage and click Show Details.
4. At the top of the device page, click More Actions for the device you want to manage, and then select Remove Cloud Backup Of Personal Settings.
5. If the Remove Cloud Backup Of Personal Settings option is not visible, ensure that sync has been turned off for all devices listed.

If you need to remove a device from your device list, perform these steps:

1. Open a web browser and sign in to your Microsoft account at *https://account.microsoft.com/devices*.
2. Go to Manage Device Limits and find the device you want to remove.
3. Select Remove to delete the device.

Implement Folder Redirection

To reduce the amount of data stored on a device—often within a user's profile—administrators can configure Group Policy to redirect individual profile folders to a new location. This location will be a file server–based folder on the network.

Once configured, the redirected folder content will be moved from the local device to the new location, and the files will be available to the user. If Folder Redirection is performed on a roaming profile, then the user can access their files and folders from any device that they log on to. Users will be unaware that the redirection takes place because there are no visible changes to the Windows Explorer user interface.

Files and folders remain located on the network file share and use Offline Files by default to ensure that a user can still use his or her files when the device is disconnected from the network. In this way, files that are being worked on by the user are cached on the device, and then they are synchronized back to the network file share.

You can configure Folder Redirection by enabling the Folder Redirection GPO settings using this procedure:

1. Launch Group Policy Management Editor, open the relevant GPO, and then navigate to the Folder Redirection settings at User Configuration\Policies\Windows Settings\Folder Redirection.

2. Right-click a folder that you want to redirect (for example, Documents), and then select Properties.

3. In the Properties dialog box, from the Setting box, select Basic–Redirect Everyone's Folder To The Same Location, as shown in Figure 2-17.

4. In the Target Folder Location section, select Create A Folder For Each User Under The Root Path.

5. In the Root Path box, type the path to the file share storing redirected folders; for example, type **\\LON-DC1.Adatum.com\Users$**.

6. Select the Settings tab, and review the settings.

7. Optionally, on the Settings tab screen in the Policy Removal section, select Redirect The Folder Back To The Local Userprofile Location When The Policy Is Removed.

8. Select OK.

9. Accept the dialog box warning if one appears and click Yes.

Three organizational benefits of using Folder Redirection are

Reduced risk of data loss   Data is no longer stored on a local device.

Centrally backed-up data   Data can be backed up centrally on the networked file server.

Set Quotas   Administrators can easily limit disk space that is used for storing redirected files and folders, and optionally, administrators can restrict the types of files stored in user profiles.

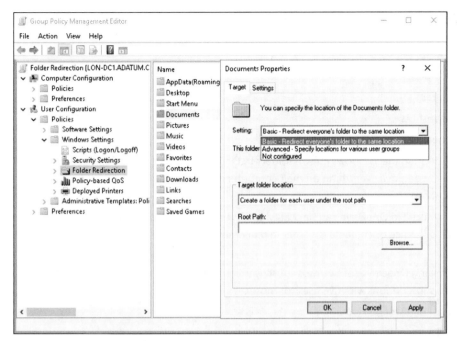

FIGURE 2-17 Folder Redirection

> **NEED MORE REVIEW?** **DEPLOY FOLDER REDIRECTION**
>
> If you want to know how to deploy Folder Redirection, use this Microsoft website: *https://docs.microsoft.com/en-us/windows-server/storage/folder-redirection/deploy-folder-redirection.*

Implement OneDrive Known Folder Move

OneDrive for Business offers personal online storage space for your staff. They can use it to store and protect work files and access them across multiple devices by using their Azure AD work credentials. Windows known folder move (KFM) for OneDrive is a feature that automatically redirects users' personal folders and important files to their OneDrive for Business account stored in the Microsoft Cloud. This redirect allows users to access their files across different devices and applications.

As more organizations are embracing the cloud, the availability of local, network-based file storage is likely to reduce. If KFM is enabled on devices prior to a migration project, it provides immediate and secure access to a user's files on the new or refreshed Windows 10 PC. All data stored in OneDrive for Business is encrypted when at rest and during transit. Using Group Policy, you can configure the synchronization to operate silently in the background.

The typical folders that are redirected as part of the Windows known folders feature include

- Desktop
- Documents
- Pictures
- Screenshots
- Camera Roll

When adopting the Windows known folders to OneDrive feature, users don't need to change their workflow; everything on their computers looks the same before, during, and after synchronization.

Any files stored in OneDrive can be shared with business colleagues, and workers can collaborate on Office documents together in real time with Office desktop, web, and mobile apps.

The following OneDrive for Business subscription licensing plans provide personal cloud storage (for subscriptions with five users or more).

- SharePoint Online Plan 2
- OneDrive for Business Plan 2
- Office 365 A1, A3, A5, E3, E5, G3, and G5 plans
- Microsoft 365 A3, A5, E3, E5, G3, and G5 plans

> **NOTE INCREASE ONEDRIVE FOR BUSINESS STORAGE**
>
> All customers will initially receive 1TB of cloud storage with OneDrive for Business. Once a user has filled 90 percent of his or her 1TB storage, an administrator can increase that user's storage to 5TB. If a user fills 90 percent of the user's 5TB storage, then an administrator can open a case with Microsoft Technical Support, who will then increase the storage space to 25TB per user. If needed, additional storage space beyond 25TB will be provided in the form of SharePoint team sites to individual users.

To configure OneDrive Known Folder Move using Group Policy, you need to ensure the following requirements are met:

- OneDrive sync build 18.111.0603.0004 or later must be installed on client devices.
- Any existing Windows Folder Redirection Group Policy settings used in the domain must be removed.
- Move users' OneNote notebooks out of their known folders because known folders, which include OneNote notebooks, won't be moved.

There are several GPO settings, shown in Table 2-14, which enterprises can use to fine tune the configuration of OneDrive Known Folder Move within an environment that uses Active Directory Domain Services.

The .adml and .admx files that contain the Group Policy settings relating to the Windows Known Folders Move feature can be found on a Windows 10 client running OneDrive sync build 18.111.0603.0004 or later here:

```
%localappdata%\Microsoft\OneDrive\<onedrive version>\adm
```

To use the OneDrive GPO settings, you will need to first import the .adml and .admx files from a client and add them to your domain's GPO Central Store in the following location:

```
\sysvol\domain\Policies\PolicyDefinitions
```

Once you have imported the .admx and .adml files, you will be able to view the Computer Configuration policies in the Group Policy Editor, found under Computer Configuration\Policies\Administrative Templates\OneDrive.

TABLE 2-14 Windows Known Folder Move GPO settings

GPO SETTING	DESCRIPTION
Prompt users to move Windows known folders to OneDrive	Use this setting to give the users a popup notification, as shown in Figure 2-18, to protect their files by automatically moving their Windows known folders to OneDrive. If users dismiss the prompt, a reminder notification will appear in the Activity Center until they complete the move. If a user has already redirected his or her known folders to a different OneDrive account, the prompt will request to direct the folders to your organization's OneDrive account.
Silently move Windows known folders to OneDrive	Use this setting to redirect known folders to OneDrive without any user interaction. Once configured, this setting redirects known-folder content to OneDrive.
Prevent users from redirecting their Windows known folders to their PC	Use this setting to disable the ability for users to change the setting, thereby forcing users to keep their known folders directed to OneDrive. Enabling this policy sets the following registry key: [HKLM\SOFTWARE\Policies\Microsoft\OneDrive]"KFMBlockOptOut"=" dword:00000001"
Prevent users from moving their Windows known folders to OneDrive	Use this setting to prevent users from moving their Windows known folders to OneDrive.

NEED MORE REVIEW? **ONEDRIVE SYNC CLIENT GROUP POLICY SETTINGS**

If you want to know more about how to manage the OneDrive sync client in a Windows Server enterprise environment, visit the Microsoft website: *https://docs.microsoft.com/en-us/ onedrive/use-group-policy.*

FIGURE 2-18 OneDrive prompt

Configure Enterprise State Roaming in Azure AD

Windows 10 users who use a Microsoft account can sync their user settings, Edge browser passwords, and application settings between devices that use the same Microsoft account.

For enterprise users, Azure Active Directory provides the roaming functionality. Administrators can enable an enterprise feature called Enterprise State Roaming to allow Azure AD to securely synchronize users' Windows settings, passwords, and Universal Windows Platform (UWP) app settings and data across their Windows devices. With their profile settings stored in the cloud, the settings can be automatically applied to a new device following sign-in.

In addition to the settings that are included in the consumer-facing Sync settings, Enterprise State Roaming offers the following additional functionality:

- **Separation of corporate and consumer data**   There is no mixing of corporate data and consumer data. Each cloud account holds data separately.

- **Enhanced security**   Using Azure Rights Management protection, data is always encrypted, both in transit and while at rest.

- **Better management and monitoring**   The Azure AD portal provides control and visibility over which users and devices have their settings synced.

- **Data retention** Enterprise State Roaming data that has been synced to Azure is retained for between 90 and 180 days after it was last accessed.

For an organization to use Enterprise State Roaming, it must meet the following requirements:

- Windows 10 Version 1511 or later, with the latest updates installed on the device.
- Devices must be Azure AD–joined or Hybrid Azure AD–joined.
- Ensure that Enterprise State Roaming is enabled for the tenant in Azure AD.
- Users must already be assigned an Azure AD Premium or Enterprise Mobility + Security (EMS) license.
- Devices must be restarted following the enabling of Enterprise State Roaming.
- Users must sign in using an Azure AD identity.

Once the Enterprise State Roaming feature is enabled, the organization is granted a free, limited-use license to use Azure Rights Management protection in Azure Information Protection. This license is limited to encrypting and decrypting enterprise settings and application data synced by Enterprise State Roaming.

To enable Enterprise State Roaming within Azure, perform this procedure:

1. Sign in to the Azure admin center using a global administrator account.
2. Select Azure Active Directory and then under Manage, click Devices.
3. On the Devices–All Devices blade, under Manage, click Enterprise State Roaming.
4. On the Devices–Enterprise State Roaming page, configure the Users May Sync Settings And App Data Across Devices option to suit your organizational needs—you can enable roaming for all users or for only a selected group of users. (See Figure 2-19.) Click Save.

FIGURE 2-19 Configure Enterprise State Roaming

Once the Azure AD settings have been configured, your Windows 10 devices need to be restarted, and the user needs to authenticate using the user's primary sign-in identity.

> **NEED MORE REVIEW?** **HYBRID AZURE ACTIVE DIRECTORY JOINED DEVICES**
>
> If you want to know how to configure Hybrid Azure Active Directory joined devices, use this Microsoft website: *https://docs.microsoft.com/azure/active-directory/devices/hybrid-azuread-join-manual-steps*.

All user settings and application settings data synced to the Microsoft cloud using Enterprise State Roaming is retained for a period based on the rules shown in Table 2-15.

TABLE 2-15 Enterprise State Roaming data retention

GPO SETTING	DESCRIPTION
Explicit deletion	■ **User Deletion** When an Azure AD user account is deleted, the user account roaming data is deleted after 90 to 180 days. ■ **Directory Deletion** After deletion of an entire directory in Azure AD, all the settings data associated with that directory is deleted after 90 to 180 days. ■ **On Request Deletion** An Azure AD admin can file a ticket with Azure support to manually delete a specific user's data or settings data.

Stale data deletion	■ User account roaming data that has not been accessed for one year will be treated as stale and may be deleted from the Microsoft cloud. The retention period is subject to change but will not be less than 90 days. The stale data is based on the following criteria:
	  ■ If no devices access a settings collection, such as a specific app setting, or Windows 10 Theme, then that collection becomes stale after the retention period and may be deleted.
	  ■ If a user disables settings sync on his or her device, then all the settings data for that user will become stale and may be deleted after the retention period.
	  ■ If Enterprise State Roaming is disabled for the entire directory, then settings syncing will stop. All settings data for all users will become stale and may be deleted after the retention period.

Deleted data recovery	The Enterprise State Roaming data retention policy is not configurable. Once the sync data is deleted it is not recoverable. The data deletion only applies to the Microsoft cloud and not from the user device. If a device later reconnects to the Enterprise State Roaming service, the device-based settings will be synced and stored in the Microsoft cloud.

> *NEED MORE REVIEW?*   **ENTERPRISE STATE ROAMING IN AZURE AD**
>
> If you want to know more about enabling Enterprise State Roaming in Azure Active Directory, visit this Microsoft website: *https://docs.microsoft.com/en-us/azure/active-directory/devices/enterprise-state-roaming-enable.*

Thought experiments

In these thought experiments, demonstrate your skills and knowledge of the topics covered in this chapter. You can find the answers to these thought experiments in the next section.

Scenario 1

Contoso has 2,000 workstations currently running Windows 10 Enterprise, which are currently managed using Group Policy and SCCM. Management has recently purchased Microsoft 365 licensing and wants IT to utilize the MDM functionality, which is included with Microsoft 365. Most users work at the head office, though about 50 members of staff work remotely.

As a consultant for Contoso, answer the following questions:

1. What software tool included within Microsoft 365 will you use to implement co-management for the organization?

2. What tool will you deploy on managed devices to evaluate and help migrate policy to MDM?

3. For the organization to synchronize their on-premises Active Directory domain users to Azure Active Directory, what tool must they first install to sync the users to the cloud?

4. Management wants to implement co-management for all devices as soon as possible. Recommend a strategy on how the organization should roll out co-management.

Scenario 2

Contoso has 500 remote workers across the country. The remote workers work from their home offices and use Surface Books. They need to access a web-based line-of-business (LOB) app and access the corporate network using a secure VPN. Contoso has recently purchased Microsoft 365 and wants to implement their corporate security and compliance requirements for remote workers using MDM. Contoso wants to de-commission the corporate VPN as soon as possible.

Answer the following questions for your manager:

1. You need to ensure that when staff members access the LOB app, they do so securely. What type of conditions should you include in a conditional access policy you will implement?

2. What type of conditions should you include in a conditional access policy you would implement to replace the outgoing VPN connection for the remote workers?

3. What information would you need from the employee to implement your solution?

4. Your manager has asked you to implement your conditional access policies for the remote workers. What should you do before you deploy the policies to the remote workers?

Scenario 3

Your organization currently runs a mixture of operating systems on its devices, including Windows 7 Pro and Windows 10 Pro. The company purchased 500 Surface Book devices running Windows 10 Pro to replace half of the Windows 7 devices. You have created a new Azure AD group called Surface Book Devices, and you've added a dynamic membership rule to add all Surface Book devices to the group. The company recently purchased Microsoft 365 Enterprise and intends to manage new devices entirely using MDM.

Answer the following questions for your manager:

1. You need to deploy a legacy Win32 application that is required by your frontline workforce. How will you deploy the application using the least administrative effort?

2. Corporate security policy requires that users are not allowed to use Microsoft accounts on corporate owned devices. What should you do to enforce corporate policy?

3. You have deployed a device configuration profile to customize the Start menu layout. The following day, Surface Book users report that the corporate Start menu layout has not been implemented on their devices. You check the profile device configuration settings and Scope (Tags) are correct. The Surface Book dynamic group has populated with the Surface Books. What else should you check?

4. You want to deploy device configuration profiles to the Windows 7 Pro devices. You create a new device configuration profile but do not see Windows 7 listed in the Platform drop down menu. Why not?

5. You need to manage all devices using MDM. What should you do? Your answer should not incur additional costs.

Scenario 4

Adatum Corporation uses Microsoft 365 Enterprise and has implemented Windows 10 Enterprise on all devices. The organization employs co-management for the devices located at the head office with users connected to the domain. Remote workers are managed via Microsoft Intune.

Answer the following questions for your manager:

1. Members of the graphics editing team at the head office complain that it takes up to 10 minutes for their devices to log on each morning. You investigate and discover that roaming profiles are used at the head office. What two options could you suggest for improving log on times? Your answers should not incur additional costs.

2. You want to enable Windows sync settings on several remote workers' devices so that browser settings such as passwords, browser favorites, top sites, and typed URLs can be kept in sync between users' devices. The pilot group containing the remote workers says sync is not working. You need to resolve the issue for just the pilot group. How will you proceed?

3. You have enabled Enterprise State Roaming for all remote workers, but one user reports that no Microsoft Edge browser settings are being synchronized between their devices. You verify that Enterprise State Roaming has been correctly configured in Azure AD and that other settings are being synchronized for the user. How will you resolve the issue?

4. Contoso uses Folder Redirection for user's profile files and folders. Management does not want to restrict disk space, but the head office file server is running low on drive space. Your manager has asked you to recommend a solution that does not incur additional costs.

5. Some users have very large profiles and complain because logon times are very slow. Contoso uses Folder Redirection to a head office file server, and when you investigate, you find that several users have been storing music and video files within their profiles. You need to recommend how you could speed up the log-on process and restrict the users from storing music and video files exceeding 500MB in their profiles.

Thought experiment answers

This section provides the solutions for the tasks included in the thought experiment.

Scenario 1

1. Microsoft Intune is included within Microsoft 365.

2. The MDM Migration Analysis Tool (MMAT) is used to evaluate which Group Policies have been set for a target user/device and cross-reference against its built-in list of supported MDM policies.

3. Azure AD Connect.

4. IT should create rollout groups for staging co-management. The groups could include a pilot group with few devices and a larger production group. Rollout groups help to identify and resolve issues that are encountered during the implementation.

Scenario 2

1. Multifactor authentication conditional access policies can be used with supported cloud-based apps.

2. You should implement a conditional access policy that uses a location-based condition.

3. You would need the employee to provide you with the IP address for his or her home network.

4. You should prepare a conditional access test plan. You then test the policies in a non-production environment or to a pilot group of remote workers to ensure that the actual result of the policies matches the expected results, as documented in the test plan.

Scenario 3

1. You can deploy Win32 apps using PowerShell to the Windows 10 devices. The PowerShell script will be remotely executed by Intune, and the Win32 apps will be installed.

2. Create and deploy a Windows 10 device configuration profile that enforces device restrictions and blocks Microsoft account use.

3. You should ensure that the device configuration profile has been correctly assigned to the Surface Book Device security group.

4. Device configuration profiles do not support the Windows 7 platform.

5. With a Microsoft 365 Enterprise subscription, you are licensed to upgrade Windows 7 devices to Windows 10 without incurring additional costs.

Scenario 4

1. Answers may vary. You could restrict the size of the users' roaming profiles using a quota on the file server that hosts the profiles. You could also recommend using folder redirection to redirect specific profile folders to a storage location on the network. The roaming profile size would be reduced because the files stored in the redirected folder would not be included in the roaming profile.

2. The sync settings feature is available to Windows 10 users when they use Microsoft accounts. It is unlikely that users have Microsoft accounts within an enterprise environment. Therefore, you should recommend Enterprise State Roaming. This involves creating an Azure AD security group and adding the pilot remote workers to the group. You will then enable Enterprise State Roaming for the pilot remote workers Azure AD security group.

3. It is likely that The Microsoft Edge app has the Sync Your Microsoft Edge Favorites, Reading List, Top Sites, And Other Settings Across Your Devices setting configured to off. Turn this setting on, which will resolve the issue.

4. With a Microsoft 365 Enterprise subscription, each user is granted unlimited personal storage within OneDrive for Business. You should recommend that the company configure OneDrive Known Folder Move and utilize OneDrive for Business storage.

5. You could implement the File Server Resource Manager role service on a Windows Server at the head office to manage and classify data stored on file servers. Once enabled, File Server Resource Manager can automatically classify files and perform tasks based on these classifications, such as set quotas on folders and create reports monitoring storage usage. You should also inform users that file-size restrictions will be implemented for user profiles.

Chapter summary

- Co-management is when you manage devices using both System Center Configuration Manager and Microsoft Intune.
- Starting with Windows 10 Version 1803 and later, Intune can take precedence over policy when both Group Policy and its equivalent Intune policy are set on the device.
- The MDM Migration Analysis Tool is used to evaluate which Group Policies have been set for a target user/device and cross-reference against its built-in list of supported MDM policies.
- Conditional access policies provide administrators with a tool that allows Azure AD to check whether conditions have been met before access to corporate resources, such as controlled apps, will be granted.
- Conditional access policies can define conditions and controls that build rules that will be evaluated by Azure AD.
- When implementing Conditional Access, you should create a test plan.

- Compliance policies are used to ensure devices meet compliance requirements, such as being encrypted, not being jailbroken and using a password for device access.

- Non-compliant devices can be blocked from accessing resources or can be offered help to become compliant.

- When multiple device compliance policies are assigned to a device, Intune calculates a compliance status based on the highest severity level of all the policies assigned to the device.

- Devices will periodically check with Intune to determine the compliance status of the device; this will be every six hours for Apple devices and every eight hours for Android and Windows devices.

- Intune device configuration policies are used to configure device settings using MDM.

- Intune can deploy PowerShell scripts to Windows devices using an MDM extension. This allows administrators to deploy Win32 apps if required.

- Scope tags are used to assign and filter Intune policies to specific Azure AD groups.

- You can configure custom policies with Intune by configuring an Open Mobile Alliance Uniform Resource Identifier (OMA-URI) policy.

- A user profile contains the user state which includes application settings and other system components settings, and per-user data, such as the user's Desktop, Start menu and Documents folder.

- User profiles can be Local, Roaming, Mandatory, Super Mandatory, and Temporary User.

- If roaming user profiles grow too large, they can have a detrimental effect by slowing down log in times for users.

- Users can sync common Windows settings, including passwords, themes, and browser settings in the cloud, which can be synced to all devices that sign in with the same Microsoft account.

- Administrators can enable Folder Redirection to store individual profile folders to a location stored on the network.

- Windows Known Folder Move for OneDrive allows users' folders and important files to be redirected to their OneDrive for Business accounts stored in the Microsoft Cloud.

- Administrators can enable Enterprise State Roaming to allow Azure AD to securely synchronize users' Windows settings and Universal Windows Platform (UWP) app settings data across their Windows devices.

CHAPTER 3

Manage and protect devices

A critical part of the job role for the modern desktop administrator (MDA) is to manage and protect their users' devices. As an MDA, you can use a number of Windows 10 components, in conjunction with Microsoft Intune features, to manage your organization's devices. This chapter explores those components and features.

Skills covered in this chapter:

- Skill 3.1: Manage Windows Defender
- Skill 3.2: Manage Intune Device Enrollment and inventory
- Skill 3.3: Monitor devices

Skill 3.1: Manage Windows Defender

Built in to Windows 10 are a number of features that are part of the Windows Defender suite of security apps. It's important that you are familiar with each of these, you can determine what they do, you know how they can help secure your organization's devices, and you know how you can enable and configure these features.

> **This skill covers how to:**
> - Implement and manage Windows Defender Credential Guard
> - Implement and manage Windows Defender Exploit Guard
> - Implement and manage Windows Defender Application Guard
> - Implement Windows Defender Advanced Threat Protection
> - Integrate Windows Defender Application Control
> - Manage Windows Defender Antivirus
> - Use Microsoft Intune for Endpoint Protection

Implement and manage Windows Defender Credential Guard

When users sign in to an Active Directory Domain Services (AD DS) domain, they provide their user credentials to a domain controller. As a result of successful authentication, the authenticating domain controller issues Kerberos tickets to the user's computer. The user's computer uses these tickets to establish sessions with servers that are part of the same AD DS forest. When a server receives a session request, it examines the Kerberos ticket for validity. If the ticket is valid in all respects and is issued by a trusted authenticating authority, such as a domain controller in the same AD DS forest, the session is allowed.

These Kerberos tickets, and related security tokens, such as NTLM hashes, are stored in the Local Security Authority, which is a process that runs on Windows-based computers and handles the exchange of such information between the local computer and requesting authorities. However, it is possible for certain malicious software to gain access to this security process and exploit the stored tickets and hashes.

Requirements

To help protect against this possibility, 64-bit versions of both Windows 10 Enterprise and Windows 10 Education editions have a feature called Windows Defender Credential Guard, which implements a technology known as *virtualization-assisted security*; this enables Windows Defender Credential Guard to block access to credentials stored in the Local Security Authority.

In addition to requiring the appropriate edition of 64-bit editions of Windows 10, the following are the requirements for implementing Windows Defender Credential Guard:

- Support for Virtualization-based security.
- UEFI 2.3.1 or greater.
- Secure Boot.
- TPM 2.0, either discrete or firmware.
- UEFI (firmware) lock.
- Virtualization features: Intel VT-x or AMD-V; SLAT must be enabled.
- An Intel VT-d or an AMD-Vi input-output memory management unit.

Enabling Windows Defender Credential Guard

After you have verified that your computer meets the requirements, you can enable Windows Defender Credential Guard by using Group Policy in an AD DS environment. On the domain controller, open the appropriate Group Policy Object (GPO) for editing and navigate to Computer Configuration > Policies > Administrative Templates > System > Device Guard. Enable Turn On Virtualization Based Security, as shown in Figure 3-1.

> *NEED MORE REVIEW?* **MANAGE WINDOWS DEFENDER CREDENTIAL GUARD**
>
> To review further details about how Windows Defender Credential Guard works, refer to the Microsoft website at *https://docs.microsoft.com/windows/security/identity-protection/credential-guard/credential-guard-manage.*

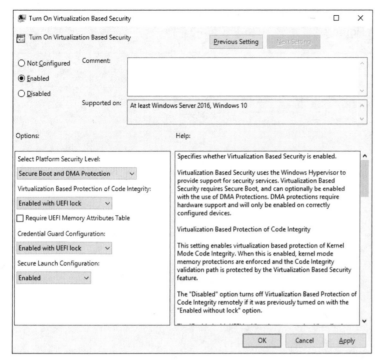

FIGURE 3-1 Enabling Windows Defender Credential Guard

Implement and manage Windows Defender Exploit Guard

You can use Windows Defender Exploit Guard, part of Windows Defender Advanced Threat Protection, to help to reduce the attack surface of your users' apps. Windows Defender Exploit Guard consists of four components:

- **Exploit protection**   Uses Windows Defender Antivirus or, if installed, third-party anti-virus software to help mitigate exploit techniques used against your organization's apps.

- **Attack surface reduction rules**   Uses rules to help prevent attack vectors implemented by scripts, email, and Office-based malware. Based on Windows Defender Antivirus.

- **Network protection**   Extends Windows Defender SmartScreen protection in Micro-soft Edge to other applications to prevent access to Internet domains that may host phishing scams, exploits, and other malicious content. Requires Windows Defender Antivirus and cloud-delivered protection enabled.

- **Controlled folder access**   Helps protect against ransomware and malware by preventing changes to files in protected folders if the app attempting to make changes is malicious or exhibits suspicious behavior. Also requires Windows Defender Antivirus.

> *NOTE* **WINDOWS DEFENDER TEST GROUND WEBSITE**
>
> You can see these features in action at the following Microsoft website at *https://demo.wd .microsoft.com/?ocid=cx-wddocs-testground.*

You can manage and report on Windows Defender Exploit Guard by using the Windows Security app, as shown in Figure 3-2.

FIGURE 3-2 Windows Security app

Table 3-1 identifies the Windows Defender Exploit Guard features available in each of the listed Windows 10 editions.

TABLE 3-1 Windows Defender Exploit Guard features

EDITION OF WINDOWS 10	FEATURES SUPPORTED
Windows 10 Home	■ Exploit protection ■ Controlled folder access
Windows 10 Pro	■ Exploit protection ■ Controlled folder access
Windows 10 Enterprise E3 & Windows 10 Education E3	■ Exploit protection ■ Controlled folder access ■ Network protection
Windows 10 Enterprise E5 & Windows 10 Education E5	■ Exploit protection ■ Controlled folder access ■ Network protection ■ Attack surface reduction rules

Implement Exploit Protection

Exploit Protection helps to protect your users' devices against malware that uses exploits to spread through your organization. Exploit Protection consists of a number of specific mitigations that you must enable and configure separately.

By default, Exploit Protection already enables several mitigations that apply to the operating system and to specific apps. However, if you want to configure these and other mitigations, use the following procedure:

1. Open the Windows Security app.

2. Select the App & Browser control tab.

3. Scroll down and select the Exploit Protection Settings link.

4. On the Exploit Protection page, shown in Figure 3-3, configure the required settings. See Table 3-2 for an overview of available settings.

5. Click the Export Settings link to export the settings to an XML file.

6. Distribute the XML file to other devices by using Group Policy Objects (GPOs).

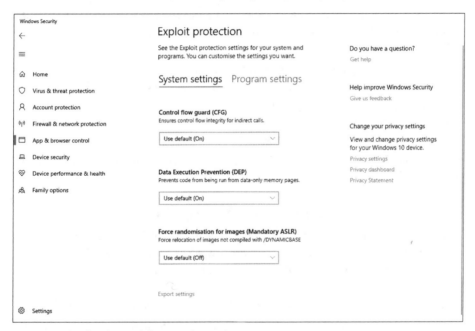

FIGURE 3-3 Configuring exploit protection settings

TABLE 3-2 Exploit protection mitigations

MITIGATION	EXPLANATION
Control Flow Guard (CFG)	Control Flow Guard combats memory corruption vulnerabilities.
Data Execution Prevention (DEP)	Help to prevent executable code from being run from pages that contain data.
Force Randomization For Images (Mandatory ASLR)	Helps prevents attacks by putting processes into memory at random locations.
Randomize Memory Allocations (Bottom-Up ASLR)	Helps prevents attacks by putting processes into memory at random locations.
Validate Exception Chains (SEHOP)	Helps prevent the use of a structured exception-handler attack.
Validate Heap Integrity	Helps to prevent attacks that seek to use memory corruption.

> **NOTE   AUDIT MODE**
>
> You can also enable mitigations in audit mode; this allows you to determine the effect of enabling a specific mitigation without affecting the user's device usage.

In addition to using the Windows Security app to configure Exploit Protection, you can also use Windows PowerShell cmdlets. You can use either the **Get** or **Set** verb with the **ProcessMitigation** cmdlet. For example, to enable the Data Execution Prevention (DEP) mitigation for the MyLOB.exe program located in the C:\Apps\LOB folder, and to prevent that executable from creating child processes, use the following PowerShell command:

```
Set-ProcessMitigation -Name C:\Apps\LOB\MyLOB.exe -Enable DEP, EmulateAtlThunks,
DisallowChildProcessCreation
```

> **NEED MORE REVIEW?   CUSTOMIZE EXPLOIT PROTECTION**
>
> To review further details about enabling and configuring Exploit Protection, refer to the Microsoft website at *https://docs.microsoft.com/windows/security/threat-protection/windows-defender-exploit-guard/customize-exploit-protection*.

To use GPOs to distribute the exported settings, use the following procedure:

1. On a domain controller, open the appropriate GPO for editing.

2. In the Group Policy Management Editor, navigate to Computer Configuration > Policies > Administrative Templates > Windows Components > Windows Defender Exploit Guard > Exploit Protection.

3. Open the Use A Common Set Of Exploit Protection Settings setting.

4. Click Enabled, as shown in Figure 3-4, and then type a valid UNC path to the XML file that contains the necessary settings.

5. Click OK, and then close the Group Policy Management Editor.

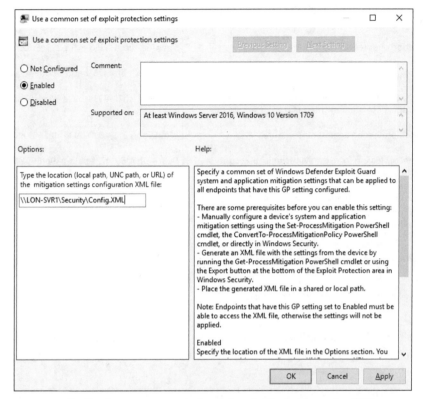

FIGURE 3-4 Configuring a common set of exploit protection settings using GPOs

Implement Attack Surface Reduction rules

You can use Attack Surface Reduction rules to help prevent actions and apps, which are often used by exploit-seeking malware to infect your organization's devices. Each rule is identified by a unique identity known as a GUID. Table 3-3 lists and describes the available Attack Surface Reduction rules and their respective GUIDs.

TABLE 3-3 Attack Surface Reduction rules

RULE AND DESCRIPTION	GUID
Block executable content from email client and webmail.	be9ba2d9-53ea-4cdc-84e5-9B1eeee46550
Block all Office applications from creating child processes.	d4f940ab-401b-4efc-aadc-ad5f3c50688a
Block Office applications from creating executable content.	3b576869-a4eC-4529-8536-b80a7769e899

(Continued)

RULE AND DESCRIPTION	GUID
Block Office applications from injecting code into other processes.	75668c1f-73b5-4Cf0-bb93-3ecf5cb7cc84
Block JavaScript or VBScript from launching downloaded executable content.	d3e037e1-3eb8-44c8-a917-57927947596d
Block execution of potentially obfuscated scripts.	5beb7efe-fd9A-4556-801d-275e5ffc04cc
Block Win32 API calls from Office macro.	92e97fa1-2edf-4476-bdd6-9dd0B4dddc7b
Block executable files from running unless they meet a prevalence, age, or trusted list criteria.	01443614-cd74-433a-b99e-2ecdc07bfc25
Use advanced protection against ransomware.	c1db55ab-c21a-4637-bb3f-a12568109d35
Block credential stealing from the Windows local security authority subsystem (lsass.exe).	9e6c4e1f-7d60-472f-ba1a-a39ef669e4b2
Block process creations originating from PSExec and WMI commands.	d1e49aac-8f56-4280-b9ba-993a6d77406c
Block untrusted and unsigned processes that run from USB.	b2b3f03d-6a65-4f7b-a9c7-1c7ef74a9ba4
Block Office communication applications from creating child processes.	26190899-1602-49e8-8b27-eb1d0a1ce869
Block Adobe Reader from creating child processes.	7674ba52-37eb-4a4f-a9a1-f0f9a1619a2c

To enable specific Attack Surface Reduction rules, you can use GPOs or Windows PowerShell. To use GPOs to manage Attack Surface Reduction rules, use the following procedure:

1. On a domain controller, open the appropriate GPO for editing.

2. In the Group Policy Management Editor, navigate to Computer Configuration > Policies > Administrative Templates > Windows Components > Windows Defender Antivirus > Windows Defender Exploit Guard > Attack Surface Reduction.

3. Open the Configure Attack Surface Reduction Rules setting.

4. Click Enabled, as shown in Figure 3-5.

5. Click Show. In the Value Name box in the Show Contents window, type the relevant GUID, as shown in Figure 3-6. (See Table 3-3 for more detail about GUIDs.)

6. In the Value box, type one of the following:

   - **0** to disable the specific rule

   - **1** to enable block mode

   - **2** to enable audit mode only

7. Click OK twice, and then close the Group Policy Management Editor.

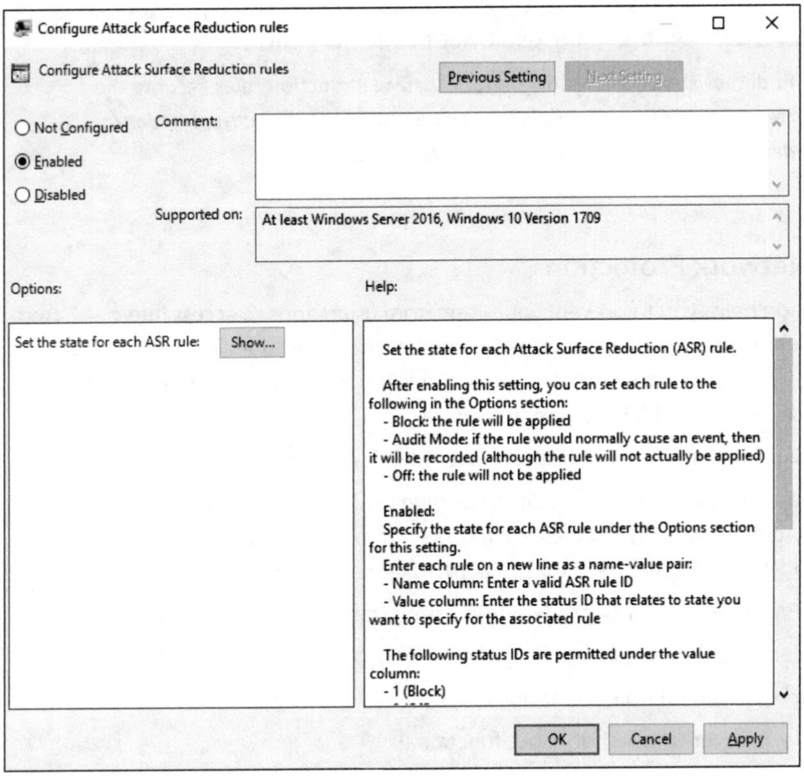

FIGURE 3-5 Configuring Attack Surface Reduction rules

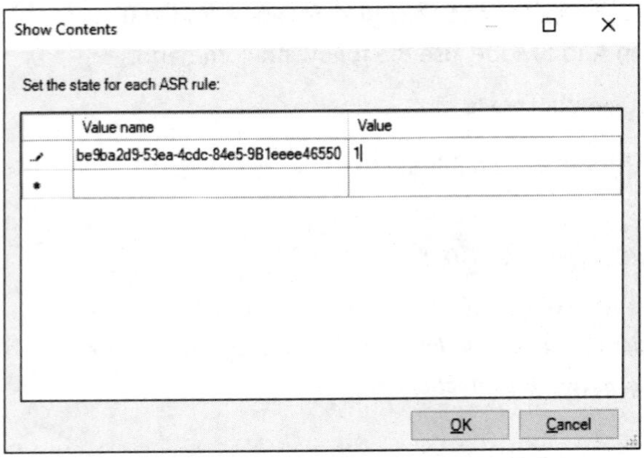

FIGURE 3-6 Specifying an ASR rule

To use Windows PowerShell (Administrator) to configure these rules, you can use the **Set-MpPreference** cmdlet, as shown in the following code snippet:

```
Set-MpPreference -AttackSurfaceReductionRules_Ids <rule ID>
-AttackSurfaceReductionRules_Actions Enabled
```

Implement Network Protection

Network Protection helps you to prevent your users from using apps to access Internet-based domains that might present a risk of malware, scams, or other malicious content. You can use GPOs, mobile device management (MDM) policies, or Windows PowerShell to enable network protection. To use GPOs, use the following procedure:

1. On a domain controller, open the appropriate GPO for editing.

2. In the Group Policy Management Editor, navigate to Computer Configuration > Policies > Administrative Templates > Windows Components > Windows Defender Antivirus > Windows Defender Exploit Guard > Network Protection.

3. Open the Prevent Users And Apps From Accessing Dangerous Websites setting.

4. Click Enabled, and then select one of the following:

   - **Block.** Users cannot access malicious sites.

   - **Disable.** Network Protection is not functional.

   - **Audit Mode.** Tracks activity but does not block access to malicious sites.

5. Click OK, and then close the Group Policy Editor.

To use Windows PowerShell (Administrator), use the **Set-MpPreference** cmdlet. For example, to enable Network Protection in Audit Mode, use the following command:

```
Set-MpPreference -EnableNetworkProtection AuditMode
```

Available options are: Disabled, AuditMode, and Enabled.

Implement Controlled Folder Access

You can use Controlled Folder Access to help prevent the spread of malicious software. Specifically, controlled folder access helps protect valuable data stored in specific folders. You can use Windows PowerShell, GPOs, or MDM to configure controlled folder access.

To use GPOs to manage Controlled Folder Access, use the following procedure:

1. On a domain controller, open the appropriate GPO for editing.

2. In the Group Policy Management Editor, navigate to Computer Configuration > Policies > Administrative Templates > Windows Components > Windows Defender Antivirus > Windows Defender Exploit Guard > Controlled Folder Access.

3. Double-click the Configure Controlled Folder Access setting, as shown in Figure 3-7, and click Enabled.

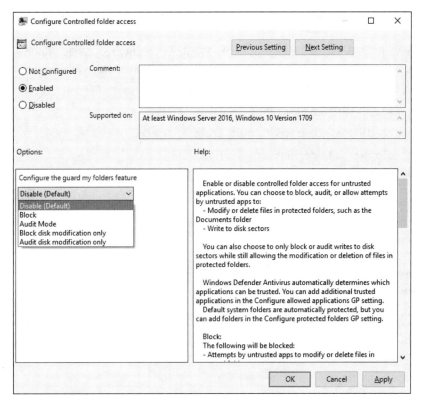

FIGURE 3-7 Enabling Controlled Folder Access

4. In the Configure The Guard My Folders Feature list, select one of the following:

   ■ **Disable.** This stops the Controlled Folder Access feature.

   ■ **Block.** Suspicious or malicious software cannot make changes to protected folders.

   ■ **Audit Mode.** Tracks rather than prevents changes to protected folders.

   ■ **Block Disk Modification Only.** Prevents untrusted apps from writing to disk sectors.

   ■ **Audit Disk Modification Only.** Audits untrusted apps that write to disk sectors.

5. Click OK and then close the Group Policy Management Editor.

To use Windows PowerShell (Administrator) to configure Controlled Folder Access, use the **Set-MpPreference** cmdlet. For example, to enable Controlled Folder Access, enter the following PowerShell command:

```
Set-MpPreference -EnableControlledFolderAccess Enabled
```

Available options are: Disabled, AuditMode, and Enabled.

After you have enabled Controlled Folder Access, you must also specify the Trusted Apps and Protected Folders settings as well. By default, Windows protects a number of folders, including system folders and default locations, such as Documents, Pictures, Movies, and Desktop.

You can configure additional folders using the Windows Security app, GPOs, Windows PowerShell, and MDM. To use the Windows Security app, use the following procedure:

1. Open the Windows Security app and select the Virus & Threat Protection tab.

2. Click the Manage Ransomware Protection link.

3. If Controlled Folder Access is not already enabled, click On.

4. Click the Protected Folders link shown in Figure 3-8.

FIGURE 3-8 Adding protected folders

5. Click Add A Protected Folder. Specify the additional folders that you want to protect.

6. Click Back.

7. To configure trusted apps, click the Allow An App Through Controlled Folder Access link.

8. Click Add An Allowed App. Specify the additional app(s) that you trust and click Open.

9. Close Windows Security.

To use GPOs to add additional folders and apps to Controlled Folder Access, use the following procedure:

1. On a domain controller, open the appropriate GPO for editing.

2. In the Group Policy Management Editor, navigate to Computer Configuration > Policies > Administrative Templates > Windows Components > Windows Defender Antivirus > Windows Defender Exploit Guard > Controlled Folder Access.

3. Select the Configure Protected Folders setting and click Enabled. Click Show and enter each folder's name.

4. Click OK.

5. Select the Configure Allowed Applications setting and click Enabled. Click Show and enter each app's path and name.

6. Click OK.

7. Close the Group Policy Editor.

To use Windows PowerShell to add protected folders, use the **Add-MpPreference** cmdlet. For example, to protect a folder named C:\MyDATA, use the following command:

```
Add-MpPreference –ControlledFolderAccessProtectedFolders "C:\MyDATA"
```

To use Windows PowerShell to add trusted apps, use the **Add-MpPreference** cmdlet. For example, to add a trusted app named C:\Apps\LOB\MyAPP.exe, use the following command:

```
Add-MpPreference –ControlledFolderAccessAllowedApplications "C:\Apps\LOB\MyAPP.exe"
```

> *NEED MORE REVIEW?* **ENABLE CONTROLLED FOLDER ACCESS**
>
> To review further details about configuring folder access, refer to the Microsoft website at *https://docs.microsoft.com/windows/security/threat-protection/windows-defender-exploit-guard/enable-controlled-folders-exploit-guard*.

Implement and manage Windows Defender Application Guard

Windows Defender Application Guard isolates browser sessions from the local device by running those sessions in a virtual machine environment; this helps prevent malicious apps or content from accessing the local device.

Requirements

The requirements for Windows Defender Application Guard are as follows:

- 64-bit version of Windows 10 Enterprise, Education, or Professional.
- 8 GB of physical memory is recommended.

- Support for Virtualization-based security.
- UEFI 2.3.1 or greater.
- Secure Boot.
- TPM 2.0, either discrete or firmware.
- UEFI (firmware) lock.
- Virtualization features: Intel VT-x, AMD-V, and SLAT must be enabled.
- A Intel VT-d or AMD-Vi input-output memory management unit.

Configuring Windows Defender Application Guard

You can configure Windows Defender Application Guard in one of two modes:

- **Standalone Mode**   In standalone mode, users can manage their own device settings.
- **Enterprise Mode**   With Enterprise mode, an administrator configures appropriate device settings using GPOs, MDM, or Windows PowerShell.

To enable Windows Defender Application Guard, use the following procedure:

1. Open Control Panel.
2. Click Programs.
3. Click Turn Windows Features On Or Off.
4. Scroll down and select the Windows Defender Application Guard check box, as shown in Figure 3-9.

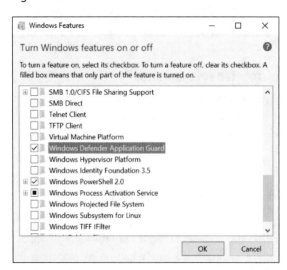

FIGURE 3-9 Enabling Windows Defender Application Guard

5. Click OK. You are prompted to restart your computer.

To use Windows Defender Application Guard in standalone mode, in Microsoft Edge, click the ellipse button and then click New Application Guard Window, as shown in Figure 3-10. The Windows Defender Application Guard service starts, and then a new instance of Microsoft Edge opens.

FIGURE 3-10 Opening a new Application Guard window

NEED MORE REVIEW? **CONFIGURE WINDOWS DEFENDER APPLICATION GUARD POLICY SETTINGS**

To learn how to configure Windows Defender Application Guard policies, refer to the Microsoft website at *https://docs.microsoft.com/windows/security/threat-protection/ windows-defender-application-guard/configure-wd-app-guard*.

Implement Windows Defender Advanced Threat Protection

Windows Defender Advanced Threat Protection (ATP) is a security platform built in to Windows 10 and integrated with Microsoft cloud-based security services. Table 3-4 describes some of the capabilities built in to Windows Defender ATP.

TABLE 3-4 Capabilities of Windows Defender ATP

CAPABILITY	DESCRIPTION
Attack surface reduction	Helps reduce the attack surface of a computer, its applications, and the data it consumes by implementing several Windows Defender ATP features.
Endpoint detection and response	Continuously monitors your organization's endpoints for possible attacks against devices or networks in your organization and provides you with the features you can use to mitigate and remediate threats.
Automated investigation and remediation	Offers automatic investigation and remediation capabilities that help reduce the volume of alerts and actions an administrator needs to perform to fix breaches.
Secure score	Enables you to assess the security posture of your organization and identify devices that might need attention, as well as recommendations for actions to improve your score
Management and APIs	Provides a means for you to interact with the platform by providing APIs.

Windows Defender ATP integrates many of the security features we have already discussed to help you secure your devices.

Requirements

To use Windows Defender ATP, you require one of the following Microsoft Volume licensing options:

- Windows 10 Enterprise E5
- Windows 10 Education E5
- Microsoft 365 E5

The Portal

You use the Windows Defender Security Center portal to manage Windows Defender ATP settings and to view reports and alerts. You can access the portal at *https://securitycenter.windows.com.*

Integrate Windows Defender Application Control

Windows Defender Application Control enables you to determine precisely which apps your users are allowed to run; it does this by blocking any unsigned apps and scripts. You configure Windows Defender Application Control with policies that specify whether a code that runs in kernel mode, such as device drivers or apps can run.

A policy typically includes rules that

- Control options such as whether audit mode is enabled
- Determine whether user mode code integrity (UMCI) is enabled
- Specify the level at which apps are be identified and/or trusted

Each Windows 10 device has a single Windows Defender Application Control policy defined for it. Typically, you configure this by using GPOs in an AD DS environment or by using MDM for enrolled devices. Either way, the policy is stored as a local file called SIPolicy.p7b that resides in the C:\Windows\System32\CodeIntegrity folder; for UEFI-based computers, the file is <EFI System Partition>\Microsoft\Boot.

Signing apps

To enable Windows Defender Application Control in your organization, you must digitally sign all the trusted apps that you want to allow to run on your devices. You can do this in a number of ways.

- **Publish your apps by using the Microsoft Store**   All apps in the Microsoft Store are automatically signed with signatures from a trusted certificate authority (CA).

- **Use your own digital certificate or public key infrastructure (PKI)**   You can sign the apps by using a certificate issued by a CA in your own PKI.

- **Use a non-Microsoft CA**   You can use a trusted non-Microsoft CA to sign your own desktop Windows apps.

- **Use the Windows Defender Application Control signing portal**   In Microsoft Store for Business, you can use a Microsoft web service to sign your desktop Windows apps.

Create a default Windows Defender Application Control policy

To create a default policy, start by creating a reference computer that is virus- and malware-free and contains the set of apps that your users require to run. It might be that you need to create several reference computers, each representing a typical device configuration within your organization. For example, you create a standard device for the research department, and perhaps you create a kiosk-type device for use in the library.

Having created the reference computer, sign in and then complete the following procedure:

1. Open an elevated Windows PowerShell command prompt.

2. Create the required variables for the process by running the following three commands:

   ```
   $CIPolicyPath=$env:userprofile+"\Desktop\"
   $InitialCIPolicy=$CIPolicyPath+"InitialScan.xml"
   $CIPolicyBin=$CIPolicyPath+"DeviceGuardPolicy.bin"
   ```

3. Scan the system for installed apps using the **New-CIPolicy** cmdlet:

   ```
   New-CIPolicy -Level PcaCertificate -FilePath $InitialCIPolicy –UserPEs 3>
   CIPolicyLog.txt
   ```

4. Convert the WDAC policy to a binary format (for import) using the **ConvertFrom-CIPolicy** cmdlet:

   ```
   ConvertFrom-CIPolicy $InitialCIPolicy $CIPolicyBin
   ```

Enabling Windows Defender Application Control

After creating the default WDAC policy, you can use GPOs to distribute the required settings. Use the following procedure to complete this process:

1. On a domain controller, open Group Policy Management.

2. Open the appropriate GPO for editing and navigate to Computer Configuration > Policies > Administrative Templates > System > Device Guard.

3. Double-click the Deploy Windows Defender Application Control setting.

4. In the Deploy Windows Defender Application Control dialog box, click Enabled.

5. Specify a value for the Code integrity policy file path and click OK. The file must be specified as a UNC path. Whichever file you point to, when downloaded to the client, it is renamed as SIPolicy.p7b.

6. Close the Group Policy Management Editor.

> **NEED MORE REVIEW?** **PLANNING AND GETTING STARTED ON THE WINDOWS DEFENDER APPLICATION CONTROL DEPLOYMENT PROCESS**
>
> To review further details about deploying Windows Defender Application Control, refer to the Microsoft website at *https://docs.microsoft.com/windows/security/threat-protection/windows-defender-application-control/windows-defender-application-control-deployment-guide*.

Manage Windows Defender Antivirus

Malicious software can do many things to your computer, such as allowing unauthorized parties remote access to your computer or collecting and transmitting information that is sensitive or confidential to unauthorized third parties.

Some types of malware include:

- **Computer viruses**   Replicate malicious code, normally with email attachments or files.

- **Computer worms**   Replicate, without direct intervention, across networks.

- **Trojan horses**   Trick the user into providing an attacker with remote access to the infected computer.

- **Ransomware**   Harms the user by encrypting user data until a ransom (fee) is paid to the malware authors to recover the data.

- **Spyware**   Tracking software that reports to the third party how a computer is used.

The most common attack vector for malware is still by email, although attacks from websites, pirated software, video, and music files are becoming increasingly common.

You can help protect against malware infection by following these guidelines.

- All software should be from a reputable source.
- Ensure that all software and operating system updates are applied without delay.
- Install and enable antimalware software on your devices. Windows Defender is automatically enabled.
- Make sure antimalware definitions are up to date.
- Avoid using or accessing pirated software or non-mainstream media-sharing sites.
- Be suspicious of out-of-the-ordinary email attachments, and don't open links in spam or phishing emails.

Although no antimalware solution can provide 100 percent safety, modern solutions can reduce the probability that malware compromises your device.

Windows Defender Antivirus can help protect your device by actively detecting spyware, malware, and viruses both in the operating system and on Windows 10 installed on Hyper-V virtual machines. Windows Defender runs in the background and automatically installs new definitions as they are released, often daily.

You can use Windows Defender Antivirus manually to check for malware with various scan options listed in Table 3-5.

TABLE 3-5 Windows Defender Antivirus scan options

SCAN OPTIONS	DESCRIPTION
Quick	Checks the most likely areas that malware—including viruses, spyware, and software—commonly infect.
Full	Scans all files on your hard disk and scans all running programs.
Custom	Enables users to scan specific drives and folders to target specific areas of your computer, such as a removable drive.
Windows Defender Offline Scan	Allows users to find and remove difficult-to-remove malicious software. The system will need to reboot, and the scan can take about 15 minutes.

Monitor for malware

You should routinely check your system for malware. If it becomes infected or you suspect malware is on your system, you can run a Full Scan.

To configure and use Windows Defender Antivirus, follow these steps.

1. Open Windows Security, as shown in Figure 3-11.
2. Click the Home item on the left and verify that your device is being protected and that Virus & Threat Protection is active. (You'll see a check mark on a green background.) Also, be sure to verify that the threat definitions are up to date.

3. Click the Shield item on the left, and in the Threat History, review the last scan results and number of files scanned.

4. Under Virus & Threat Protection updates, click the Check For Updates link and verify that the definitions are up to date. If they are not, ensure that you are connected to the Internet and click the Check For Updates button.

5. Under Current Threats, click the Threat History link. Here, you can view Current, Quarantined, and Allowed Threats. Review the results of any Quarantined or Allowed items that were on your PC.

6. If you want to remove all quarantined threats, click Remove All.

7. You can also highlight each item and choose Remove (to remove a single item); choose Restore to restore the file if you believe this is not malware.

8. When it is removed, the item is deleted, and the Quarantined Threats list is cleared.

9. Close Windows Security app.

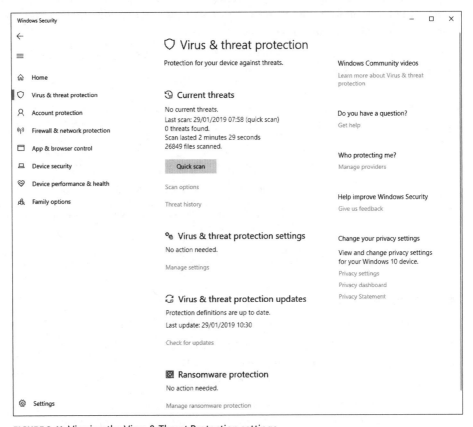

FIGURE 3-11 Viewing the Virus & Threat Protection settings

Configure Windows Defender Advanced Threat Detection

Windows Defender Antivirus can detect, and then report directly to Microsoft, details of suspicious or malicious activity on devices across the world. This provides an effective early warning system that allows near-instant detection and subsequent blocking of new and emerging threats by Windows Defender Antivirus. Telemetry from Windows Defender Antivirus is sent automatically and can include samples of malicious code. This code is then analyzed and helps reduce the threat and likelihood of "zero-day" exploits, which can affect millions of users worldwide. Microsoft can see activity and react much earlier than with traditional threat notification, which would involve manual interventions to forward samples of malware.

You can customize this option to turn off the feature that sends data to Microsoft by selecting Turn Off Telemetry Options in the Settings app, using these steps.

1. Open the Windows Security app.
2. Click on the Virus & Threat Protection item on the left.
3. Select the Manage Settings link under the Virus & Threat Protection Settings heading.
4. Under the Cloud-Delivered Protection, toggle the setting to Off, which prevents Windows from automatically sending sample submissions of malware to Microsoft.

You can also configure these settings by using Group Policy. The settings are found in the following node: Computer Configuration > Policies > Administrative Templates > Windows Components > Windows Defender Antivirus > MAPS.

The Microsoft Active Protection Service (MAPS) is the cloud service that Microsoft uses to collect and analyze key telemetry events and suspicious malware queries from computers running Windows Vista or later. The service also provides real-time blocking responses back to client devices for suspicious items that do not match published definitions. As a cloud service, it uses distributed resources and machine learning to deliver the endpoint protection. This results in malware analysis and remediation including signature updates delivered to the user much faster than with traditional methods.

You can manage Windows Defender Antivirus settings either locally, by using GPOs, with MDM endpoint protection policies, or with Windows PowerShell.

Using Microsoft Intune for Endpoint Protection

Throughout this skill, we have discussed ways in which you can enable and configure the various Windows Defender security features and components. The focus has been on using GPOs or Windows PowerShell. However, it is also possible to use the Microsoft 365 Mobile Device Management portal, as shown in Figure 3-12.

Typically, you use Intune and the Microsoft 365 Device Management portal to manage enrolled devices within your organization; these devices are not members of your on-premises AD DS forest.

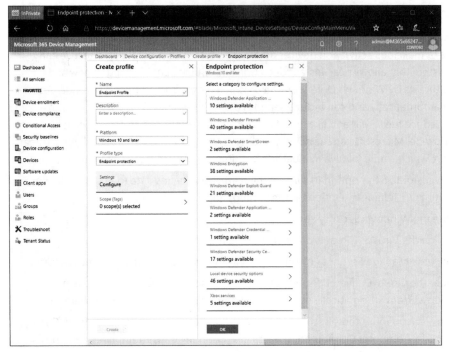

FIGURE 3-12 Using the Microsoft 365 Device Management portal to create endpoint protection profiles

To create and edit Windows Defender settings using Microsoft 365 MDM, use the following procedure:

1. Open the Microsoft 365 Device Management portal.

2. Sign in using your global admin account.

3. Select Device Configuration from the Navigation pane.

4. Select Profiles.

5. Click Create Profile.

6. Enter a name and description and select Windows 10 And Later from the Platform list.

7. In the Profile Type list, click Endpoint Protection.

8. On the Endpoint Protection blade, you can configure the following settings:

   - Windows Defender Application Guard

   - Windows Defender Firewall

   - Windows Defender SmartScreen

   - Windows Encryption

   - Windows Defender Exploit Guard

   - Windows Defender Application Control

   - Windows Defender Credential Guard

   - Windows Defender Security Center

- Local device security options
- Xbox services

9. After you have configured the desired settings, click OK and then click Create.

10. Assign the policy to the appropriate groups of devices.

We will discuss using Intune and the Microsoft 365 Device Management portal in more detail in the next skill.

Skill 3.2: Manage Intune Device Enrollment and inventory

MDM enables administration of remote mobile devices across multiple platforms. Microsoft Intune supports MDM for managing remote mobile devices. However, before you can start managing devices, you must enroll them in Intune. Once enrolled, you can perform various management tasks using Intune on your mobile devices, as shown in Table 3-6.

TABLE 3-6 Management tasks

CATEGORY	DETAILS
App management	<ul><li>App deployment</li><li>App restrictions</li><li>Mobile application management</li></ul>
Device security and configuration	<ul><li>Configuration policies</li><li>Password management</li><li>Remote wipe and lock</li><li>Custom policies</li></ul>
Company resource access	<ul><li>VPN profiles</li><li>WiFi profiles</li><li>Email profiles</li><li>Certificate profiles</li><li>Conditional access profiles</li></ul>
Inventory and reporting	<ul><li>Hardware inventory</li><li>Application inventory</li><li>Reporting</li></ul>
Endpoint protection	<ul><li>Windows Defender Application Guard</li><li>Windows Defender Firewall</li><li>Windows Defender SmartScreen</li><li>Windows Encryption</li><li>Windows Defender Exploit Guard</li><li>Windows Defender Application Control</li><li>Windows Defender Security Center</li><li>Windows Defender Advanced Threat Protection</li><li>Windows Information Protection</li></ul>

In this skill, you will learn how to configure and enable enrollment. You'll also learn how to use Intune to enroll various device types in MDM.

> **This skill covers how to:**
> - Configure enrollment settings
> - Enable Device Enrollment
> - Configure Intune automatic enrollment
> - Enroll Windows devices
> - Enroll non-Windows devices
> - Generate custom device inventory reports and review device inventory

Configure enrollment settings

You enable MDM for devices by enrolling them. The enrollment process is different for each platform, and each platform has a specific set of requirements, as shown in Table 3-7.

TABLE 3-7 Enrollment requirements

DEVICE PLATFORM	ENROLLMENT REQUIREMENTS
■ Apple iOS 9.0 and later ■ Mac OS X 10.9 and later	Obtain an Apple Push Notification service certificate. This enables Microsoft Intune to communicate securely with iOS devices.
■ Android 4.4 and later (including Samsung KNOX Standard 4.4 and higher) ■ Android for Work	Download the Microsoft Intune Company Portal app from the Google Play store on each device.
■ Windows 10 (Home, S, Pro, Education, and Enterprise versions) ■ Windows 10 Mobile ■ Devices running Windows 10 IoT Enterprise (x86, x64) ■ Devices running Windows 10 IoT Mobile Enterprise ■ Windows Holographic & Windows Holographic Enterprise ■ Windows Phone 8.1, Windows 8.1 RT, PCs running Windows 8.1 (Sustaining mode)	If direct enrollment is not possible (for example, with older versions of Windows), you can install the Microsoft Intune software client from the Intune classic portal. The Intune software client can be used to manage Windows 7 and later PCs (except Windows 10 Home edition).

For Windows devices, there is an existing trust relationship between the device operating system and Intune; therefore, you can configure and enable automatic enrollment. The following list provides a high-level explanation of the enrollment process for each platform:

- **Windows 7 and Windows 8** Install the Microsoft Intune client. The Company Portal app is not available.

- **Windows 8.1 or Windows RT 8.1**   On the device, tap Settings > PC Settings > Network > Workplace, enter your credentials, and click Join. Turn on Device Management.

- **Windows 10**   If users sign into the device using their corporate credentials, their account is added to Azure Active Directory (Azure AD) and the device is then managed with Intune.

- **iOS—BYOD (Bring Your Own Device) iPads, iPhones, and Mac computers**
  An MDM Push certificate is required for Intune to manage iOS and Mac devices. Install the Company Portal app from the App Store, open the app, and follow the Enrollment wizard.

- **iOS—Company-owned devices**   For bulk enrollments, you can use the following methods:
  - Apple's Device Enrollment Program (DEP)
  - Apple School Manager
  - Apple Configurator Setup Assistant enrollment
  - Apple Configurator direct enrollment
  - Intune Device Enrollment Manager account

- **Android and Samsung Knox Standard devices**   Users must enroll their devices by downloading the Intune Company Portal app from Google Play.

> **NOTE   ANNUAL CERTIFICATE RENEWAL**
>
> The Apple MDM push certificate is valid for one year and must be renewed annually to maintain iOS and macOS device management. If your certificate expires, enrolled Apple devices cannot be contacted or managed.

Before you can configure enrollment, you must first make Intune your MDM authority. This is a one-time activity. To enable Intune as your MDM authority, perform the following procedure:

1. Open Microsoft Edge and navigate to *https://devicemanagement.microsoft.com*.
2. Sign in with the global admin account associated with your Microsoft 365 subscription.
3. In Microsoft 365 Device Management, click Device Enrollment, and then under MDM Authority, select Intune MDM Authority and click Choose.
4. In the upper-right part of the details pane, verify that MDM authority is now set to Intune.

After this step is complete, you can begin the process of configuring enrollment settings.

To enable Device Enrollment, click Device Enrollment in the Microsoft 365 Device Management portal's Navigation pane, as shown in Figure 3-13.

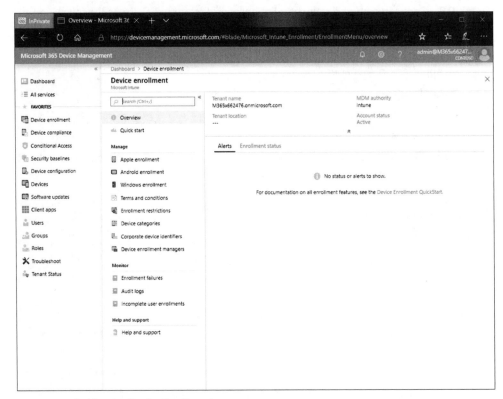

FIGURE 3-13 Configuring Device Enrollment

You can select the Quick Start option, as shown in Figure 3-14, to help guide you through the process of configuring Device Enrollment. Quick Start identifies the steps you must take to enable and configure Device Enrollment. If you click any of the unticked links, then Intune opens the required configuration blade.

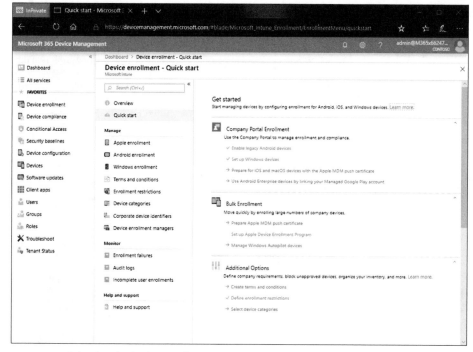

FIGURE 3-14 Selecting the Device Enrollment Quick Start option

Alternatively, you can select from the available options in the Manage section of the Device Enrollment blade. These options are described in Table 3-8.

TABLE 3-8 Enrollment Configuration options

OPTION	DESCRIPTION
Apple Enrollment	From this node, you can configure the Apple MDM Push Certificate. You can also configure bulk enrollment methods for iOS devices.
Android Enrollment	By default, all Android devices can be enrolled as conventional devices. Link your managed Google Play account to Intune from this blade. You can also configure Android Enterprise settings from here: ■ Personal Devices With Work Profile ■ Corporate-Owned Dedicated Devices ■ Corporate-Owned, Fully Managed User Devices
Windows Enrollment	From this blade, you can access the following settings to configure Windows Device Enrollment: ■ Automatic Enrollment. Configure Windows devices to enroll automatically when they join or register with Azure AD. ■ Windows Hello For Business. Replace passwords with two-factor authentication. ■ CNAME Validation. Verify that your company's custom domain name registration is successful.

(Continued)

OPTION	DESCRIPTION
	■ Enrollment Status Page. Configure the app and profile installation status to users during their device setup. ■ Windows Autopilot deployment profiles. Configure how provisioning works with Windows Autopilot. ■ Windows Autopilot devices. Manage and configure devices deployed through Windows Autopilot. ■ Intune Connector for Active Directory. Configure the behavior of enrolled hybrid Azure AD–joined devices.
Terms And Conditions	Create and configure Terms And Conditions statements for enrolled devices. These are messages users see during Device Enrollment.
Enrollment Restrictions	■ Create new Enrollment Restriction. There are device type and device limit restrictions. There is a default restriction for both device types and for device limits. ■ The default device type restriction enables all users to enroll any type of device. ■ The default device limit restriction enables all users to enroll no more than 15 devices. ■ You can modify these two default restrictions (but you cannot delete them), or you can create additional restrictions. A device must comply with the highest-priority Enrollment Restriction assigned to its user. You can drag a device restriction to change its priority.
Device Categories	Create Device Categories from which users must choose during Device Enrollment. You can filter reports and create Azure Active Directory device groups based on Device Categories.
Corporate Device Identifiers	You can enter (or upload) Device Identifiers for corporate-owned devices. The identifier might be an IMEI number or a serial number.
Device Enrollment Managers	Add one or more users with the ability to enroll multiple devices.

Configure Terms And Conditions

Terms And Conditions display to users during their Device Enrollment. To configure custom terms and conditions, from the Microsoft 365 Device Management portal, select the Device Enrollment node, and then use the following procedure:

1. On the Device Enrollment blade, select Terms And Conditions.
2. Click Create.
3. In the Create Terms And Conditions window, in the Display Name box, type a name.
4. In the Description box, type a meaningful description.
5. Click Define Term Of Use.
6. As shown in Figure 3-15, enter a Title, Summary Of Terms, and Terms And Conditions.

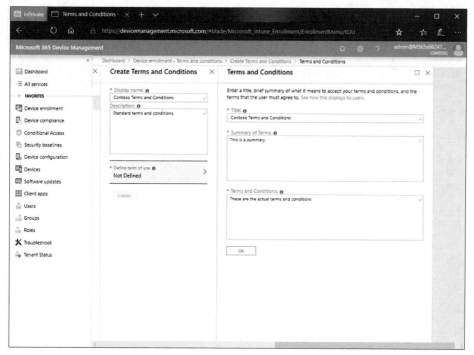

FIGURE 3-15 Defining terms and conditions for enrolling devices

7. Click Ok, and then click Create.

8. On the Device Enrollment—Terms And Conditions blade, your new terms and conditions are listed. However, they are not assigned. To assign, click the new Terms And Conditions object.

9. Click Assignments and then choose whether to assign to All Users, as shown in Figure 3-16, or to assign to Selected Groups. If you choose the latter, then select the desired groups.

10. Click Save.

Your terms and conditions will now display during enrollment.

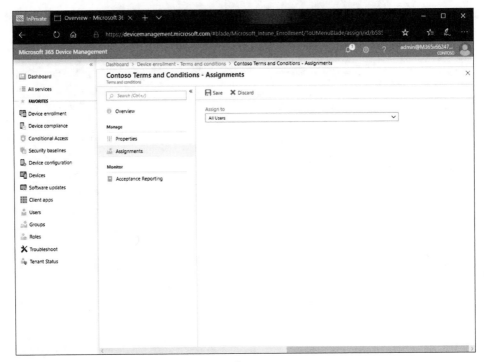

FIGURE 3-16 Assigning terms and conditions to All Users

Configure Enrollment Restrictions

Enrollment Restrictions determine the type and number of devices users can enroll to Intune. To configure Enrollment Restrictions, from the Microsoft 365 Device Management portal, select the Device Enrollment node and use the following procedure:

1. On the Device Enrollment blade, select Enrollment Restrictions.

2. To create a new type of restriction, click Create Restriction.

3. On the Create Restriction page, enter a Name and Description and select the Device Type Restriction option.

4. Click Select Platforms.

5. On the Select Platforms blade, choose the appropriate device types, as shown in Figure 3-17, and then click OK.

6. Click Configure Platforms.

7. On the Configure Platforms blade, select the appropriate minimum and maximum version information for each device type, as shown in Figure 3-18, and then click Ok. Define versions as major.minor.build. Note that version restrictions only apply to devices enrolled with the Company Portal app.

8. Click Create and then click Assignments.

9. Click Select Groups and then choose the appropriate group for which the restriction(s) will apply. Click Save.

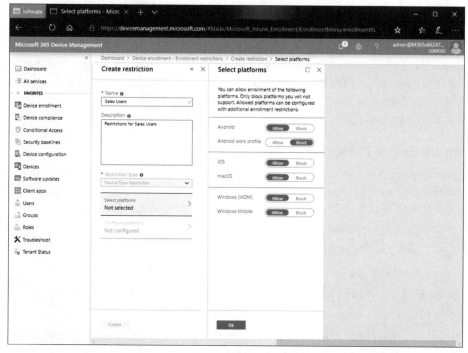

FIGURE 3-17 Selecting device platforms for enrollment

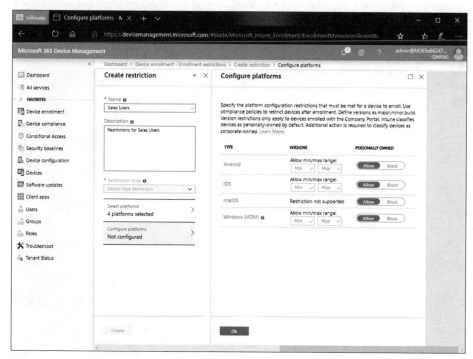

FIGURE 3-18 Specifying versions for platforms for Device Enrollment

To create a device limit restriction, the process starts the same. However, when you specify the restriction type as Device Limit Restriction, you can then only configure a Device Limit, which can be any number between 1 and 15 (the default). Again, after creating the restriction, you must assign it to a group as described above.

When you have multiple Enrollment Restrictions configured, you can drag and drop them to change priority. Remember that the device must comply with the highest priority Enrollment Restriction assigned to its user.

Configure Device Categories

Categories help you when you are using reporting tools. Users select a suitable category during enrollment. To configure Device Categories, from the Microsoft 365 Device Management portal, select the Device Enrollment node, and then use the following procedure:

1. On the Device Enrollment blade, select Device Categories.

2. Click Create Device Category.

3. On the Create Device Category blade, type a suitable name in the Category box.

4. In the Description box, type a meaningful description of your category.

5. Click Create.

After you have created all the appropriate Device Categories, as shown in Figure 3-19, when users enroll devices, they must select from the listed categories.

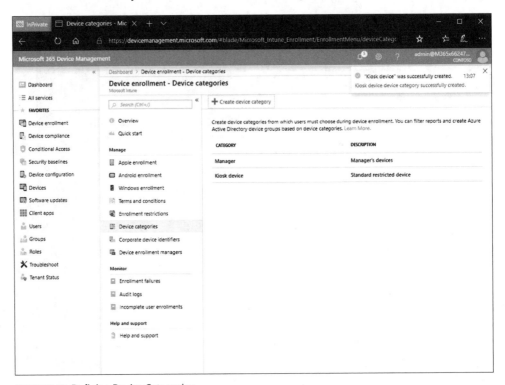

FIGURE 3-19 Defining Device Categories

You can also use these categories to create dynamic groups in Azure AD. Dynamic groups have a membership based on the result of a query. For example, you could create a dynamic group called "Kiosk device" that had a membership based on the result of the following query:

```
device.deviceCategory -eq "Kiosk device"
```

Configure Device Identifiers

Device identifiers enable you to identify specific devices as being corporate-owned devices. This is done by entering the serial number or IMEI into Intune. To configure Device Identifiers, from the Microsoft 365 Device Management portal, select the Device Enrollment node and use the following procedure:

1. On the Device Enrollment blade, select Device Identifiers.
2. Click Add and select either Upload CSV file or Enter Manually.
3. If you select to upload a CSV file, specify the identifier type (choose between Serial Number or IMEI) in the CSV file. Browse to the CSV file location, select the CSV file for upload, and click Add.
4. If you choose to manually enter the identifiers, for each identifier, select the type (choose between serial number or IMEI), enter the identifier and details information for each device, and click Add.

Configure Enrollment Managers

If you want to enroll a large number of devices in an enterprise scenario, you can use the Device Enrollment Manager (DEM) account in Microsoft Intune. The DEM is a special account in Microsoft Intune that allows you to enroll up to 1,000 devices. (Standard users can manage and enroll up to 15 devices.) For security reasons, the DEM user should not also be an Intune administrator. Each enrolled device requires a single Intune license. By default, there is no Device Enrollment account user present in Microsoft Intune.

Typically, these DEM accounts might be IT personnel. To configure Enrollment Managers, from the Microsoft 365 Device Management portal, select the Device enrollment node and use the following procedure:

1. On the Device Enrollment blade, select Enrollment Managers.
2. Click Add, type the user name (for example, **user@contoso.com**) in the User Name box, and click Add.

The complete list of Enrollment Managers is displayed, as shown in Figure 3-20.

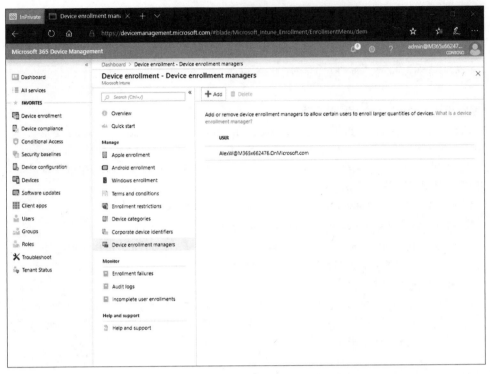

FIGURE 3-20 Defining Device Enrollment Managers

Enable Device Enrollment

After you have configured Device Enrollment settings, you must enable Device Enrollment before you can start enrolling devices. Precisely what you must do varies depending on the device types you want to be able to enroll.

For all device types, you must first define Intune as your MDM. This process was described earlier. See "Configure enrollment settings" in Skill 3.2: Manage Intune Device Enrollment and inventory.

For Windows devices, you can now go on to configure automatic enrollment, if desired. For non-Windows devices, there are additional preparation steps required. These are described in the following sections. You can see what preparatory steps remain by visiting the Device Enrollment tab in the Microsoft 365 Device Management portal, and selecting the Quick Start node, as shown in Figure 3-21.

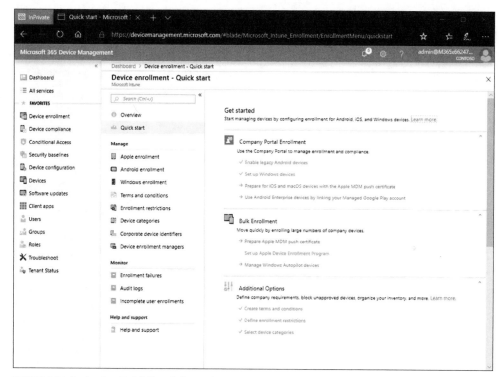

FIGURE 3-21 Reviewing Quick Start information

Configure Intune automatic enrollment

To configure automatic enrollment for Windows devices, complete the following procedure in the Microsoft 365 Device Management portal:

1. Select the Device Enrollment node.

2. Select Windows Enrollment.

3. In the Windows Enrollment blade, click Automatic Enrollment.

4. On the Configure blade, shown in Figure 3-22, choose one of the following MDM User Scope options:

   - **None** Prevent automatic enrollment for Windows devices. This is the default value.

   - **Some** Specify the appropriate groups that have automatic enrollment permissions.

   - **All** Enable all users to automatically enroll their devices.

5. If you selected Some, then click Select Groups. Browse and select the necessary groups that will have automatic enrollment privileges.

6. Click Save.

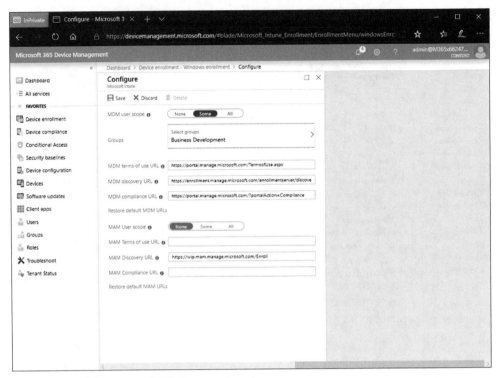

FIGURE 3-22 Enabling automatic Windows enrollment

Enroll Windows devices

There are several different ways to enroll devices in Intune. These are:

- **Add Work Or School Account**   Use this method to register the device with Azure AD or join the device to Azure AD. If you have an Azure AD Premium subscription and you have enabled Windows Automatic Enrollment, this method also enrolls the device in Intune. This method is user initiated.

- **Enroll In MDM Only (User Driven)**   Select this option if you want to enroll your device(s) in Intune only, without registering or joining to Azure AD. This might be appropriate if your organization does not have an Azure AD premium subscription. This method is user initiated.

- **Azure AD Join During OOBE**   This method is very similar in terms of the end result to what happens when you perform an Add Work Or School Account procedure. However, the process is launched and managed during the initial setup of the device; this initial setup is referred to as out-of-box experience (OOBE). This is a user-initiated method.

- **Azure AD Join Using Windows Autopilot**   This enrollment method works in a similar way to the preceding method; however, using Windows Autopilot enables you to partially or completely automate the OOBE process for your users. Again, the process is launched and managed through OOBE; your Windows Autopilot settings will determine the precise level of user interaction. You can choose between user-driven mode and self-deploying; these options are configured as part of the Windows Autopilot deployment profile. Windows Autopilot is discussed in Chapter 1, "Deploy and update operating systems." This is the preferred method of enrolling using OOBE because it is a more managed approach. It does, however, assume that your organization has an Azure AD premium subscription and that you have enabled Windows Automatic Enrollment.

- **Enroll In MDM Only Using A Device Enrollment Manager** This method is similar to the Add Work Or School Account method above. However, rather than use a standard user account to enroll in your organization's MDM, you use a Device Enrollment Manager Account. These accounts can enroll up to 1,000 devices.

MORE INFO **ENROLL DEVICES USING DEVICE ENROLLMENT MANAGER**

For more information on the DEM in Microsoft Intune—together with example scenarios and limitations of devices that are enrolled with a DEM account—visit the following URL: *https://docs.microsoft.com/intune/device-enrollment-manager-enroll.*

- **Azure AD Join Using Bulk Enrollment** This method enables you to use provisioning packages to enroll a large number of devices. You create a provisioning package using Windows Configuration Designer and apply this package either during OOBE, or by distributing and running the package after a device has completed its initial setup process.

The following sections discuss some of these methods in more detail.

Add work or school account

To enroll a Windows device using this method, use the following procedure:

1. Enable Windows Automatic Enrollment for either all users or for an appropriate group to whom the designated account (which you use in step 6) belongs.
2. Sign in to your Windows 10 computer and open Settings.
3. Click Accounts.
4. Select the Access Work Or School tab.
5. Click Connect.
6. Perform one of the following actions:
   - **To register the device with Azure AD and enroll the device in Intune** In the Microsoft Account dialog box shown in Figure 3-23, in the Email Address box, type the organizational email address and then click Next.
   - **To join the device to Azure AD and enroll the device in Intune** In the Microsoft Account dialog box, click Join This Device To Azure Active Directory. Then, in the Let's Get You Signed In To Windows, type the organizational email address and then click Next.
7. When prompted, enter the user's password, and click Sign In.
8. If prompted, set up additional account verification options, such as a text message confirmation.

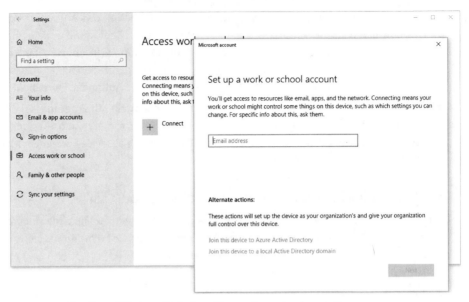

FIGURE 3-23 Enrolling a Windows 10 device with a work or school account

9. If configured, your Terms And Conditions are displayed. Click Accept.

10. If configured, your user will be prompted to select a device category, as shown in Figure 3-24.

FIGURE 3-24 Selecting a device category

11. In the Make Sure This Is Your Organization dialog box, as shown in Figure 3-25, click Join.

12. Your device is registered with/joined to your organization and enrolled in Intune. Click Done when prompted.

FIGURE 3-25 Confirming the Device Enrollment

You can verify that the device is properly registered and enrolled from the Microsoft 365 Device Management portal. Use the following procedure:

1. Sign in as global admin and navigate to the Device node.

2. Select All Devices. The new device should be listed.

3. Select Azure AD Devices. The new device is listed as either Azure AD–registered or Azure AD–joined, as shown in Figure 3-26, depending on the option you selected during enrollment.

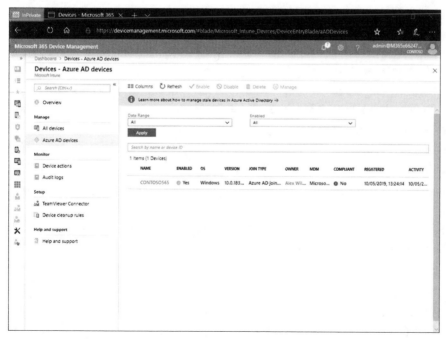

FIGURE 3-26 Verifying the presence of the newly enrolled device

Enroll in MDM only

If you want to enroll a Windows device using this method, use the following procedure:

1. Enable Windows Automatic Enrollment for either all users or for an appropriate group to whom the designated account (which you use in step 6) belongs.

2. Sign in to your Windows 10 computer and open Settings.

3. Click Accounts.

4. Select the Access Work Or School tab.

5. On the Access Work Or School tab, click Enroll Only In Device Management.

6. In the Microsoft Account window, enter the organizational email account.

7. The Connecting To A Service window opens. Enter the user's password and click Sign In.

8. In the Setting Up Your Device Window, click Got It.

9. Your device is enrolled in Intune.

You can verify that the device is properly enrolled from the Microsoft 365 Device Management portal. Use the following procedure:

1. Sign in as global admin and navigate to the Device node.

2. Select All Devices. The new device should be listed.

3. Select Azure AD devices. The new device is listed, but because you chose not to register with or join to Azure AD, the Join Type column is blank.

Azure AD Join during OOBE

To enroll a Windows device using this method, use the following procedure:

1. Turn on the new Windows device. The OOBE starts and guides the user through the process of configuring his or her device. This involves selecting a region and keyboard layout(s).

2. When prompted on the Sign In With Microsoft page shown in Figure 3-27, enter the appropriate Microsoft 365 account and click Next.

3. Enter the password when prompted and click Next.

4. Set up continues, and you are prompted to configure supplemental options, such as Privacy settings, Cortana, and other settings.

5. If prompted, set up additional account verification options such as a text message confirmation.

6. You might be prompted to set up a PIN for sign in, depending on your organizational security settings.

7. Your device is registered with or joined to your organization and enrolled in Intune. Click OK when prompted.

8. Your desktop is built.

As before, you can use the Microsoft 365 Device Management portal to view the enrolled device. Assuming you have an Azure AD Premium subscription and have enabled Windows Automatic Enrollment for Intune, the device should appear under both the Devices and Azure AD Devices nodes. It should also show as Azure AD–joined rather than Azure AD–registered.

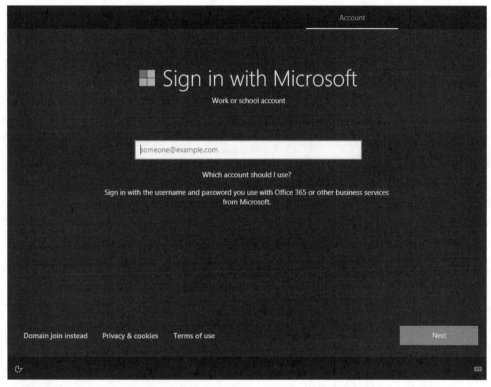

FIGURE 3-27 Sign in to your organization during OOBE

Azure AD Join using Windows Autopilot in user-driven deployment mode

To enroll a Windows device using this method, use the following procedure:

1. Open the Microsoft 365 Device Management portal and sign in with a global admin account.

2. Navigate to the Device Enrollment node and select Windows Enrollment.

3. Enable Windows Automatic Enrollment for either all users or for an appropriate group to whom the designated account belongs.

4. Navigate to the Device Enrollment node, and under the Windows Autopilot Deployment Program heading, shown in Figure 3-28, click Devices.

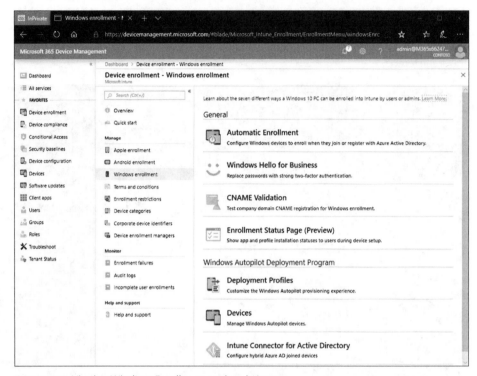

FIGURE 3-28 Viewing Windows Enrollment settings in Intune

5. Complete the procedure discussed in Chapter 1, "Deploy and update operating systems" (Skill 1.2: Plan and implement Windows 10 by using dynamic deployment, Section: Import device hardware information to cloud service) to upload the device IDs for your organization's new Windows devices.

6. On the Device Enrollment—Windows Enrollment blade, under the Windows Autopilot Deployment Program heading, select Deployment Profiles.

7. Complete the procedure discussed in Chapter 1, "Deploy and update operating systems" (Skill 1.2: Plan and implement Windows 10 by using dynamic deployment, Section: Create, validate, and assign deployment profile) to create and configure the necessary Windows Autopilot profiles. When configuring your profile, choose between User-Driven and Self-Deploying, as shown in Figure 3-29. With the former, users see a configurable

number of setup screens during OOBE setup. With the latter, the users see no setup screens during OOBE because the process is completely automated.

8. Assign the profiles.

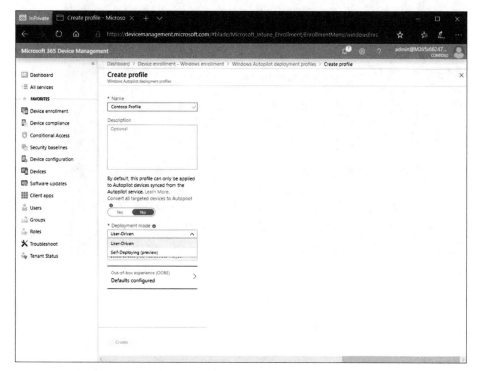

FIGURE 3-29 Configuring a Windows Autopilot deployment profile

9. When you have created, configured, and assigned the necessary Windows Autopilot deployment profiles, turn on the new Windows device(s).

10. The OOBE starts and guides the user through the process of configuring his or her device. The details vary based on how you have set up your Windows Autopilot deployment profiles. In User-Driven mode, the user(s) will see a customized sign-in screen, shown in Figure 3-30. Enter the required account information and setup will continue and complete, according to the Windows Autopilot profile settings.

After deployment, use the Microsoft 365 Device Management portal to view the enrolled device. The device should appear under both the Devices and Azure AD Devices nodes. It should also show as Azure AD–joined rather than Azure AD–registered.

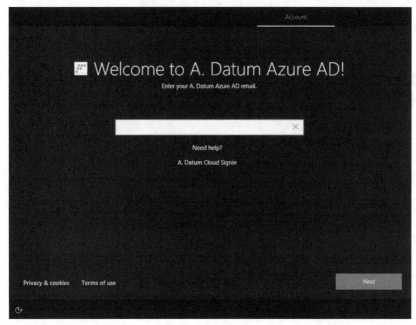

FIGURE 3-30 Sign in to your organization during Windows Autopilot OOBE

Enroll non-Windows devices

To enroll non-Windows devices, the approach is similar. Let's examine the process for Android and iOS.

Enrolling Android devices

To enroll Android devices, use the following procedure:

1. On the Android device, open the Google Play store.
2. Search for and install the Intune Company Portal app.
3. Launch the Intune Company Portal app.
4. Tap Sign In and then sign in using the appropriate user account from your Microsoft 365 subscription.
5. Follow any instructions given in the portal; these will vary based on the configured settings in Intune. Typically, you are asked to accept new settings on your device. Tap Continue on each screen to proceed through setup and enrollment.
6. Finally, you are asked to activate device administrator. Tap Activate. Your device is registered.
7. If configured, you are asked to define a device category. Tap Done.
8. When the process is complete, tap Done.

After deployment, use the Microsoft 365 Device Management portal to view the enrolled device. The device should appear under the Devices node. It should also show as Azure AD–registered rather than Azure AD–joined. You should be able to see the operating system listed in the OS column as Android.

Enrolling iOS devices

Enrolling iOS devices, such as iPads, is a similar process to that used for Android. However, there is one additional step. You must first configure and deploy an Apple MDM Push certificate. Use the following procedure to complete this step:

1. Open the Microsoft 365 Device Management portal.

2. Navigate to Device Enrollment and select Apple Enrollment.

3. Click Apple MDM Push certificate.

4. On the Configure MDM Push Certificate blade, complete the following steps:

    a. Select the I Grant Microsoft Permission To Send Both User And Device Information To Apple check box.

    b. Click the Download Your CSR Link. When prompted, click Save to save the IntuneCSR.csr file to a local folder.

    c. Click the Create Your MDM Push Certificate link. A new tab opens. On the Apple Push Certificates Portal, sign in using an Apple ID. A verification code is usually required. Create a certificate and download it.

    d. Switch to the browser tab with the Microsoft 365 Device Management portal, and in the Apple ID box, enter the Apple ID used to create your Apple MDM push certificate.

    e. Browse and locate the Apple MDM push certificate you just downloaded.

5. Click Upload.

After you have completed the process, use the following procedure to enroll an iOS device:

1. On the Apple device, sign in to the Apple Store.

2. Search for and install the Intune Company Portal app.

3. Launch the Intune Company Portal app.

4. Tap Sign In and then sign in using the appropriate user account from your Microsoft 365 subscription.

5. Follow any instructions given in the portal; these will vary based on the configured settings in Intune.

After deployment, use the Microsoft 365 Device Management portal to view the enrolled device. The device should appear under the Devices node. It should also show as Azure AD–registered rather than Azure AD–joined. You should be able to see the operating system listed in the OS column as iOS.

Generate custom device inventory reports and review device inventory

It's important to know what devices are enrolled in your organization's MDM. To access device inventory reports, in the Microsoft 365 Device Management portal, select the Devices node. As shown in Figure 3-31, you can see a summary of enrolled devices.

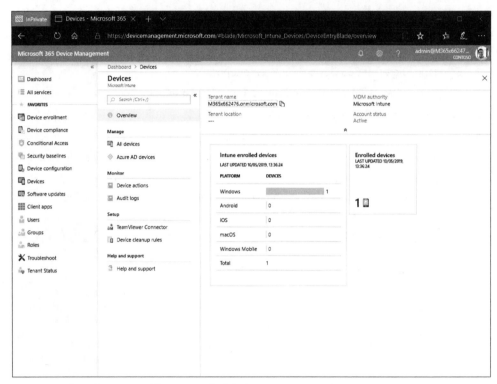

FIGURE 3-31 Overview report of Intune enrolled devices

To view additional information about enrolled devices, click the All Devices tab. As shown in Figure 3-32, you can see a list of all devices.

Select columns

Using the Columns button, as shown in Figure 3-33, you can determine exactly what information displays. Select from the available columns and click Apply.

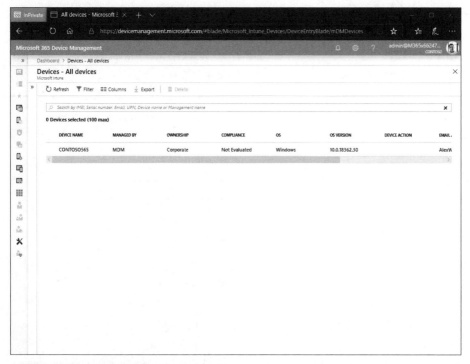

FIGURE 3-32 Viewing all devices

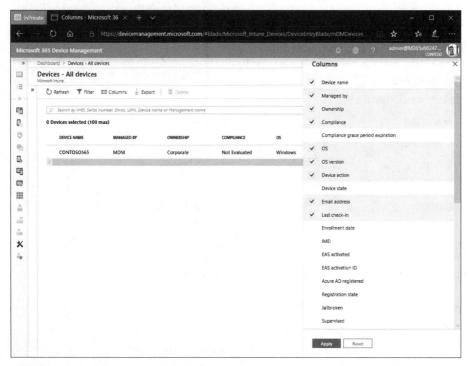

FIGURE 3-33 Selecting reporting columns for All Devices node

Available options are

- Device name
- Managed By
- Ownership, Compliance
- Compliance Grace Period
- OS
- OS version
- Device Action
- Device State
- Email Address
- Last Check-In
- Enrollment Date
- IMEI
- EAS Activated
- EAS Activation ID
- Azure AD Registered
- Registration State
- Jailbroken
- Supervised

- Category
- Last EAS Sync Time
- EAS Status
- EAS Reason
- User Principal Name
- Model
- Manufacturer
- Serial Number
- Phone Number
- User Display Name
- Security Patch Level
- WiFi MAC
- MEID
- Subscriber Carrier
- Total Storage
- Free Storage
- Management Name
- Azure AD Device ID

Filtering results

You can also use filtering. Click Filter. As shown in Figure 3-34, you can select criteria on which to filter.

Filtering categories are

- Managed By
- Device Action
- Category
- Ownership
- Compliance
- Jailbroken
- OS

- Model
- Manufacturer
- OS Version
- Phone Number
- Last Check-In Date And Time Ranges
- Enrollment Date And Time Ranges

Select and/or type the required categories and click Apply.

Export

After you have optionally filtered the devices in the list, click Export. When prompted, click Save to create a CSV file, as shown in Figure 3-35. You can then open the CSV file in Microsoft Excel to review the information.

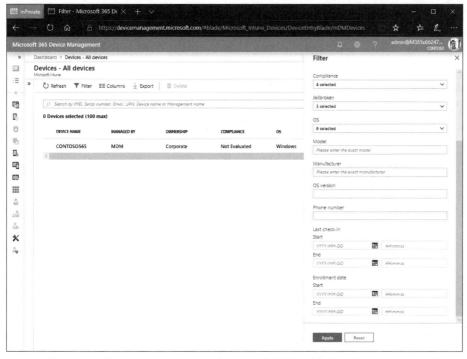

FIGURE 3-34 Filtering results for All Devices display

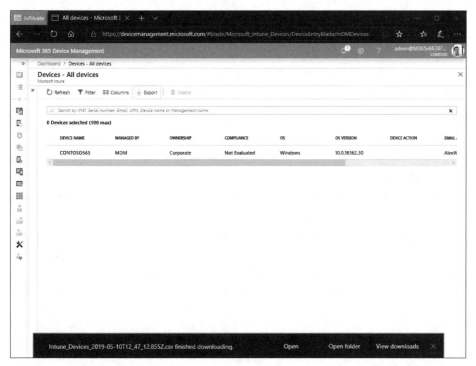

FIGURE 3-35 Exporting a report

Configure monitoring and alerts

You can also use the classic Microsoft Intune portal to monitor and report on your managed devices. The classic portal provides for a number of monitoring and reporting tools.

> **NOTE CLASSIC PORTAL**
>
> The classic portal requires Silverlight, and therefore, you must use Internet Explorer to access it. You can access the classic portal at *https://admin.manage.microsoft.com*.

There are two primary ways that you can monitor the status of your Microsoft Intune environment:

- **Reports** You can use reports to monitor the status of devices, including detected software and device history.
- **Alerts** You can use alerts to provide notifications based on Microsoft Intune events or status parameters.

USING REPORTS

Reports can provide information about events in Microsoft Intune, and they can help to forecast future needs and confirm the current state of your environment.

There are two types of reports available in Microsoft Intune as shown in Figure 3-36:

- **Detected Software Reports** This report shows software installed on computers in your organization and includes the software versions. You can filter the information that displays based on the software publisher and the software category. By clicking the directional arrow next to the list item, you can expand the updates in the list to show more detail (such as the computers on which it is installed).
- **Device History Reports** This report shows a historical log of retire, wipe, and delete actions. Use this report to see who initiated actions on devices in the past.

After you have created a report, you can save, print, or export it. The report criteria can also be loaded from a previously saved report.

CREATING A REPORT

1. In the classic Microsoft Intune administrator console, click the Reports workspace.
2. Select the report type you want to generate.
3. On the Create New Report page, accept the default values or customize them to filter the results that will be returned by the report. (For example, you could decide that only software published by Microsoft will be displayed in the detected software report.)
4. Click View Report to open the report in a new window.

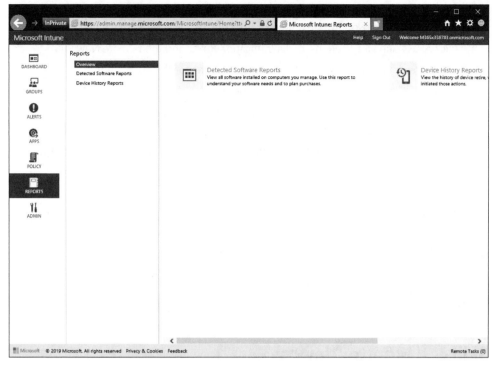

FIGURE 3-36 The Reports workspace in Microsoft Intune's classic portal

USING ALERTS

Alerts provide notification based on Microsoft Intune status events. You can use alerts in several ways in Microsoft Intune, including

- View all recent alerts to obtain a high-level view of device health.
- Identify specific issues that are occurring in your environment regarding timing and scope.
- Use Filter Alerts to target specific events or issues in your environment.

There are several alert categories available in Microsoft Intune, including

- **Notices** Informs you about configuration tasks that need to be performed (such as configuring automatic approvals for updates) and service announcements that display on the Notice Board on the System Overview page.
- **System** Informs you when client deployments have failed. Also contains a subcategory of Mobile Device Management, which informs you when mobile device issues occur, including Exchange connectivity.

> **NOTE ADD RECIPIENT EMAIL ADDRESS**
>
> If you want to be emailed when a notification rule is triggered, you need to enter a recipient email address in the Recipients area within the Admin workspace.

CREATING A NEW NOTIFICATION RULE

1. In the classic Microsoft Intune administrator console, click the Admin workspace.

2. Click Alerts And Notifications, click Notification Rules, and then Create New Rule.

3. In the Create Notification Rule Wizard, enter a Name for the notification rule.

4. Select the Categories and Severity for the notification rule, and then click Next.

5. If presented with the Select Device Groups page, select the device groups to which this rule will apply and click Next.

6. If you have previously added a notification recipient, select an email address on the Select Email Recipients page, and click Save.

7. Close the wizard.

8. The rule now appears in the Notification Rules.

> **NOTE   CLASSIC PORTAL SUPPORT TO CEASE IN 2020**
>
> At the time of writing, Microsoft has suggested that support for the classic portal will be stopped in 2020.

Skill 3.3: Monitor devices

It is important that you understand what's happening on your users' devices within your organization. You must be able to identity situations in which a device has configuration problems, is experiencing device health issues, or represents a potential security risk to your organization. Intune provides a number of monitoring tools that can help you make these determinations.

> **This skill covers how to:**
> - Monitor device health
> - Monitor device security

Monitor device health

Device health can be measured in a number of different ways. You can use the Microsoft 365 Device Management portal to:

- Monitor device actions
- Review device audit logs
- Use Log Analytics
- Use Windows Analytics
- Report on Windows Health Attestation

Monitoring Device Actions

You can perform a number of actions on your organization's enrolled devices including

- **Remote Lock**   Force a lock on supported devices, even if you do not have the device in your possession.

- **Reset Passcode**   Force the user to reset the passcode on supported devices.

- **Sync**   Forces the selected device to immediately check in with Intune and receive any pending actions or policies that have been assigned to it.

- **Retire/Wipe**   When you choose this option, you are given two options:
  - **Selective Wipe / Remove Company Data**   This option will remove only company data managed by Intune, leaving personal data intact. The type of company data removed varies by platform and includes profiles, applications, policies, and the Intune Endpoint Protection software.
  - **Full Wipe/Factory Reset**   This option will wipe the device and return it to its factory default settings by removing all data, including user personal data, from the device.

- **Delete**   This command removes the device from Microsoft Intune but does not modify device settings or software.

- **Run A Full Scan**   This command runs a full malware scan by using Microsoft Intune Endpoint Protection on the selected device.

- **Run A Quick Scan**   This command runs a quick malware scan by using Microsoft Intune Endpoint Protection on the selected device.

- **Restart Computer**   This command restarts the remote device.

- **Fresh start**   This command removes any apps that were installed on a Windows 10 PC running the Creators Update and updates the PC to the latest version of Windows.

- **Update Malware Definitions**   This command initiates an update of malware definitions for the Microsoft Intune Endpoint Protection client.

- **Refresh Policies**   This command requests a manual refresh of the client policies from the Microsoft Intune site.

- **Refresh Inventory**   This command requests updated inventory information to be sent from the device to Microsoft Intune.

- **Remote Assistance Session**   Use the TeamViewer software to give remote assistance to your users who are running the Intune software client.

The available actions depend on the type of device and whether the device is personal or organizational.

To monitor actions that have been performed on your devices, use the following procedure:

1. In the Microsoft 365 Device Management portal, select the Devices node and select All Devices.

2. On the Devices blade, under Monitor, select Device Actions. Figure 3-37 shows the various Device Actions that have been performed or are pending.

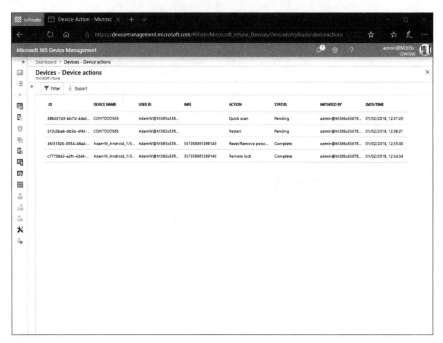

FIGURE 3-37 A list of recent and pending device actions

3. If you want to filter the results, click Filter, and select the criteria. You can choose to filter based on Action, as shown in Figure 3-38, or by Status (Pending, Complete, Failed, Not supported, Unknown, or All).

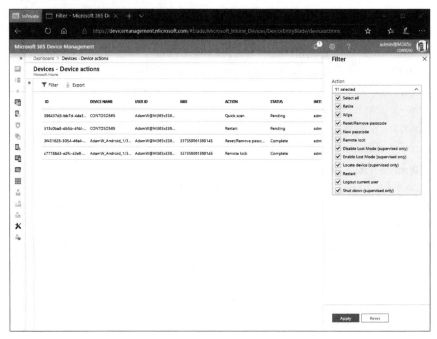

FIGURE 3-38 Filtering device actions

4. After choosing the appropriate actions and status, you can export the results to a CSV file for later analysis.

Reviewing device audit logs

You can also use the device audit logs in Microsoft 365 Device Management to view and analyze recent device actions, as shown in Figure 3-39.

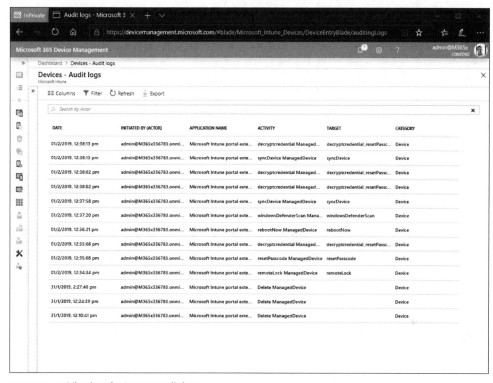

FIGURE 3-39 Viewing the Intune audit logs

If there are many actions, or you are interested in specific devices, you can filter and export the returned results. When filtering, you can filter based on Category, Activity, and Date Range.

> ### NEED MORE REVIEW? AUDIT LOGS FOR INTUNE ACTIVITIES
>
> To review further details about using logs to analyze Intune activities, refer to the Microsoft website at *https://docs.microsoft.com/intune/monitor-audit-logs*.

Using Log Analytics

While there is some analysis possible using the Microsoft 365 Device Management portal, you might want more. One option is to use the Log Analytics workspace in Intune. By using Log Analytics, you can send the logging data from Intune to Azure Monitor.

Requirements

To use Log Analytics, you require

- An Azure subscription
- A Microsoft Intune tenant in Azure
- A global admin or Intune Service Administrator account

You might also need one of the following services:

- An Azure storage account, ideally a general storage account
- An Azure event hubs namespace to integrate with third-party solutions
- An Azure log analytics workspace to send logs to Log Analytics

To send the log data to Azure monitor, use the following high-level procedure:

1. Open Microsoft Edge and navigate to *https://portal.azure.com/*.
2. Sign in as global admin.
3. To open the Microsoft 365 Device Management portal, type **Intune** in the Search box and click Intune in the returned list.
4. In the navigation pane, under Monitoring, click Diagnostics Settings, as shown in Figure 3-40.

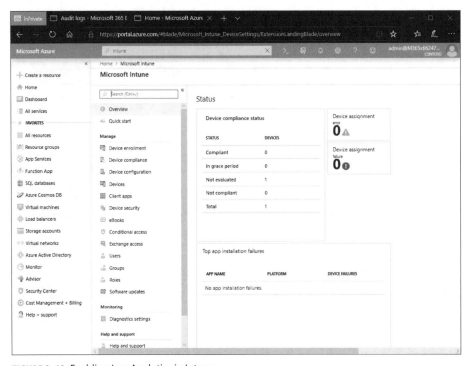

FIGURE 3-40 Enabling Log Analytics in Intune

5. Click Turn On Diagnostics and enter the following properties:

- Enter a name for the Diagnostic Settings.

- Specify whether you want to archive to a storage account. This saves log data to an Azure storage account.

- Select whether you want to stream to an Azure event hub.

- Choose whether to send diagnostics to Log Analytics. If you choose this option, the data is sent to Azure Log Analytics. Choose this option if you want to use visualizations or monitoring and alerting for your logs.

- Choose whether to send the Intune audit logs to your storage account, event hub, or Log Analytics.

- Choose whether to send Operational logs (which show the success or failure of users and devices that enroll in Intune) to your storage account, event hub, or Log Analytics.

When you have completed the set up, you should have a dialog box that looks similar to Figure 3-41.

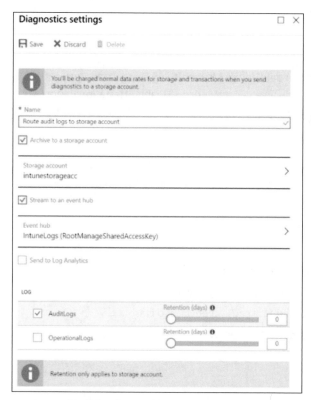

FIGURE 3-41 Verifying diagnostics settings in Intune

NEED MORE REVIEW? **SEND LOG DATA TO STORAGE, EVENT HUBS, OR LOG ANALYTICS IN INTUNE**

To review further details about Azure monitor, refer to the Microsoft website at *https://docs .microsoft.com/intune/review-logs-using-azure-monitor.*

Windows Health Attestation Report

Using Windows Health Attestation in Intune enables you to view the health status of enrolled Windows devices, using a number of factors. These include

- BitLocker
- Code integrity
- Early launch malware
- Boot debugging
- Secure boot
- Data execution prevention policy
- Virtual security mode
- Boot manager version

To access Windows Health Attestation data, in the Microsoft 365 Device Management portal, select the Device Compliance node and select Windows Health Attestation Report. As with many of the other reporting features in Intune, you can filter the listed results and export the unfiltered or filtered results to a CSV file.

Using Windows Analytics

Windows Analytics is a cloud-based service that provides the following three solutions:

- Device Health
- Update Compliance
- Upgrade Readiness

Using Windows Analytics Device Health enables you to

- Identify any of your users' devices that frequently crash
- Identify any device drivers that might be causing devices to crash

Figure 3-42 shows output from Windows Analytics Device Health.

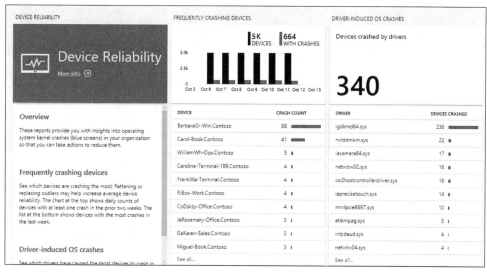

FIGURE 3-42 Device Reliability in Device Health

Requirements

To use Windows Analytics to assess device health, you require

- An Azure subscription
- One of the following Windows 10 licensing options:
    - Windows 10 Education or Enterprise editions with active Software Assurance
    - Windows 10 Enterprise E3 or E5 per-device or per-user subscription
    - Windows 10 Education A3 or A5
    - Windows VDA E3 or E5 per-user or per-device subscription

You can use Device Health to view the information about the devices in your organization, as shown in Table 3-9.

TABLE 3-9 Device Health information

INFORMATION	EXPLANATION
Device Reliability	■ Identifies devices that are unreliable ■ Displays reliability history for a device ■ Identifies crashes that might relate to devices and drivers
App Reliability	■ Displays app usage and behavior information ■ Enables you to identify apps that are unreliable
Login Health	■ Provides data about sign-in attempts within your organization ■ Identifies sign-in methods used ■ Identifies rates and patterns of sign-in success or failure ■ Indicates reasons sign-ins have failed

Monitor device security

It is important that you can verify that all your users' devices that connect to resources in your organization meet the appropriate minimum-security standards. You can use Intune to make this determination.

Monitor Device Compliance

In Chapter 2, "Manage policies and profiles," you explored how to create and configure Device Compliance (and conditional access) policies in Intune to configure and enforce security settings on your enrolled devices.

As an MDA, it's important you know which of your devices are conformant with your organization's security policies. You can use the Microsoft 365 Device Management portal to ascertain this.

In the Microsoft 365 Device Management portal, navigate to the Device Compliance node and select Device Compliance beneath the Monitoring heading. As shown in Figure 3-43, you can see a list of enrolled devices and their respective Compliance statuses.

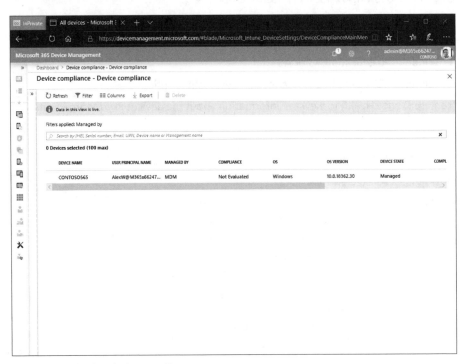

FIGURE 3-43 Viewing device compliance status

You can filter the output based on the following characteristics:

- Managed by
- Device action
- Category
- Ownership
- Compliance
- Jailbroken
- OS
- Model
- Manufacturer
- OS Version
- Phone Number
- Last Check-In
- Enrollment Date

You can also export the output to a CSV file for analysis.

NEED MORE REVIEW? **MONITOR INTUNE DEVICE COMPLIANCE POLICIES**

To review further details regarding the monitoring of compliance policies, refer to the Microsoft website at *https://docs.microsoft.com/intune/compliance-policy-monitor*.

Monitor Threat Agent Status

Earlier in this chapter, we looked at Windows Defender. You can use Intune to monitor current Windows Defender status for your enrolled devices. To do so, in the Device Compliance node, under Monitor, select the Threat Agent Status node, as shown in Figure 3-44. Then view and analyze the current threat agent status on your enrolled Windows devices. You can view

- Pending Signature Update
- Pending Full Scan
- Pending Restart
- Pending Manual Steps
- Pending Offline Scan
- Critical Failures
- Inactive Threat Agent
- Unknown Threat Agent
- Clean

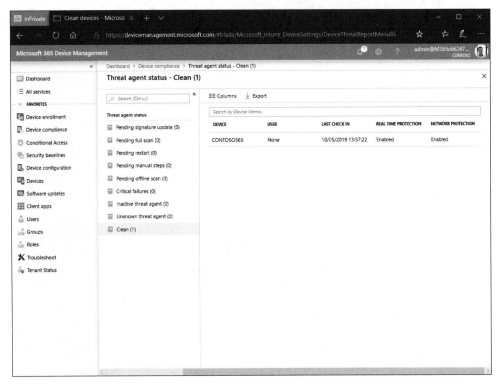

FIGURE 3-44 Assessing threat agent status

Thought experiments

In these thought experiments, demonstrate your skills and knowledge of the topics covered in this chapter. You can find the answers to these thought experiments in the next section.

Scenario 1

Your organization has 500 employees and has implemented a bring your own device (BYOD) strategy that enables users to use their personal mobile phones and tablets for corporate purposes as long as they comply with company policy regarding security and management features. After consulting an employee survey, you find that the users in your organization have iOS, Android, or Windows 10 devices.

1. What technology should you use to manage the devices?

2. You want to simplify enrollment for your Windows device users. What should you do?

3. To support your iOS devices, what additional step is required to enable MDM?

Scenario 2

Like many large organizations, security is a big concern at Contoso. You decide to implement MDM with Intune to help to manage and secure your users' devices.

1. What feature of Intune could you use to verify the current status of Windows Defender on your users' Windows 10 devices?

2. You want to be able to configure Windows Defender Application Guard settings for enrolled Windows 10 devices. How can you achieve this in Intune?

3. You don't want users with Android devices to be able to enroll them. How could you enforce this restriction?

Scenario 3

You want to streamline the Intune enrollment process for your Windows 10 device users. When users turn on a new computer for the first time, you want the enrollment process to be automatic.

1. How could you achieve this?

2. You want to largely automate the process of enrollment, but you would like users to configure some aspects of their device settings during setup. What should you do?

Thought experiment answers

This section provides the solutions for the tasks included in the Thought Experiments section.

Scenario 1

1. Microsoft Intune with Mobile Device Management enabled.

2. Enable and configure Windows Autoenrollment.

3. You require an Apple MDM Push Certificate for your organization.

Scenario 2

1. You can monitor Threat Agent Status to determine the current status of Windows Defender on your users' enrolled Windows devices.

2. You can use the Microsoft 365 Device Management portal and select the Device Configuration node. Create an Endpoint Protection Profile that contains the necessary Windows Defender Application Guard settings and assign the profile to the appropriate group(s) of devices.

3. In the Microsoft 365 Device management portal, select the Device Enrollment node. Create a Device Enrollment Restriction and define a Platform Restriction that prevents the enrollment of Android devices.

Scenario 3

1. Enable and configure Windows Autopilot to automate enrollment during the OOBE phase of device setup.

2. Configure User-Driven Windows Autopilot profiles. You can partially customize the OOBE and require a small amount of user input during device setup.

Chapter summary

- Windows Defender Credential Guard requires a TPM and virtualization features to be enabled in a 64-bit edition of either Windows 10 Enterprise or Windows 10 Education.

- Windows Defender Exploit Guard consists of four components: Exploit Protection, Attack Surface Reduction Rules, Network Protection, and Controlled Folder Access.

- Windows Defender Application Guard has similar requirements to Credential Guard and enables you to open new browser windows in a virtualized environment.

- Windows Defender Application Control enables you to determine which apps are safe to run in your organization.

- Most of these Windows Defender features are managed through Windows PowerShell, Group Policy, and Microsoft Intune.

- The Quick Start node in the Device Enrollment blade of the Microsoft 365 Device Management portal enables you to view the completed steps to enable enrollment for different device types.

- Automatic enrollment enables you to enroll Windows devices when they register with or join Azure AD.

- Device Enrollment Manager Accounts enable a specified account to enroll up to 1,000 devices.

- There are a number of ways to enroll Windows devices:

  - Add a Work Or School account
  - Enroll In MDM Only (user-driven)
  - Azure AD Join during OOBE
  - Azure AD Join using Windows Autopilot
  - Enroll In MDM only (using a Device Enrollment Manager)
  - Azure AD Join using bulk enrollment

- Windows Autopilot can be configured to be user-driven or self-deploying, depending on how much user interaction you want.

- To enroll Android and iOS devices, you can download the Company Portal app from the relevant device store, and then sign in to the app using an organizational or school account.

- Both Windows Analytics and Log Analytics require an Azure subscription.

- Threat Agent Status monitoring enables you to verify the status of Windows Defender on enrolled devices.

CHAPTER 4

Manage Apps and Data

Using Microsoft Intune or the Microsoft Store for Business, you can deploy and configure apps for your organization's enrolled devices. You can use Intune's Mobile Application Management (MAM) features to manage apps on your users' devices. In addition, you can implement features, such as Windows Information Protection (WIP) and Azure Information Protection policies, to help to protect organizational data on your users' devices. This chapter explores these app and data management capabilities.

Skills covered in this chapter:

- Skill 4.1: Deploy and update applications
- Skill 4.2: Implement Mobile Application Management

Skill 4.1: Deploy and update applications

Within an organization, you can use on-premises tools, such as System Center Configuration Manager (SCCM) and the Microsoft Deployment Toolkit (MDT), to manage Windows 10 desktop images. Using these tools, you can integrate your organization's applications into standard desktop builds. You can also deploy additional applications and manage application updates using these tools.

For devices that are not part of your Active Directory Domain Services (AD DS) environment, you might consider using Microsoft Intune to deploy and manage apps. You can deploy apps to devices running Windows 10, iOS, Android, and macOS as long as these devices are enrolled into Intune. The Microsoft Store for Business provides another method for the distribution of apps for your organizational users.

Windows Configuration Designer, part of the Windows Assessment and Deployment Toolkit, enables you to create provisioning packages for your Windows 10 devices; you can use these packages to add, remove, and configure applications on your users' Windows 10 devices.

This skill covers how to:

- Deploy apps by using Intune and assign apps to groups
- Deploy apps by using Microsoft Store for Business
- Enable sideloading of apps into images
- Using Windows Configuration Designer to deploy apps
- Configure and implement assigned access or public devices
- Deploy O365 ProPlus
- Gather Office readiness data
- Configure IE Enterprise Mode

Deploy apps by using Intune and assign apps to groups

You deploy, configure, and manage apps in Intune by using the Client apps node in the Microsoft 365 Device Management console, which is shown in Figure 4-1.

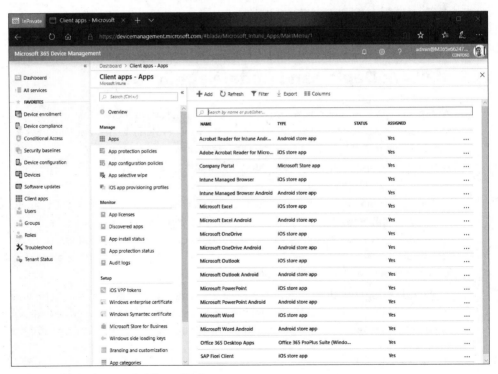

FIGURE 4-1 Managing apps in Microsoft Intune

From the Client apps node, the following options are visible under the Manage heading:

- **Apps**   Use this node to add and assign apps to your enrolled devices.

- **App Protection Policies**   Use this node to configure policies that help to protect against data leakage from deployed apps. Settings include Data Protection, Access Requirements, and Conditional Launch Properties.

- **App Configuration Policies**   You can create app configuration policies to configure apps on both iOS and Android devices, enabling you to customize the targeted app.

- **App Selective Wipe**   Enables you to remove only organizational data from a targeted device's apps.

- **iOS App Provisioning Profiles**   When you deploy apps to iOS devices by using Intune, you must use an enterprise signing certificate. This certificate helps to ensure the integrity of apps that you deploy and typically has a lifetime of three years. However, the provisioning profile used to deploy the app lasts for a year. You can only assign and use a new app provisioning profile while the certificate is still valid.

The following options are available beneath the Monitor heading:

- **App Licenses**   Enables you to identify volume-purchased apps from the app stores.

- **Discovered Apps**   Displays information about apps assigned by Intune or installed on devices.

- **App Install Status**   Reports on the status of assigned apps.

- **App Protection Status**   Displays information about app protection policy status.

- **Audit Logs**   Enables you to view the app-related activity for all Intune administrators.

Beneath the Setup heading, the following options are available:

- **iOS VPP Tokens**   Enables you to view and apply your iOS Volume Purchase Program (VPP) licenses.

- **Windows Enterprise Certificate**   Enables you to view and apply your code-signing certificate. This certificate is used to distribute your line-of-business (LOB) apps to managed Windows devices.

- **Windows Symantec Certificate**   Enables you to view and apply a Symantec code-signing certificate. This certificate is used to distribute XAP and WP8.x appx files to enrolled Windows 10 Mobile devices. XAP and WP8.x appx files are used to distribute apps to phone devices running Windows 10 Mobile.

- **Microsoft Store For Business**   Use to integrate Intune with the Microsoft Store for Business. Once configured, enables you to track license usage for apps distributed through the store.

- **Windows Side Loading Keys**   Enables you to distribute a side-loading key to devices. Allows users to install apps without needing to visit the Microsoft Store.

- **Branding And Customization**   Allows for customization of the Intune Company Portal app. Because this is often the first thing users with enrolled devices see, it's important to configure branding to help identify your organization.

- **App Categories**   Enables you to define app category names to help your users locate suitable apps.

- **Managed Google Play** Enables you to approve Google Android apps for your organization.

NEED MORE REVIEW? **WHAT IS MICROSOFT INTUNE APP MANAGEMENT?**

To review further details about using Intune for app management, refer to the Microsoft website at *https://docs.microsoft.com/intune/app-management*.

When you deploy apps to your devices, there are a number of different app types that you can select, as shown in Figure 4-2.

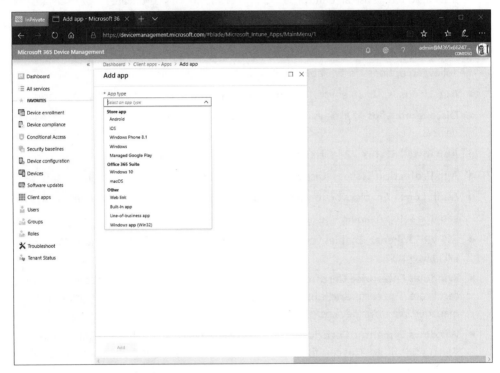

FIGURE 4-2 Adding a new client app

These are

- **Store Apps** Use this option to deploy apps to your users' devices to avoid the need for the users to deploy the apps from the specified store directly. Available options are

    - **Android** Enter the Google Play Appstore URL for the app, and then define minimum operating system level for the app.

    - **iOS** Enter a search string, and search the Apple Store directly for the appropriate app. Then configure the requirements for the app, including operating system version.

    - **Windows Phone 8.1** Enter the app's URL.

    - **Windows** Enter the app's URL.

- **Managed Google Play** Approve apps in Managed Google Play, and then assign the apps.

- **Office 365 Suite** Use this option to assign Office 365 ProPlus apps to your users' devices. Available options are

  - **Windows 10** Specify which apps within Office 365 ProPlus you want to deploy. Then define a suite name and description and options, such as whether the app suite will display in the Company Portal. You also must choose the architecture (32-bit or 64-bit), Update channel [Monthly, Monthly (Targeted), Semi-Annual, or Semi-Annual (Targeted)], and other options (Force Removal Of Other Versions, License Agreement Acceptance, and OS Languages).

  - **macOS** You cannot control which apps are deployed from the suite. However, you must define a name and description, and whether the app displays in the Company Portal.

- **Other** Use for any other type of app. Options are

  - **Web Link** Use to assign a web app for which you have a valid URL. These are client-server apps, and the URL identifies the server that contains the web app.

  - **Built-In App** Use to assign curated apps to iOS or Android devices. After you assign the app(s), it appears as either a Built-in iOS app or a Built-in Android app.

  - **Line-Of-Business App** Use to assign a Line-Of-Business (LOB) app. You can use this approach to sideload apps for which you have the application package file. Windows devices use .appx packages. Browse and select the package file and then configure supplemental options, such as category and description.

  - **Windows app (Win32)** Use to assign apps to Windows devices. Similar to an LOB app, you browse and select the package file (in this case, a file with an .intunewin file extension), and then complete configuration as above. Note that to create a file with the appropriate extension, you must convert your Win32 app to the Intune format using the Microsoft Win32 Content Prep Tool. This tool packages the app correctly for upload to Intune and is available at https://github.com/Microsoft/Microsoft-Win32-Content-Prep-Tool.

Adding a Windows store app

To add a store app, use the following procedure:

1. Open the Microsoft 365 Device Management console and select the Client Apps node.
2. Click Apps > Add.
3. On the Add App blade, shown in Figure 4-2, in the App Type list, under the Store App heading, select Windows.
4. Click App Information, and then enter the following information on the App information blade, as shown in Figure 4-3:

   - Name (required)
   - Description (required)

- Publisher (required)
- Appstore URL (required)

- Category (Business, Productivity, Photos & Media, and so on)
- Display This As A Featured App In The Company Portal (Yes/No)
- Information URL
- Privacy URL
- Developer
- Owner
- Notes
- Logo Image

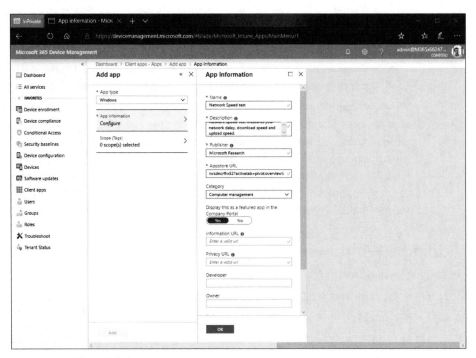

FIGURE 4-3 Adding a Windows store app

5. Click OK, and then on the Add App blade, click Add.

6. Within the properties of your newly added app, click Assignments, as shown in Figure 4-4.

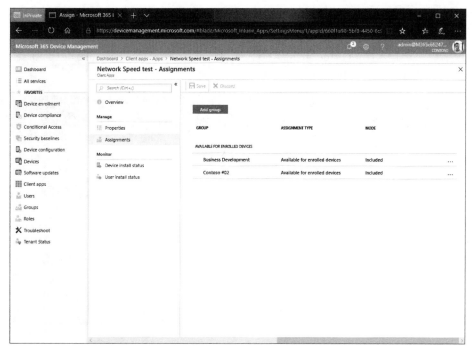

FIGURE 4-4 Assigning a Windows store app

7. Click Add Group.

8. On the Add Group blade, in the Assignment type list, select Available For Enrolled Devices.

9. Click Included Groups.

10. You can now choose to make the app available to everyone by selecting Yes next to the Make This App Available To All Users With Enrolled Devices. If you want to be more specific, click Select Groups To Include.

11. On the Select Groups blade, select one or more groups, and then click Select.

12. On the Assign blade, click OK.

13. If you want to exclude specific groups, on the Add Group blade, click Excluded Groups and then repeat the steps above to select specific groups.

14. Click OK, and then click Save.

You can use the Monitor Options to monitor device installation and user installation status for the selected app. The process for installing store apps for iOS, Android, and Windows 8.1 are fairly similar to this process.

Adding an Office 365 suite app

To add an Office 365 suite app to Windows devices, use the following procedure:

1. Open the Microsoft 365 Device Management console and select the Client Apps node.

2. Click Apps > Add.

3. On the Add App blade, in the App Type list, under the Office 365 Suite heading, select Windows 10, as shown in Figure 4-5.

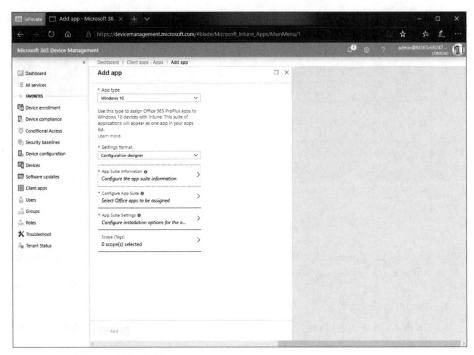

FIGURE 4-5 Adding an Office Suite app

4. Click Configure App Suite, and then on the Configure App Suite blade, select the Office 365 apps that you want to deploy (see Figure 4-6). Click OK.

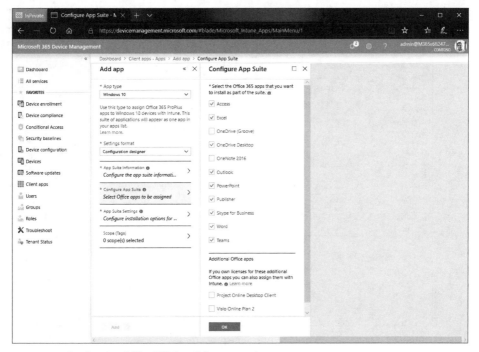

FIGURE 4-6 Configuring Office 365 App Suite properties

5. Click App Suite Information.

6. On the App Suite Information blade, shown in Figure 4-7, enter the following information, and then click OK:

- Suite Name (required)
- Suite Description (required)
- Publisher (pre-configured)
- Category (Business, Productivity, Photos & Media, and the like)
- Display This As A Featured App In The Company Portal (Yes/No)
- Information URL
- Privacy URL
- Developer (pre-configured)
- Owner (pre-configured)
- Notes
- Logo Image (pre-configured)

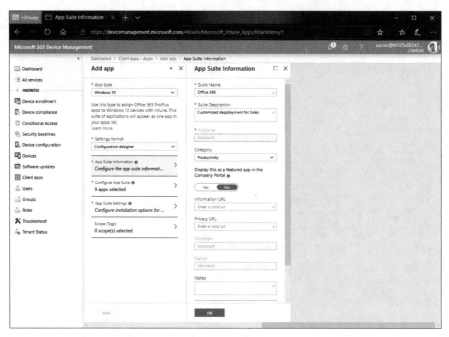

FIGURE 4-7 Configuring Office 365 App Suite properties

7. Click App Suite Settings.

8. As shown in Figure 4-8, select the appropriate Architecture and Update Channel. Both these settings are mandatory.

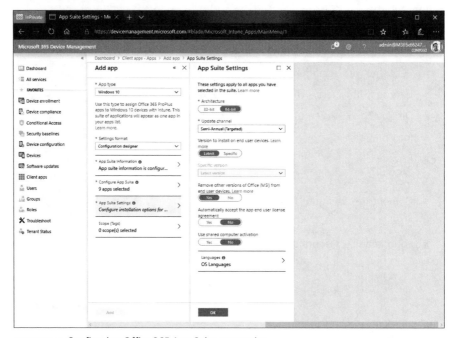

FIGURE 4-8 Configuring Office 365 App Suite properties

9. Then configure the following options and click OK:
   - **Version To Install On End User Devices**   Either choose Latest or Select A Specific Version.
   - **Remove Other Versions Of Office (MSI) From End User Devices (Yes/No).**
   - **Automatically Accept The App End User License Agreement (Yes/No).**
   - **Use Shared Computer Activation (Yes/No).**
   - **Select OS Languages.**
10. On the Add App blade, click Add.
11. Within the properties of your newly added app, click Assignments.
12. Click Add Group.
13. On the Add Group blade, in the Assignment Type list, select one of the following options:
    - **Available For Enrolled Devices**   This option enables users to choose whether to install the app.
    - **Required**   Ensures that all users (in selected groups) receive the app.
    - **Uninstall**   Used to remove the app from selected groups.
14. Click Included Groups.
15. You can now choose to make the app available to everyone by selecting Yes next to the Make This App Available To All Users With Enrolled Devices. If you want to be more specific, click Select Groups To Include. If you chose the Uninstall option, you can specify
    - Uninstall This App For All Users (Yes/No)
    - Uninstall This App For All Devices (Yes/No)
16. If you chose the Required option, you can specify
    - Make This App Required For All Users (Yes/No)
    - Make This App Required For All Devices (Yes/No)
17. On the Select Groups blade, select one or more groups and click Select.
18. On the Assign blade, click OK.
19. On the Add Group blade, if you want to exclude specific groups, click Excluded Groups, and then repeat the steps above to select specific groups.
20. Click OK and Save.

You can use the monitoring options to view installation status for both devices and users. The process for assigning Office365 to macOS varies in as much as you cannot control which components of Office you deploy, nor can you define app suite settings, such as Update and Architecture settings.

Adding a Line-of-Business (LOB) app

To add an Office 365 suite app to Windows devices, use the following procedure:

1. Open the Microsoft 365 Device Management console and select the Client Apps node.

2. Click Apps > Add.

3. On the Add App blade, in the App Type list, under the Other heading, select Line-Of-Business App.

4. On the Add App blade, shown in Figure 4-9, click App Package File.

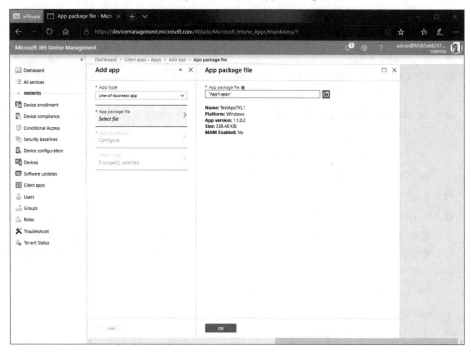

FIGURE 4-9 Adding a Windows 10 Line-Of-Business app

5. In the App Package File box, browse, locate the LOB app package file (which has an .APPX extension), and click OK.

6. Click App Information and enter the following information on the App Information blade:

   - Name (required)
   - Description (required)
   - Publisher (required)

- Category (Business, Productivity, Photos & Media etc.)
- Display This As A Featured App In The Company Portal (Yes/No)
- Information URL
- Privacy URL
- Developer
- Owner
- Notes
- Logo Image

7. On the Add App blade, click Add.

8. Click Assignments, and then assign the app using the procedure previously described.

> **NEED MORE REVIEW?**   **ADD APPS TO MICROSOFT INTUNE**
>
> To review further details about using Intune to assign apps, refer to the Microsoft website at https://docs.microsoft.com/intune/apps-add.

Deploy apps by using Microsoft Store for Business

In addition to using Intune, you can use Microsoft Store for Business to deploy apps to your users' devices. The Microsoft Store for Business provides a convenient storefront for your users. You can create a private storefront using the Microsoft Store for Business, and your users can access the store through the Windows 10 Store app.

Sign up for Microsoft Store for Business

Before you can use Microsoft Store for Business to deploy and manage apps, you must first sign up. Use the following procedure to sign up for Microsoft Store for Business:

1. Open a web browser and navigate to *https://www.microsoft.com/business-store*.

2. In the upper-right, click Sign In.

3. Enter the credentials for your organization's global admin account.

4. On the Microsoft Store For Business webpage, click Manage.

5. Accept the **Microsoft Store For Business And Your Data** warning, as shown in Figure 4-10.

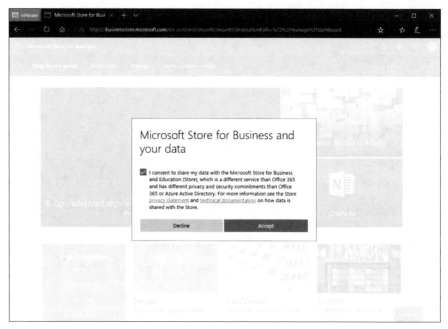

FIGURE 4-10 Accepting the Microsoft Store for Business And Your Data warning

6. On the Overview page, click Products & Services in the navigation pane.

After your store is provisioned, you will see Sway, OneNote, PowerPoint Mobile, Excel Mobile, and Word Mobile apps listed. When they do appear, you can deploy these apps to your users.

> **NOTE**
>
> Note that provisioning can take up to 36 hours.

Managing administrative roles

Although you can choose to administer everything in Microsoft Store for Business using your Azure AD global admin account, you can also assign administrative roles to your organization's users. The relevant available roles are:

- **Billing Account Owner**   Can perform all tasks.
- **Billing Account Contributor**   Can edit the store account and sign agreements.
- **Billing Account Reader**   Can only view the account information.
- **Signatory**   Can sign agreements for the organization.
- **Purchaser**   Can acquire and distribute products for your organization.
- **Basic Purchaser**   Can acquire and distribute products they own.

Table 4-1 lists the administrative abilities each role has.

TABLE 4-1 Microsoft Store for Business administrative and purchasing roles

ABILITY	BILLING ACCOUNT OWNER	BILLING ACCOUNT CONTRIBUTOR	BILLING ACCOUNT READER	SIGNATORY	PURCHASER	BASIC PURCHASER
Buy from the Microsoft Store	Yes				Yes	Yes
Assign permissions	Yes					
Edit account	Yes	Yes				
Sign agreements	Yes	Yes		Yes		
View account	Yes	Yes	Yes	Yes		
Manage all items	Yes				Yes	
Manage items I buy	Yes					Yes

To assign a role to a user, use the following procedure:

1. In the Microsoft Store for Business, click the Permissions tab in the navigation pane.

2. In Permissions, click the Roles tab, and then click Assign Roles.

3. In the Enter A Name Or Email Address box, type the name or email address for the user to which you want to assign a specific role and press Enter.

4. Select the appropriate role or roles and then click Save, as shown in Figure 4-11.

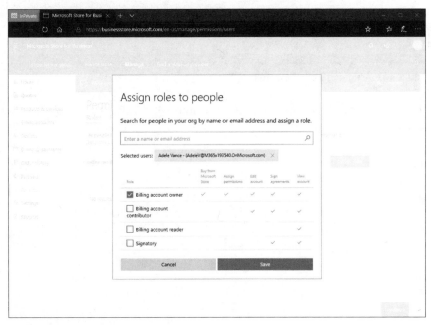

FIGURE 4-11 Assigning an admin role

To assign a purchasing role, use the following procedure:

1. In the Microsoft Store For Business, click the Permissions tab in the navigation pane.

2. In Permissions, click the Purchasing Roles tab and click Assign Roles.

3. In the Enter A Name Or Email Address box, type the name or email address for the user to which you want to assign a specific role and press Enter.

4. Select the required roles, as shown in Figure 4-12, and then click Save.

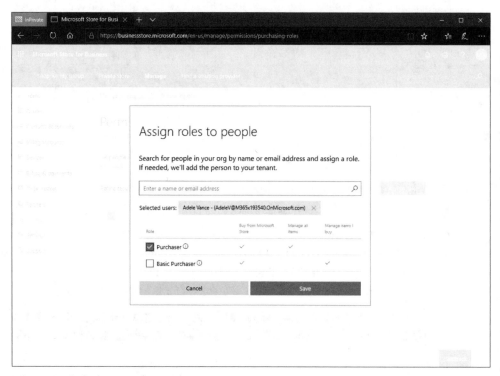

FIGURE 4-12 Assigning a purchaser role

You can review the assigned roles, as shown in Figure 4-13, by clicking the Roles or Purchasing Roles tabs.

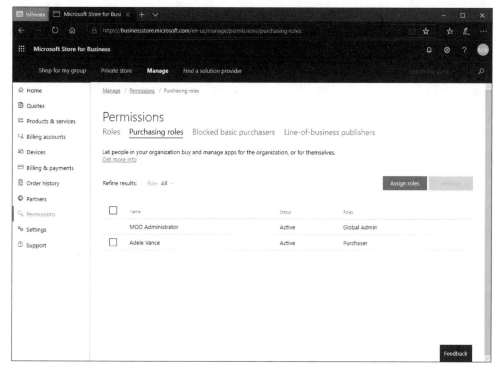

FIGURE 4-13 Reviewing assigned roles

Enabling the Private Store

You can create a Private Store for your users with the Microsoft Store for Business. When your users open the Store app in Windows 10, they will be able to see a Private Store tab. You can configure this tab with your organization name if you wish.

To configure and enable the Private Store, use the following procedure:

1. In Microsoft Store For Business, click Settings, and then click the Distribute tab.
2. Under the Private Store heading, click the Change link.
3. In the Private Store window, type the name of the private store and click Save.
4. As shown in Figure 4-14, the store name is changed in the menu.

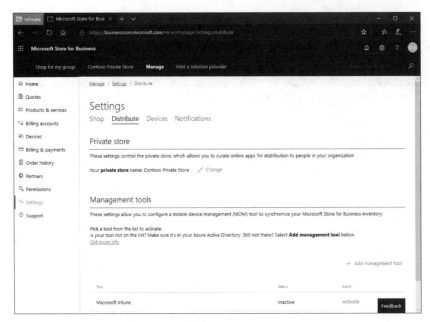

FIGURE 4-14 Editing the private store details

5. In the menu bar, click the link for your private store, and then click Activate Private Store, as shown in Figure 4-15.

6. Accept the Microsoft Store For Business and Education Services Agreement.

The private store is provisioned and enabled.

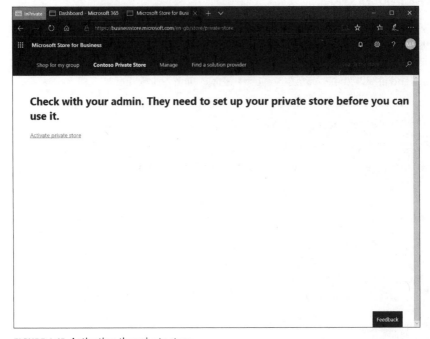

FIGURE 4-15 Activating the private store

Licensing Store apps

For a user to install and use an app, the app must be licensed. The Microsoft Store for Business supports two methods for licensing apps:

- **Online** All apps in the Store support online licensing, and this is the default licensing mode. Users require an Azure AD account and must authenticate with the Store before they can acquire online licensed apps. You can either distribute online licensed apps by using the Store or by using Microsoft Intune or System Center Configuration Manager (SCCM).

- **Offline** Only certain apps support this licensing mode. Using offline licensing enables an organization to obtain the app and install it on the organizational network for distribution to users' devices. These apps can be deployed using Intune or SCCM, and they can even be embedded into a standard Windows 10 desktop image. Using the offline mode requires that you purchase the required licenses from the software vendor. Note that this mode enables you to make apps available to users who do not have an Azure AD account and/or cannot connect to the Store.

Offline apps can be made visible in the Store by using the following procedure:

1. In the Microsoft Store For Business, on the Settings node, click Shop.
2. As shown in Figure 4-16, under Shopping Experience, beneath the Show Offline Apps option, click On.

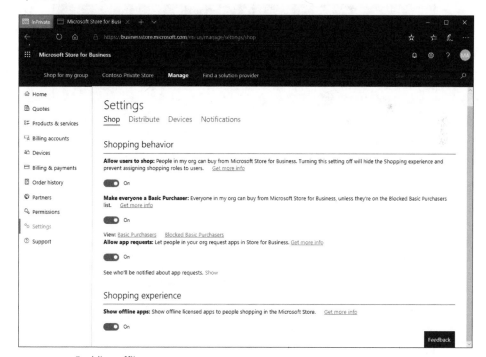

FIGURE 4-16 Enabling offline apps

Adding apps to the Store

After you have provisioned and configured the Microsoft Store For Business, you can deploy and manage apps. To do this, you must add apps to your private store. Next, you must determine how the apps will be made available to your users. There are three approaches you can take when adding apps to the store:

- **Use the Store** Instruct your users to sign in to the store, select the Private Store tab, and then browse and select the appropriate app.

- **Assign apps from the Store** Assign apps using the Store. Users will receive an email that provides a link to the app. Users who follow the link must authenticate with the Store, and then the app deploys without further user intervention.

- **Use a management tool** You can use Intune (or SCCM) to deploy the app. You can sync the list of apps that you want to make available for deployment to Intune. The Intune administrator can then deploy the app like any other app.

ACQUIRE AN APP AND DISTRIBUTE FROM THE PRIVATE STORE

To acquire an app and make it available in the private store, use the following procedure:

1. Sign in to Microsoft Store For Business and search for the desired app.

2. Select the app, as shown in Figure 4-17, and then select Get The App.

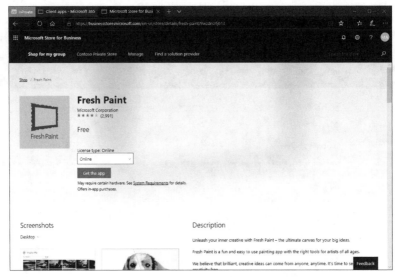

FIGURE 4-17 Selecting an app for inclusion in the Private Store

3. In the Thanks For Your Order window, select Close.

4. Select the ellipsis (...), and then select Manage.

5. Click the Private Store Availability link.

6. In the Choose Groups Of People Who Can See This App list, select No One or Everyone, as shown in Figure 4-18, or else select Specific Groups. In Figure 4-18, Everyone is selected; if you choose Everyone, then select the appropriate groups.

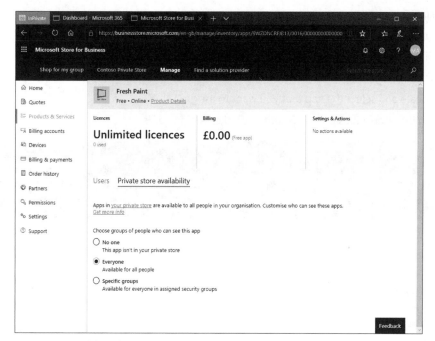

FIGURE 4-18 Enabling all users to see the Fresh Paint app

7. Verify that the private store is updated by selecting the Private Store link on the menu bar. The newly acquired app should display, as shown in Figure 4-19.

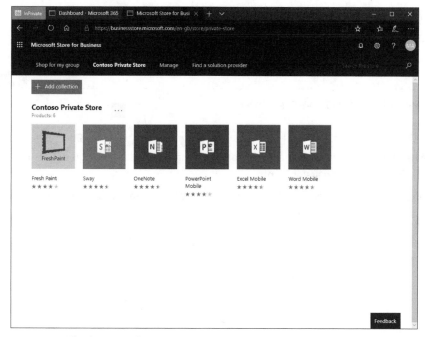

FIGURE 4-19 The Contoso private store

ASSIGNING APPS FROM THE PRIVATE STORE

To assign apps from the Private Store, use the following procedure:

1. Sign in to Microsoft Store For Business and select Manage from the menu bar.

2. In the navigation pane, select Products & Services.

3. Locate and select the app that you want to assign.

4. On the Users tab, shown in Figure 4-20, click Assign To Users.

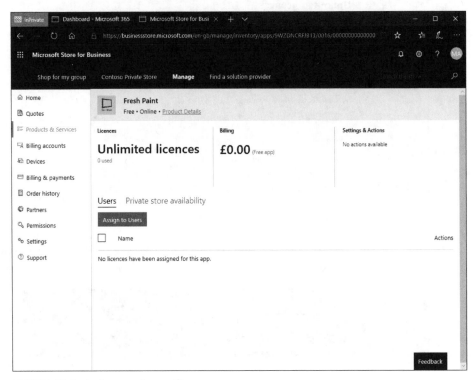

FIGURE 4-20 Assigning apps to specific users

5. Select one or more users, as shown in Figure 4-21, and then click Assign.

6. When the process is complete, click Close. You can also click Download Results to view a CSV file detailing the assignments.

7. On the preceding screen, you should now see that the license count has increased by the number of assignments made.

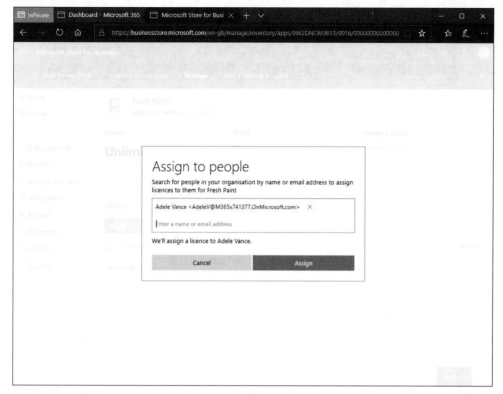

FIGURE 4-21 Assigning a Store app to users

USE INTUNE TO DISTRIBUTE THE APP

To distribute an app with Intune, use the following procedure:

1. Sign in to Microsoft Store For Business and get the desired app.

2. Sign in to the Microsoft 365 Device Management console and select the Client Apps node in the navigation pane.

3. Select the Microsoft Store For Business node from Setup and click Enable.

4. Click the Open The Business Store link.

5. In Microsoft Store For Business, select Manage and click the Distribute tab.

6. Scroll down, and under Management Tools next to Microsoft Intune, click Activate (see Figure 4-22). You might need to wait a while until you can see the link.

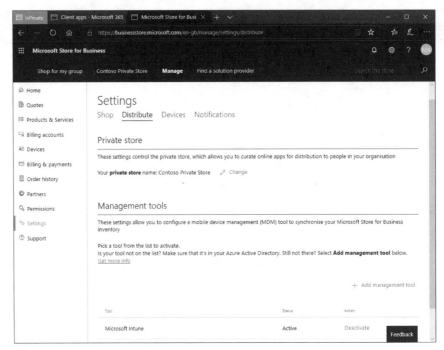

FIGURE 4-22 Activating Intune for Microsoft Store For Business management

7. Switch back to Microsoft 365 Device Management and click Save. Refresh the page.

8. Click Sync, as shown in Figure 4-23.

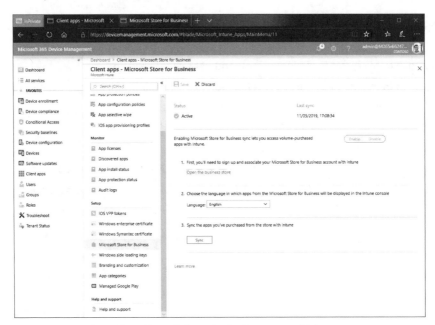

FIGURE 4-23 Synchronizing Microsoft Store For Business apps with Intune

9. Depending on the number of apps, this might take some time. When the process is complete, select the Apps node. Your Store apps should be listed, as shown in Figure 4-24.

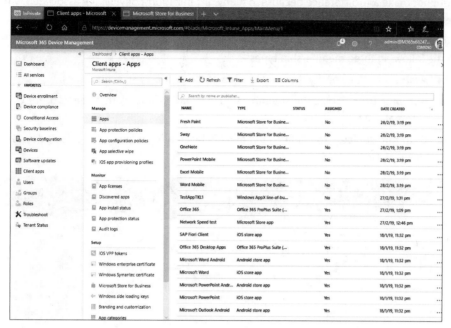

FIGURE 4-24 Viewing Store apps in Intune

10. You must now assign the app(s) in the usual way. Select the app, click Assignments, and then define to which users/devices the app will be deployed. This process was described in "Adding a Windows store app," earlier in this chapter.

> **NEED MORE REVIEW?** **DISTRIBUTE APPS TO YOUR EMPLOYEES FROM MICROSOFT STORE FOR BUSINESS AND EDUCATION**
>
> To review further details about deploying apps with the Microsoft Store For Business, refer to the Microsoft website at *https://docs.microsoft.com/microsoft-store/distribute-apps-to-your-employees-microsoft-store-for-business.*

Creating and managing groups for app assignment

We have already looked at the process of assigning apps to groups, thereby making the app available to users. However, it's important that you also know how to create groups. You can then assign apps to those groups.

In Intune, there are a number of different group types. These groups are stored in Azure AD. These groups are

- **Security** These groups are used for assigning permissions on Office 365 resources.
- **Office 365** These groups are used for collaboration between users.

From the app distribution perspective, the only significant difference is that Security groups can contain devices as members, while Office 365 groups can only contain users; that might not make any difference because in many organizations, devices are associated with a specific user.

After you have selected the type of the group, you must select the membership type. There are the following three membership types:

- **Assigned** You specify the membership of the group by selecting users.
- **Dynamic user** You define membership by creating a query that selects users automatically.
- **Dynamic device** You define membership by creating a query that selects devices, as shown in Figure 4-25.

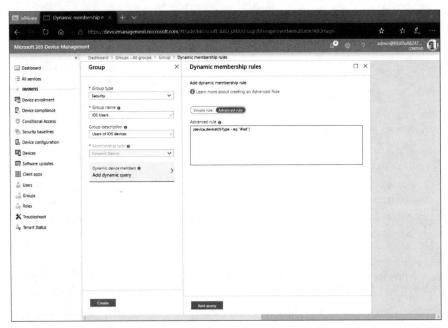

FIGURE 4-25 Creating a dynamic device group

Remember, only security groups can contain devices. To create groups, in the Microsoft 365 Device Management console, use the following procedure:

1. Select the Groups node in the navigation pane, and then select All Groups.
2. Click New Group.
3. Select the Group Type from the list.
4. Enter a Group Name.
5. Enter a Group Description (optional).

6. Select the Membership Type, and complete one of the following steps:

- If you choose Assigned, click the Members link, and add the members to the group. Then click Create.

- If you choose Dynamic User, click Add Dynamic Query, and create either simple or advanced rule, click Add Query, and then click Create.

- If you choose Dynamic Device, then click Add Dynamic Query, and create either simple or advanced rules click Add Query, and then click Create.

After you create the group, you can assign apps to the group, as described in the "Adding a Windows store app" section earlier in this chapter.

> **NEED MORE REVIEW?   COMPARE GROUPS**
>
> To review further details about groups in Intune, refer to the Microsoft website at *https://docs.microsoft.com/office365/admin/create-groups/compare-groups?view=o365-worldwide.*

Enable sideloading of apps into images

Sideloading is the process of installing an LOB app in Windows 10 without needing to use a Store to deploy the app to users' devices. The app might originate in the Microsoft Store, but so long as the app supports offline licensing and you have purchased adequate licenses for your needs, you can then choose to sideload the app.

Also, organizations sometimes create their own apps. These apps have the same characteristics as the Universal Windows Platform (UWP) apps you find in the Microsoft Store. As noted earlier, enterprise administrators can make these apps available publicly if they want to go through the Microsoft Store certification process, or they can make them available to their enterprise users through a process known as sideloading. Also, universal apps can be deployed by using provisioning packages created with the Windows Configuration Designer.

Enabling sideloading in Windows 10

By default, the sideloading option in Windows 10 is disabled. To enable sideloading, you can use a Group Policy setting. To configure Group Policy so that computers can accept and install sideloaded apps that you created for your organization, open the appropriate GPO for editing, navigate to Computer Configuration\Administrative Templates\Windows Components\App Package Deployment. Double-click Allow All Trusted Apps To Install.

You can also enable sideloading through the Settings app. Click Settings > Update And Security, and on the For Developers tab, shown in Figure 4-26, click Sideload Apps. Click Yes at the security warning message. After sideloading is enabled, any line of business (LOB) Microsoft Store app that is signed by a Certification Authority (CA) that the computer trusts can be installed.

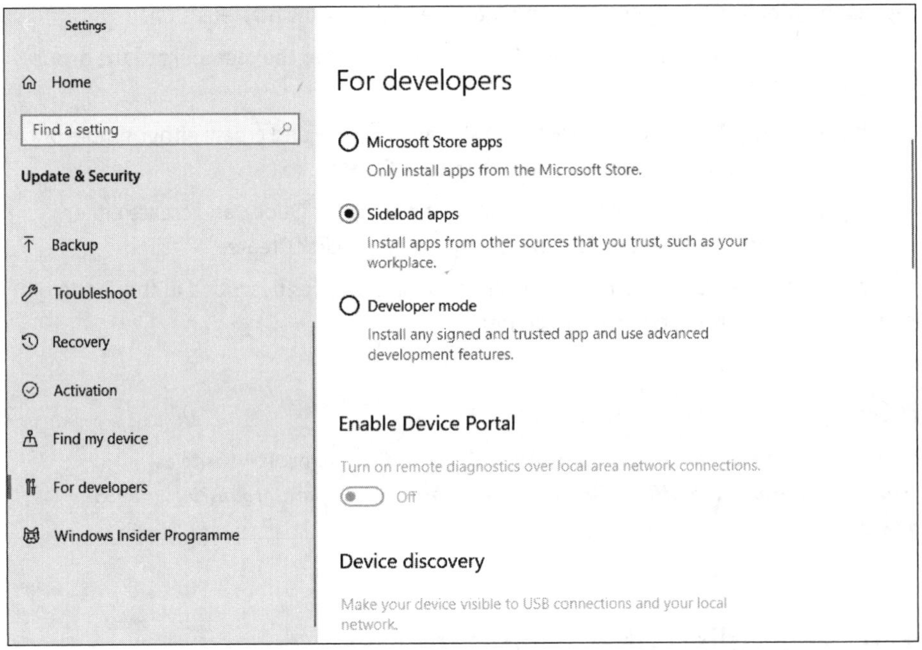

FIGURE 4-26 Enabling sideloading

Sideloading an app

After sideloading is enabled, you can sideload the app using the AppX Windows PowerShell module and the associated cmdlets. To manually sideload an app for the currently logged in user, perform the following steps from a Windows PowerShell prompt:

Type **Add-appxpackage "path and name of the app"** to add the app and press Enter. Table 1-1 shows the available AppX cmdlets. If you need to add app dependencies, use this command: **Add-appxpackage C:\MyApp.appx DependencyPath C:\appplus.appx**.

The app installs and then is available to the user. If multiple users share a single computer, follow the process for each user. The AppX module for Windows PowerShell includes several cmdlets that you can use to install and manage LOB Microsoft Store apps, some of which are shown in Table 4-2.

TABLE 4-2 Cmdlets in the AppX module for Windows PowerShell

CMDLET	DESCRIPTION
Add-AppxPackage	Add a signed app package to a single user account
Get-AppxLastError	Review the last error reported in the app package installation logs
Get-AppxLog	Review the app package installation log
Get-AppxPackage	View a list of the app packages installed for a user profile
Get-AppxPackageManifest	Read the manifest of an app package
Remove-AppxPackage	Remove an app package from a user account

Using DISM to sideload apps into Windows images

If you want to sideload the apps to multiple computers, use Deployment Image Servicing and Management (DISM) commands. You can use DISM commands to manage app packages in a Windows image. When you use DISM to provision app packages, those packages are added to a Windows image and are installed for the desired users when they next log on to their computers.

You should be familiar with the DISM syntax when servicing a Windows image, whether a computer is offline or online. Table 4-3 lists a few cmdlets to keep in mind.

TABLE 4-3 Commands for use with DISM

COMMAND	DESCRIPTION
DISM.exe {/Image:<path_to_image_directory> | /Online} [dism_global_options] {servicing_option} [<servicing_argument>]	To service a Windows image with DISM
DISM.exe /Image:<path_to_image_directory> [/Get-ProvisionedAppxPackages | /Add-ProvisionedAppxPackage | /Remove-ProvisionedAppxPackage | / Set-ProvisionedAppxDataFile]	To service an app package (.appx or .appxbundle) for an offline image
DISM.exe /Online [/Get-ProvisionedAppxPackages | /Add-ProvisionedAppxPackage | /Remove-ProvisionedAppxPackage | /Set-ProvisionedAppxDataFile	To service an app package (.appx or .appxbundle) for a running operating system

Other command-line service options include /Get-ProvisionedAppxPackages, /FolderPath, /PackagePath, /LicensePath, and /Add-ProvisionedAppxPackage. Becoming familiar with these is very important because you'll likely be tested on them. You can learn about all available commands and options at *https://docs.microsoft.com/previous-versions/windows/it-pro/windows-8.1-and-8/hh824882(v=win.10)*. Review this article and make sure that you can make sense of commands you might come across, such as

```
Dism /Online /Add-ProvisionedAppxPackage /FolderPath:C:\Test\Apps\MyUnpackedApp /
SkipLicense
```

Another example is

```
Dism /Image:C:  est\offline /Add-ProvisionedAppxPackage /FolderPath:c:\Test\Apps\
MyUnpackedApp /CustomDataPath:c:\Test\Apps\CustomData.xml
```

Using Windows Configuration Designer to deploy apps

You can use the Windows Configuration Designer tool, shown in Figure 4-27, to reconfigure your deployed Windows 10 devices by creating and distributing provisioning packages.

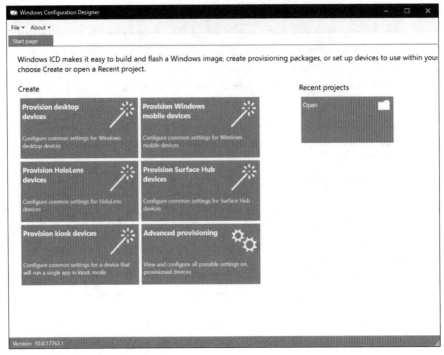

FIGURE 4-27 The Windows Configuration Designer home page

To install Windows Configuration Designer, download and install Windows ADK.

Create provisioning packages to deploy apps

You can use provisioning packages to perform a number of management tasks, including deploying apps. To deploy apps, start by opening Windows Configuration Designer. On the Start page, click the option that best describes the type of provisioning that you want to do. If you are uncertain, choose Advanced Provisioning. Use the following procedure to create your provisioning package to deploy a universal LOB app.

1. Click Advanced Provisioning.

2. In the New Project wizard, on the Enter Project Details page, in the Name box, type the name for your provisioning package and a meaningful description. For example, type **LOB apps,** add a suitable description, and then click Next.

3. On the Choose Which Settings To View And Configure page, choose whether the package is applicable to

   - All Windows editions

   - Only to desktop editions

   - Only to mobile editions

   - Only to IoT editions

4. Click Next.

5. On the Import A Provisioning Package (Optional) page, click Finish. You can use this option to import settings from a previously configured package that mostly, but not entirely, meets your needs.

6. On the Available Customizations page, shown in Figure 4-28, in View, click Common IT Pro Settings and expand Runtime Settings.

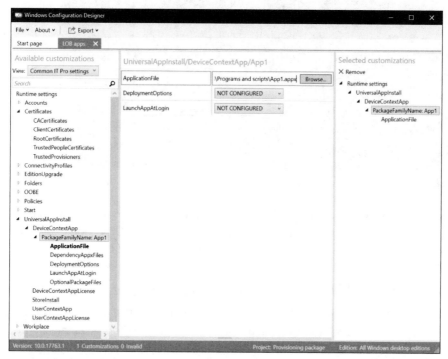

FIGURE 4-28 Available customizations for your package

7. On the Available Customizations page, in the navigation pane, expand UniversalAppInstall and click DeviceContextApp.

8. In the details pane, in the PackageFamilyName text box, type a name for this collection of apps. For example, type **LOB App1**.

9. Select the PackageFamilyName: LOB App1 node.

10. Click the ApplicationFile node and in the ApplicationFile text box, click Browse, and navigate to and select the .appx file that represents your app.

11. In the File menu, click Save.

You have created a customization for your app. You are now ready to deploy this customization by applying the provisioning package.

Apply provisioning packages

To apply a provisioning package, you must start by exporting the package. Then distribute the package to your users' devices. A simple way to apply a provisioning package is locate the package file and double-click it. When prompted, as shown in Figure 4-29, click Yes, Add It.

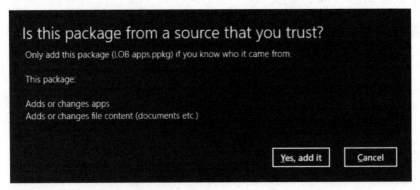

Is this package from a source that you trust?

Only add this package (LOB apps.ppkg) if you know who it came from.

This package:

Adds or changes apps
Adds or changes file content (documents etc.)

Yes, add it   Cancel

FIGURE 4-29 Installing a provisioning package

From the Settings app, you can view installed packages and add or remove additional packages. Select the Accounts node, and then on the Access Work Or School Account page, click Add Or Remove A Provisioning Package. Installed packages are displayed.

Configure and implement assigned access or public devices

Often, organizations have special-use devices, which are devices that perhaps run only a single app. These devices might be available in public areas for use by visitors. Alternatively, these devices might be available for use by organizational users in a restricted location, such as a library.

Windows 10 supports the notion of assigned access or public devices, sometimes referred to as "kiosk mode." You can configure kiosk mode in several ways.

Enabling kiosk mode in Windows 10 using the Settings app

In Windows 10, you can use the Settings app to define kiosk mode. Use the following procedure:

1. Open the Settings app.
2. Select Account > Family & Other Users.
3. Scroll down and beneath the Set Up A Kiosk heading, click Assigned Access (see Figure 4-30).
4. On the Set Up A Kiosk page, click Get Started.
5. In the Create An Account window, type the name of an account to create. This account is used for assigned access. Click Next.
6. In the Choose A Kiosk App window, select the single assigned app that the kiosk account will use, as shown in Figure 4-31. Click Next.

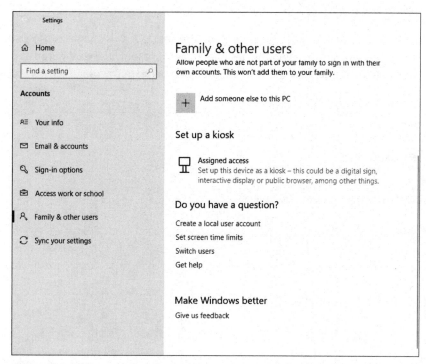

FIGURE 4-30 Setting up assigned access

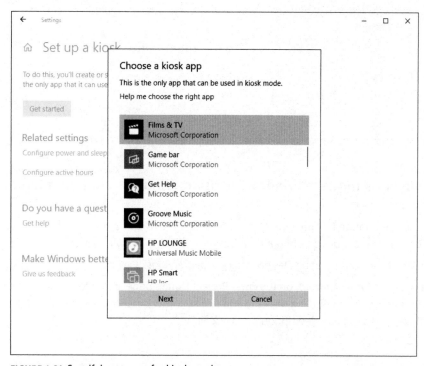

FIGURE 4-31 Specifying an app for kiosk mode

7. Click Close to complete the procedure.

You can review or edit the selected settings on the Set Up A Kiosk page, as shown in Figure 4-32. When you sign in using the designated account, only the configured app will run. To remove kiosk mode, click the selected user, and beneath the user, click Remove Kiosk.

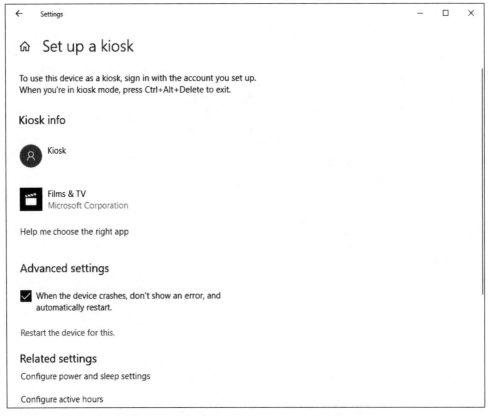

FIGURE 4-32 Reviewing the kiosk mode settings

Enabling kiosk mode in Windows 10 using Windows Configuration Designer

Windows Configuration Designer enables you to create provisioning packages to configure kiosk mode. To use Windows Configuration Designer, use the following procedure:

1. In Windows Configuration Designer, click Provision Kiosk Devices.

2. In the New Project wizard, on the Enter Project Details page, in the Name box, type the name for your provisioning package and a meaningful description. For example, type **Kiosk,** add a suitable description, and click Finish.

3. In the new tab window, click the Configure Kiosk Account And App button, as shown in Figure 4-33.

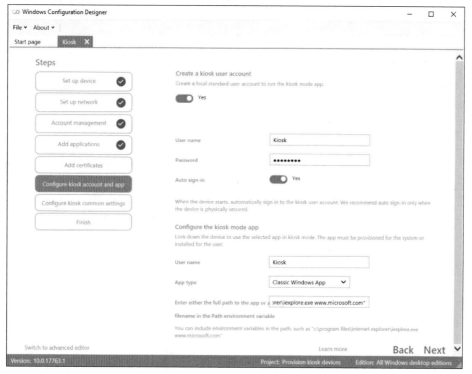

FIGURE 4-33 Creating a kiosk configuration provisioning package

4. Under the Create A Kiosk User Account heading, enter the following information:

- **User Name** This is the account that will be created for use as the kiosk user account.

- **Password** Enter the password for the user account.

- **Auto Sign-In** Specify whether the user will sign in automatically when the computer is started.

5. Under the Configure The Kiosk Mode App heading, enter the following information:

- **User Name** This is the account that will be used as the kiosk user account.

- **App Type** Choose between Classic Windows App or Universal Windows App. If you choose the former, specify the path to the filename for the desktop app. If you choose the latter, enter the Application User Model Identity (AUMID) of the app. You can determine the AUMID of an app using Windows PowerShell, File Explorer, or by editing the registry. To use Windows PowerShell, run the **Get-StartApps** cmdlet. The AppID is returned.

6. Click Next.

7. As shown in Figure 4-34, on the Configure Kiosk Common Settings page, configure the following options:

   - **Set Tablet Mode** Display In Tablet Mode With The On-Screen Keyboard When The Kiosk User Signs In.

   - **Customize User Experience** If you choose Yes for Configure Welcome And Shutdown Screens, you must then define branding options.

   - **Configure Power Settings** If you choose Yes for Turn Off Timeout Settings, you can then define Screen Timeout and Sleep Timeout options.

FIGURE 4-34 Completing kiosk mode setup with provisioning package configuration

8. Click Next.

9. On the final page of the wizard, you can optionally password protect your package. Click Create when you have finished.

10. Click the displayed link to open the folder that contains the exported package.

   You can now distribute the package to the required computer devices.

Deploy Office 365 ProPlus

Microsoft 365 includes Office 365 ProPlus. Office 365 ProPlus includes the following apps: Access, Excel, OneNote, Outlook, PowerPoint, Publisher, Skype for Business, and Word. Office 365 ProPlus installs as a single package, although you do have some control over the details.

Users who have an Office 365 license associated with their accounts can download and install Office 365, depending on the subscription. To do this, they must sign in to *www.office .com* using their Office 365 accounts. Then on the Office 365 homepage, they can click the link to Install Office (see Figure 4-35).

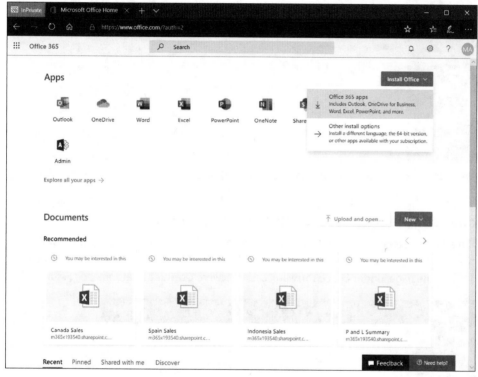

FIGURE 4-35 Installing Office 365 ProPlus manually from the Office 365 portal

They can select either

- Office 365 Apps, which installs the default apps. The defaults are configurable by the Office 365 administrator.
- Other Install Options, which enables users to choose additional options, as shown in Figure 4-36.

As you can see in Figure 4-36, users can choose to install Office and Skype For Business in either 32-bit or 64-bit versions; optionally, users can install Office on their iOS, Android, or Windows phones.

FIGURE 4-36 Choosing the Office 365 components for installation

Administrative control over deployment options

As an administrator, you can control what users can install. Open the Microsoft 365 admin center by navigating to *admin.microsoft.com* and signing in using your global admin account. On the Home page, under Office software, click Software Download Settings (see Figure 4-37).

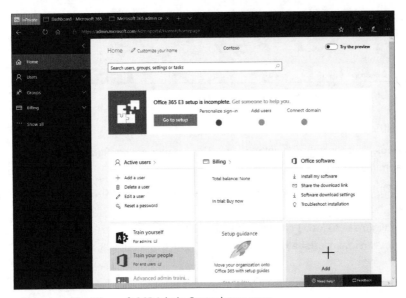

FIGURE 4-37 The Microsoft 365 Admin Center home page

On the Software Download Settings blade, shown in Figure 4-38, select the components of Office 365 that your users can deploy from Office 365. You can also configure the update interval for Office 365 app updates. When you have finished configuring the options, click Save at the bottom of the display.

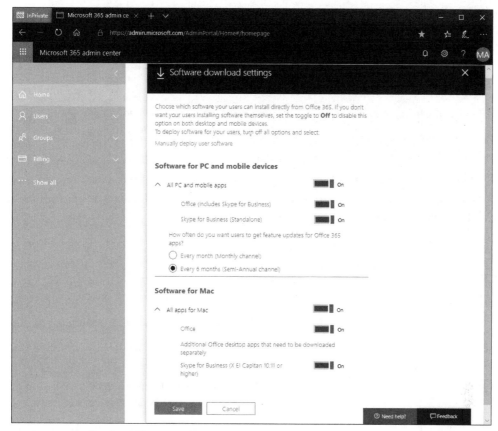

FIGURE 4-38 Configuring Office 365 software download settings

Using Intune to deploy Office 365

You can also use Intune to deploy Office 365 ProPlus, but this skill was already covered earlier in this chapter in "Adding an Office 365 suite app."

Gather Office readiness data

Before you can deploy Office 365 to your users' devices, you must ensure that their devices are ready for Office 365. Office 365 ProPlus currently aligns with Office 2019 applications. Consequently, before you can deploy Office ProPlus, you should verify that your users' devices support the newer version. Also, there might be compatibility issues with older versions of Office documents and newer versions of the apps.

Many organizations use Office add-ins to help automate Office-based tasks. These add-ins might not be compatible with Office 365 ProPlus. To help you identify potential add-in compatibility issues within your organization, you can use the Readiness Toolkit to assess your organization's readiness for Office 365 ProPlus.

NOTE   **READINESS TOOLKIT FOR OFFICE ADD-INS AND VBA**

To download the Readiness Toolkit, visit the following website at *https://www.microsoft.com /en-us/download/details.aspx?id=55983.*

To use the Readiness Toolkit, your computers must meet the following requirements:

- Running Windows 7 SP1 or a newer operating system
- Microsoft .NET Framework 4.5.1 or newer
- Excel 2010 or newer to view the reports

After installing the Readiness Toolkit, you can decide what type of report you want to run. Available options are detailed in Table 4-4.

TABLE 4-4 Readiness Toolkit reporting options

REPORTING OPTIONS	DESCRIPTION
Most recently used Office documents and installed add-ins on this computer	- Scans Office documents in the user's list of most recently used files. - Also looks for any Add-Ins for Office that are installed. - Report type: VBA and Add-In.
Office documents in a local folder or network share	- Scans the Office documents in the folder or network share that you specify. - Report type: VBA only. Does not scan for Add-Ins.
Previous readiness results saved together in a local folder or network share	- Enables you to create a consolidated report comprised of individual readiness results from multiple computers. Useful for departmental analysis. - Report type: Configurable depending on what you previously scanned for.
Add-in data from Office Telemetry dashboard	- Scans data from the Office Telemetry dashboard. - Report type: Add-In only.

NEED MORE REVIEW?   **TELEMETRY DASHBOARD TOPOLOGY, SIZING, AND BANDWIDTH PLANNING**

To find out about the Telemetry Dashboard, visit the Microsoft website at *https://docs.microsoft .com/deployoffice/compat/plan-telemetry-dashboard-deployment.*

You can then choose either a basic or an advanced report. Advanced reports are recommended because they provide more complete information on which to base your decisions. The Readiness Report Creator tool generates an Excel spreadsheet comprised of a number of worksheets. Each worksheet contains information about different aspects of your existing devices' compatibility.

Depending on the report type, the following worksheets are available:

- VBA Overview
- VBA Summary
- VBA Results
- VBA Remediation
- VBA References
- Add-In Summary
- Add-In Details
- By Computer Name

> **NEED MORE REVIEW?** **USE THE READINESS TOOLKIT TO ASSESS APPLICATION COMPATIBILITY FOR OFFICE 365 PROPLUS**
>
> To learn how to use the Readiness Toolkit, visit the Microsoft website at *https://docs.microsoft.com/deployoffice/use-the-readiness-toolkit-to-assess-application-compatibility-for-office-365-pro.*

Configure Internet Explorer Enterprise Mode

Windows 10 ships with two Internet browsers: Internet Explorer and Microsoft Edge. For most situations, Microsoft Edge offers a more streamlined, efficient browsing experience. This browser is also available on other platforms, including iOS and Android, making it ideal for users with multiple devices.

However, not all websites function correctly when accessed with Edge. This is especially true for apps that are developed to run using ActiveX controls, or with certain add-ins for Internet Explorer. To help to address this problem, you can use Internet Explorer Enterprise mode, which enables you to define which browser to use when accessing specific websites.

To use Internet Explorer Enterprise Mode, you must download and install the Enterprise Mode Site List Manager tool. This is accessible from the Microsoft website at *https://www.microsoft.com/en-us/download/details.aspx?id=49974.*

After you have downloaded and installed the Enterprise Mode Site List Manager tool, launch it. Enter the URLs for websites for which you want to specify an appropriate compatibility mode or specific browser, as shown in Figure 4-39.

When you are finished, click File > Save To XML. Browse and enter a location to save the XML file. You should save the file to a website that is accessible to your users. For example, save the file to the web root on the web server *https://LON-WEB1.Adatum.com/Enterprisemode.xml*. Note that the specific local file location might vary.

FIGURE 4-39 Configuring websites for Enterprise Mode Site Lists

When you have saved the file, you must configure your Windows 10 computers to use the XML file. You can do this by using Group Policies. Open the Group Policy Management console. Create and link a Group Policy Object (GPO) to the appropriate container in AD DS. Then use the following procedure:

1. Open the GPO for editing.

2. Navigate to Computer Configuration\Administrative Templates\Windows Components, and then click Internet Explorer.

3. In the details pane, double-click Let Users Turn On And Use Enterprise Mode from the Tools menu.

4. Click Enabled and then click OK. This lets users choose to use Enterprise Mode.

5. In the details pane, double-click Use The Enterprise Mode IE Website List.

6. Click Enabled, and then in the Type The Location (URL) Of Your Enterprise Mode IE Website list box, type the URL for the location of the XML file, as shown in Figure 4-40, and then click OK.

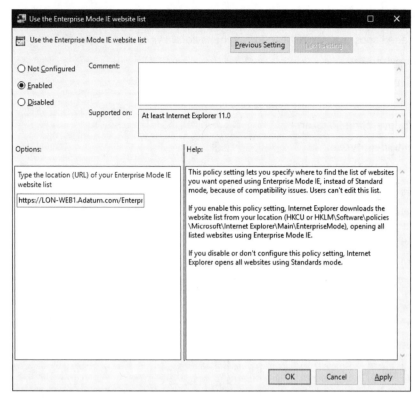

FIGURE 4-40 Configuring the XML file location for Enterprise Mode

Skill 4.2: Implement Mobile Application Management

Using Microsoft Intune, you can implement Mobile Application Management (MAM) to assign, configure, update, secure, and monitor your users' apps. In addition to using MAM to manage app usage on your users' devices, you can also implement a number of security features that can help secure corporate data on those devices. These features include Data Loss Prevention (DLP) policies, Window Information Protection (WIP), and Azure Information Protection.

> **This skill covers how to:**
> - Plan MAM
> - Implement and manage MAM policies
> - Secure data by using Intune
> - Configure Windows Information Protection
> - Implement Azure Information Protection templates

Plan MAM

You can use managed apps to enforce the following behaviors in your users' apps:

- Restrict Copy and Paste
- Restrict Save As
- Specify a managed browser for opening web links
- Define app-level conditional access
- Enable multi-identity use
- Apply DLP policies to devices that are not enrolled
- Provide app protection without device enrollment

The precise details of management options vary based on the type of device being managed. Table 4-5 identifies the key functions.

TABLE 4-5 Management options in Intune MAM

MANAGEMENT FUNCTION	ANDROID	IOS	MACOS	WINDOWS 10	WINDOWS PHONE 8.1
Add and assign apps to devices and users	Yes	Yes	Yes	Yes	Yes
Assign apps to devices not enrolled with Intune	Yes	Yes	No	No	No
Use app configuration policies to control the startup behavior of apps	No	Yes	No	No	No
Use mobile app provisioning policies to renew expired apps	No	Yes	No	No	No
Protect company data in apps with app protection policies	Yes	Yes	No	No1	No
Remove only corporate data from an installed app (app selective wipe)	Yes	Yes	No	Yes	Yes
Monitor app assignments	Yes	Yes	Yes	Yes	Yes
Assign and track volume-purchased apps from an app store	No	No	No	Yes	No
Mandatory install of apps on devices (required)	Yes	Yes	Yes	Yes	Yes
Optional installation on devices from the Company Portal (available installation)	Yes	Yes	Yes	Yes	Yes

(Continued)

MANAGEMENT FUNCTION	ANDROID	IOS	MACOS	WINDOWS 10	WINDOWS PHONE 8.1
Install shortcut to an app on the web (web link)	Yes	Yes	Yes	Yes	Yes
In-house (line-of-business) apps	Yes	Yes	Yes	Yes	No
Apps from a store	Yes	Yes	No	Yes	Yes
Update apps	Yes	Yes	No	Yes	Yes

Implement and manage MAM policies

To create and manage MAM policies, open the Microsoft 365 Device Management portal, and sign in as a global admin. Navigate to the Client Apps node, as shown in Figure 4-41. Under Manage, select the App Protection Policies node.

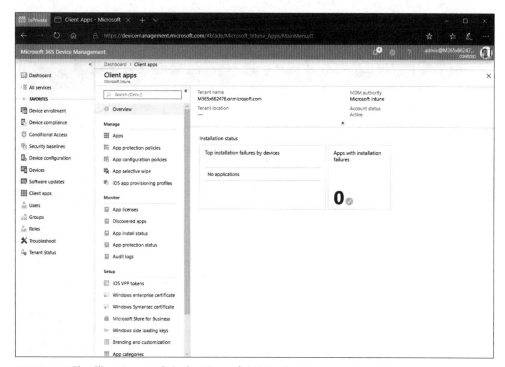

FIGURE 4-41 The Client Apps node in the Microsoft 365 Device Management portal

Implement an iOS app protection policy

To create an iOS app protection policy, use the following procedure:

1. Navigate to the Microsoft 365 Device Management portal and sign in using your global admin account.

2. In the navigation pane, select Client Apps.

3. In the Client Apps blade, select App Protection Policies.

4. Click Create Policy.

5. Enter the following values:

   - **Name**   Type a name for your new policy.

   - **Description**   Type an optional description.

   - **Platform**   Select iOS.

   - **Target To All App Types**   The options are Yes or No. If you choose Yes, all apps, regardless of management state, are targeted. If you choose No, then you must specify the next value.

   - **App Types**   Select one or both of the following:

     - Apps On Unmanaged Devices

     - Apps On Intune Managed Devices

6. Select the Apps node. In the list of apps shown in Figure 4-42, select one or more apps.

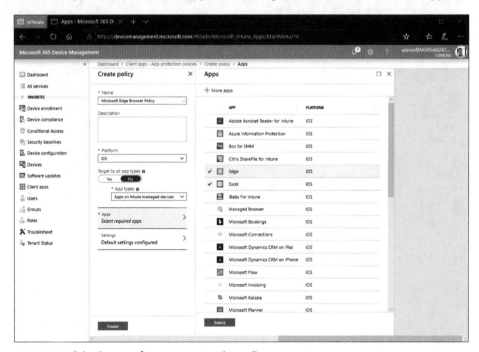

FIGURE 4-42 Selecting apps for an app protection policy

7. Click Select.

8. On the Create Policy blade, click Default Settings Configured.

9. On the Settings blade, select and configure the following:

- Data protection settings, shown in Figure 4-43, including data transfer, encryption, and functionality
- Access requirements settings, including
  - PIN For Access
  - Work Or School Account Credentials For Access
  - Recheck Access Requirements After Inactivity
- Conditional Launch Settings, including
  - Minimum OS Version
  - Maximum PIN Attempts
  - Offline Grace Periods
  - Whether jailbroken/rooted devices are allowed.

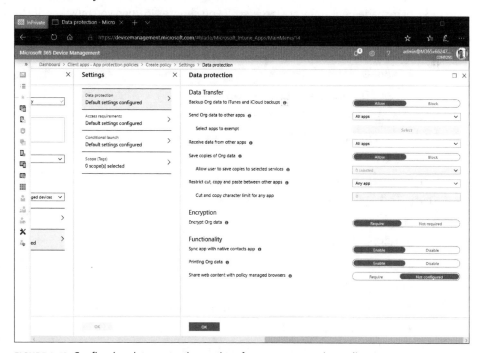

FIGURE 4-43 Configuring data protection options for an app protection policy

10. Click OK twice and then click Create.

You must now assign the policy to group(s), as described in the "Creating and managing groups for app assignment" section earlier in this chapter.

Implement an Android app protection policy

To create an Android app protection policy, use the following procedure:

1. Navigate to the Microsoft 365 Device Management portal and sign in using your global admin account.

2. In the navigation pane, select Client Apps.

3. In the Client Apps blade, select App Protection Policies.

4. Click Create Policy.

5. Enter the following values:

   - **Name**   Type a name for your new policy.

   - **Description**   Type an optional description.

   - **Platform**   Select Android.

   - **Target To All App Types**   Choose Yes or No. If you choose Yes, all apps, regardless of management state, are targeted. If you choose No, then you must specify the next value.

   - **App Types**   Select all that apply from the following:

     - Apps On Unmanaged Devices

     - Apps On Intune Managed Devices

     - Apps In Android Work Profile

6. Then select the Apps node. In the list of apps, select one or more apps.

7. Click Select.

8. On the Create policy blade, click Default settings configured.

9. On the Settings blade, select and configure the following:

   - Data protection settings, including

     - Data Transfer

     - Encryption

     - Functionality

   - Access Requirements Settings, shown in Figure 4-44, including

     - PIN For Access

     - Work Or School Account Credentials For Access

     - Recheck Access Requirements After Inactivity

   - Conditional Launch Settings, including

     - Maximum PIN Attempts

     - Offline Grace Periods

     - Jailbroken/rooted devices are allowed

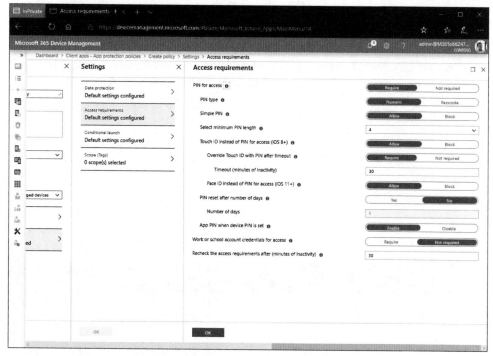

FIGURE 4-44 Configuring Access Requirements in an app protection policy

10. Click OK twice and then click Create.

You must now assign the policy, as described earlier.

Implement a Windows 10 app protection policy

To create a Windows 10 app protection policy, use the following procedure:

1. Navigate to the Microsoft 365 Device Management portal and sign in using your global admin account.

2. In the navigation pane, select Client Apps.

3. In the Client Apps blade, select App Protection Policies.

4. Click Create Policy.

5. Enter the following values:

   - **Name**   Type a name for your new policy.
   - **Description**   Type an optional description.
   - **Platform**   Select Windows 10.
   - **Enrollment State**   Choose Without Enrollment or With Enrollment.

6. Then select the Protected Apps node. These are apps that must adhere to the policy.

7. Click Add Apps, select one or more apps, and click OK twice.

8. Optionally, you can click Exempt Apps and define one or more apps that do not need to adhere to the policy settings.

9. Click Required Settings. To enable WIP, under the Windows Information Protection heading, click Block. This prevents corporate data from leaving protected apps. The default value, Off, enables users to move data freely from protected apps. Click OK. Note that WIP app protection policies are examined in more detail later in this chapter in "Configure Windows Information Protection."

10. On the Create Policy blade, click Advanced Settings.

11. On the Advanced Settings blade, shown in Figure 4-45, select and configure the following:

   ■ Network Perimeter

   ■ Data Protection

12. Click OK > Create.

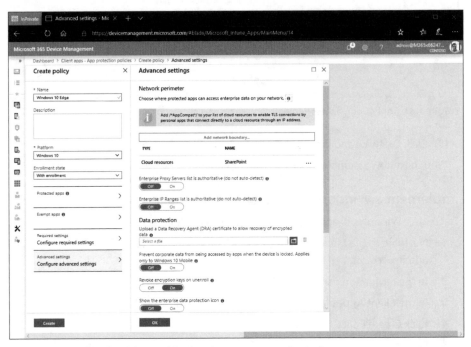

FIGURE 4-45 Configuring Advanced Settings in an app protection policy

You must now assign the policy, as described in the "Adding a Windows store app" section.

Implement an iOS app configuration policy

You can use iOS app configuration policies to configure selected apps. For example, you can use an app configuration policy to configure:

   ■ Security settings

- Language or locale settings
- Branding, such as a company logo

To create an iOS app configuration policy, use the following procedure:

1. Navigate to the Microsoft 365 Device Management portal and sign in using your global admin account.
2. In the navigation pane, select Client Apps.
3. In the Client Apps blade, select App Configuration Policies.
4. Click Add.
5. Enter the following values:
   - **Name** Type a name for your new policy.
   - **Description** Type an optional description.
   - **Device Enrollment Type** Choose Managed Devices or Managed Apps.
     - If you choose Managed Apps, when you select the apps, you can select either or both iOS and Android apps.
     - If you choose Managed Devices, you must choose the device platform—iOS or Android.
6. Assuming you choose iOS, click Associated App.
7. Select the appropriate app and click OK, as shown in Figure 4-46.

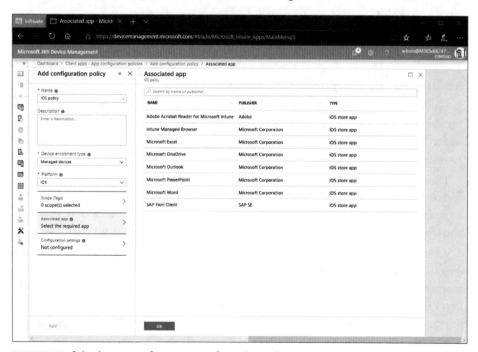

FIGURE 4-46 Selecting an app for an app configuration policy

8. Click Configuration Settings, and then, in the Configuration Settings Format list, choose either Use Configuration Designer or Enter XML Data. Populate the field with the XML data to configure the app's settings.

NEED MORE REVIEW? **ADD APP CONFIGURATION POLICIES FOR MANAGED IOS DEVICES**

To find out more about the configurable properties, refer to the Microsoft website at *https://docs.microsoft.com/intune/app-configuration-policies-use-ios.*

9. Click OK, and then click Add.

You must now assign the policy in the usual way.

Implement an Android app configuration policy

To create an Android app configuration policy, the process is almost identical to the process for iOS.

NEED MORE REVIEW? **DEPLOYING OUTLOOK FOR IOS AND ANDROID APP CONFIGURATION SETTINGS**

You can find out how to use app configuration policies to configure a specific app (in this case, Outlook for iOS and Android), by referring to the Microsoft website at *https://docs.microsoft.com /exchange/clients-and-mobile-in-exchange-online/outlook-for-ios-and-android/outlook-for-ios-and-android-configuration-with-microsoft-intune.*

Securing data by using Intune

Regardless of business size and industry, all companies have data that they consider sensitive. Microsoft aims to protect your corporate data from being lost, stolen, or getting into the wrong hands with their Information Protection Solutions built into Office 365, Windows, Azure, and across the Microsoft Cloud.

Information protection is a huge issue for many enterprises, and some are bound by law and regulations, which stipulate how data should be protected and for how long it must be safeguarded before secure deletion. We will introduce many of the solutions from Microsoft and see how they can be configured and deployed to protect your data.

Office 365 offers businesses an integrated solution with many popular features, such as email, Office apps, SharePoint, and OneDrive for Business. There is a full data protection suite that allows businesses to comply with industry regulations and laws that require organizations to protect sensitive information, such as personally identifiable information (PII), and prevent its inadvertent disclosure. Leaks of sensitive information can have a huge negative impact on businesses. This can include sizable fines and lost goodwill.

Following the Health Insurance Portability and Accountability Act (HIPAA) in the USA, which aims to ensure protection for individually identifiable health data, officers in charge of running the business that loses PII can be jailed for not ensuring adequate safeguards are in place.

With a DLP policy in place, using the Office 365 Compliance Center, you can identify, monitor, and automatically protect sensitive information across the Office 365 suite of products, including Exchange Online, SharePoint Online, and OneDrive for Business.

A DLP policy can help

- Identify sensitive information in Exchange Online, SharePoint Online, and OneDrive for Business.
- Prevent the accidental sharing of sensitive information.
- Monitor and protect sensitive information in Office 2019—Word, Excel, and PowerPoint.
- Help train users to stay compliant with their work.
- View DLP compliance reports.

With Office 365, you can create and manage DLP policies in the Compliance Center. A DLP policy can be configured on one of the Office 365 locations mentioned above, and then you need to establish rules that will protect the content. These are comprised mainly of

- **Conditions**   The content monitored by the DLP must match the conditions in place for the rule to be enforced.
- **Actions**   These are the actions that you want the rule to take when the conditions are met. For example, the action could block access to the document and send an email notification to the compliance team.

Office 365 includes more than 40 ready-to-use templates containing rules that you can use or customize to meet your organization's compliance requirements.

There are DLP policy templates that can be used to help with the compliance requirements for the following industry regulations and legislations, and many others:

- Gramm-Leach-Bliley Act (GLBA)
- Payment Card Industry Data Security Standard (PCI-DSS)
- United States Personally Identifiable Information (U.S. PII)
- United States Health Insurance Portability and Accountability Act (HIPAA)

Create a DLP policy from a template

1. Open the Microsoft 365 Admin Center and sign in using your global admin account.
2. In the navigation pane, expand Admin Centers and then click Compliance, as shown in Figure 4-47.
3. On the Compliance Center home page, in the navigation pane, click Policies.
4. In the details pane, under Data (2), click Data Loss Prevention. A new tab opens.
5. In the details pane, click +Create A Policy.

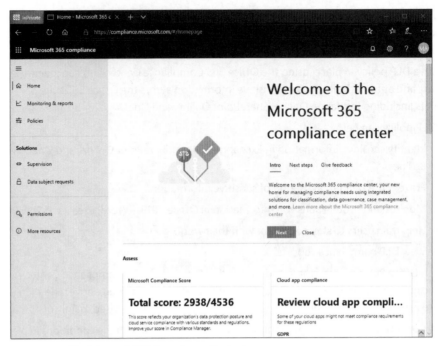

FIGURE 4-47 The Microsoft 365 Compliance Center homepage

6. Choose one of the DLP policy templates. For this example, we will select a Privacy template covering U.S. Personally Identifiable Information (PII) Data, as shown in Figure 4-48, and then click Next.

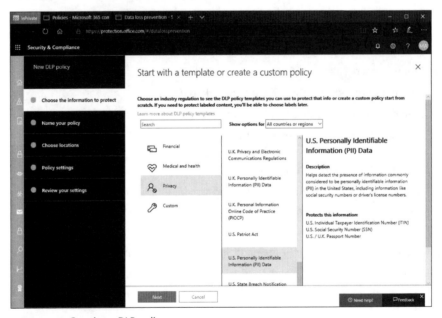

FIGURE 4-48 Creating a DLP policy

7. Enter a name and description for the policy and click Next.

8. Choose the locations that you want the DLP policy to protect. As shown in Figure 4-49, you can choose custom locations, or select All locations in Office 365. We will choose Let Me Choose Specific Locations and click Next.

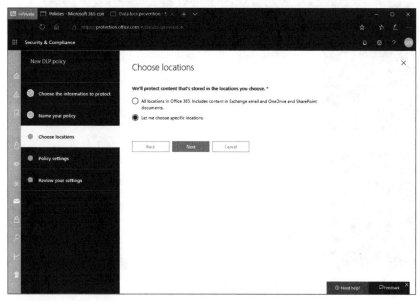

FIGURE 4-49 Defining data locations for protection with a DLP policy

9. On the Choose Locations page, as shown in Figure 4-50, you can fine tune the locations, accounts, and sites. Click Next.

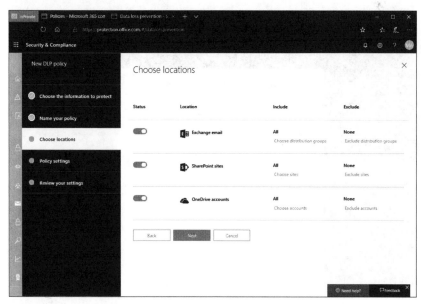

FIGURE 4-50 Enabling specific data locations for protection with a DLP policy

10. On the Policy Settings page, shown in Figure 4-51, you can view the options to customize the type of content that the U.S. PII Data template looks for, and then click Next. (You can modify the rule conditions and actions by clicking the Use Advanced Settings link on the Policy Settings page.)

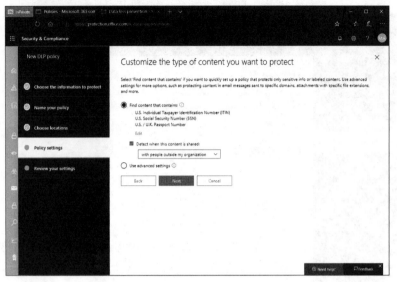

FIGURE 4-51 Customizing the content type for DLP protection

11. On the What Do You want To Do If We Detect Sensitive Info? page, shown in Figure 4-52, review the options and click Next. Note that you can

- Notify users when content matches the policy settings
- Detect when a specific amount of sensitive info is being shared at one time

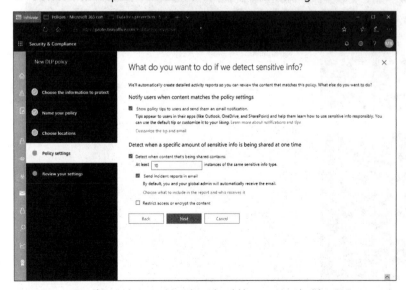

FIGURE 4-52 Specifying what sensitive data should be protected with a DLP protection policy

12. On the Do You Want To Turn On The Policy Or Test Things Out First? page, there are three options:

- Yes, Turn It On Right Away
- I'd Like To Test It Out First (Show Policy Tips While In Test Mode)
- No, Keep It Off. I'll Turn It On Later

13. Select the appropriate option and click Next.

14. Review your settings for this policy and click Create.

15. Click Close.

Depending on the size of your organization, you should consider rolling your DLP policies out gradually to assess their impact and test their effectiveness. A DLP policy could unintentionally block access to documents that staff require for their daily work. It is therefore recommended that you initially pilot the deployment of DLP policies and initially limit the location and scope.

Once the initial test deployment is successful, you can roll them out to a wider audience. Throughout the process, you should monitor the DLP reports, incident reports, and any notifications to make sure that the results are what you intend.

Configure Windows Information Protection

Built into Windows 10 are tools that allow businesses to protect data, contain data, and prevent data leakage when it is both shared internally and externally outside of an organization. The key pillars of information protection are shown in Figure 4-53.

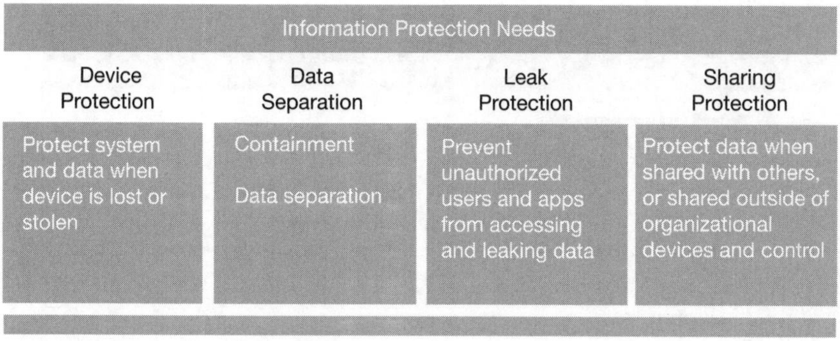

Information Protection Needs			
Device Protection	Data Separation	Leak Protection	Sharing Protection
Protect system and data when device is lost or stolen	Containment Data separation	Prevent unauthorized users and apps from accessing and leaking data	Protect data when shared with others, or shared outside of organizational devices and control

FIGURE 4-53 The four information protection needs

Windows Information Protection is the inclusion of many of the above needs, being incorporated directly into the information protection stack within Windows. Windows 10 caters for Device Protection with BitLocker, which protects your data while it's at rest on the device, even if the device is lost or stolen. If the hard drive is removed from the device, all data is encrypted and unreadable.

The separation of data allows administrators to identify personal versus corporate data. With Microsoft Intune, it is possible to separate data into these categories and securely wipe business data from a device remotely, on demand. This is also possible within the Windows 10 operating system.

Windows 10 also contains capabilities to prevent business data from leaking out of the organization (for example, posting data from a corporate Word document to a non-corporate location, such as Facebook or Twitter). You can now make sure that only authorized apps have access to business data and employ Copy and Paste restrictions where needed.

The last pillar requirement is to help ensure that business data can be shared with others within and outside of their organization in a secure way. An example of this would be allowing corporate documents to be emailed to authorized colleagues, with controls on who can view or edit the document and with the ability to revoke permissions as needed.

If you have a Microsoft 365 subscription, you can use policies in Intune to remotely manage WIP. An example of WIP in action using Intune would be to enforce a Windows 10 device compliance policy to require that BitLocker is used and reported through the Windows Health Attestation Service.

Create a WIP policy within Intune

With Intune, you can create a WIP-specific policy through the Microsoft 365 Device Management portal.

1. Navigate to the Microsoft 365 Device Management portal and sign in using your global admin account.

2. In the navigation pane, select Client Apps.

3. In the Client Apps blade, select App Protection Policies, as shown in Figure 4-54.

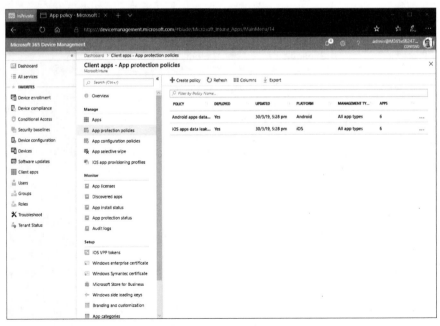

FIGURE 4-54 Listing app protection policies

4. Click Create Policy.

5. Enter the following values:

   - **Name** Type a name for your new policy.

   - **Description** Type an optional description.

   - **Platform** From the drop down, select Windows 10.

   - **Enrollment State** Choose Without Enrollment.

6. Click Protected Apps and choose Add Apps. The Add Apps blade opens, shown in Figure 4-55, which shows you all apps that are currently available and can access your enterprise data.

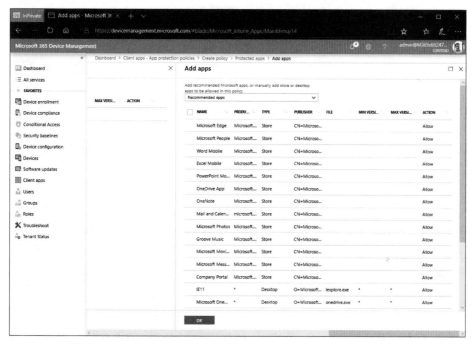

FIGURE 4-55 Adding apps to an app protection policy

NOTE ADD A DESKTOP APP

If you want to add a desktop app to your allowed apps list, use the drop-down menu and select Desktop Apps. You will then need to enter the info into the fields and choose OK to add the app to your Allowed Apps list.

7. Select Microsoft Edge and click OK twice.

8. Click the Configure Required Settings. You can apply a protection mode as shown in Figure 4-56. If this is a pilot or test, choose Silent or Allow Overrides because this setting will permit WIP breaches. If you want to enforce WIP, change the setting to Block.

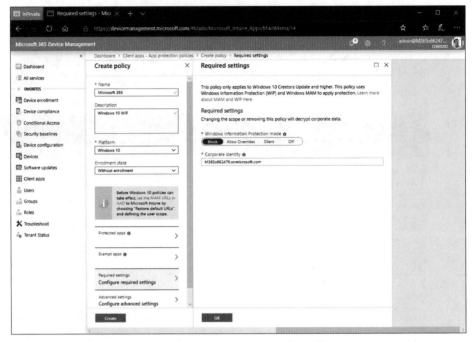

FIGURE 4-56 Configuring required settings for an app protection policy

9. Click OK.

10. If you want to configure advanced settings, shown in Figure 4-57, click the Configure Advanced Settings link. You can define the following advanced settings:

   - **Network Perimeter**   Enables you to define from where corporate data can be accessed

   - **Data Protection**   Includes data recovery agent (DRA) settings and Azure RMS options

   - **Access**   Defines sign-in options

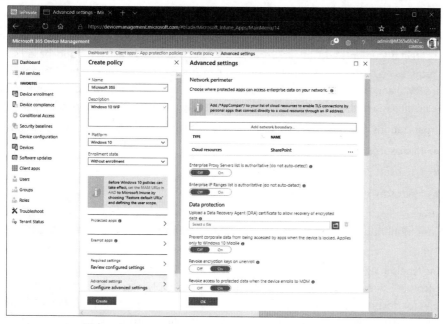

FIGURE 4-57 Modifying the advanced settings in a Windows 10 app protection policy

11. Click OK, and then click Create.

To deploy the policy to Windows 10 devices, open the policy, as shown in Figure 4-58, and then assign the policy to the appropriate group(s).

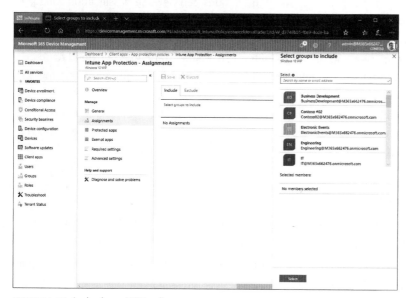

FIGURE 4-58 Assigning a WIP policy

Implement Azure Information Protection templates

Azure Information Protection continues the protection of information by helping classify, label, and protect documents and emails. Because this is an Azure service, it is a cloud-based solution that requires no on-premises infrastructure. The technology uses Azure Rights Management (Azure RMS) and allows administrators to define rules and conditions, which then automatically add classification to the data. (Also, users can manually add the classification to their files.)

Organizations with one of the following Microsoft 365 subscriptions include Azure RMS:

- Microsoft 365 Enterprise E3, or E5
- Microsoft 365 Education A3, or A5
- Microsoft 365 Government G3 or G5

After content is classified, administrators can then track and control how it is used. This includes monitoring data flows, tracking access to documents, and preventing data leakage or misuse.

The labels in Azure Information Protection are not the same as the labels available in Microsoft 365 Security & Compliance. AIP labels let you apply classification and protection policies for documents and emails. The Microsoft 365 Security & Compliance labels are used to classify documents and emails for auditing and retention purposes within Microsoft 365 services.

Documents and emails use labels to apply classification which always stays with the document or email, regardless of where the data is stored or if it is shared. The labels are visible to the user, and metadata is also attached to files and email headers in clear text, which ensures that other services, such as data loss–prevention solutions, can view the classification and take appropriate action.

With the technology being cloud-based, it is integrated with Microsoft 365 and Azure Active Directory. Developers and software vendors can use the Graph APIs to extend Azure RMS to work with third-party information protection solutions, both on-premises or in the cloud.

The Azure Information Protection solution keeps you in control of your data by using encryption, identity, and authorization policies. Within the Azure Rights Management service, there are default templates that you can use to restrict data access to users within your organization.

Configure Azure Information Protection

To use or evaluate Azure Information Protection, you will need the following pre-requisites:

- A Microsoft 365 subscription that includes Azure Information Protection
- A global administrator account or security administrator account to sign in to the Azure portal and configure the Azure Information Protection policy
- A computer running Windows (minimum of Windows 7 with Service Pack 1) with Office installed

Activate the Azure Rights Management service

The first stage in configuring Azure Information Protection is to activate the Azure Rights Management service by using the following steps:

1. Sign in to the Azure portal as a global admin or security admin at *https://portal .azure.com*.

2. In the search box, type Azure Information Protection and then click Azure Information Protection in the returned results.

3. On the Azure Information Protection blade, shown in Figure 4-59, click Protection Activation.

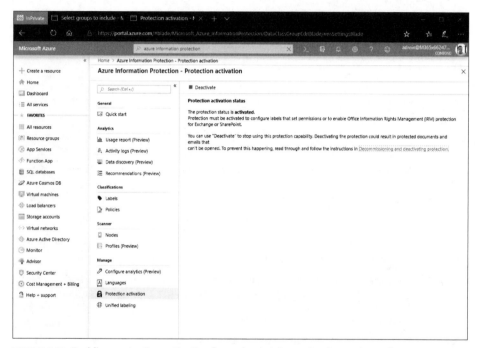

FIGURE 4-59 Enabling protection activation for an Azure Information Protection policy

4. On the Protection Activation page, select Activate.

Explore Azure Information Protection policies

Azure Information Protection comes with a default policy called Global policy, which you can use without modification. Also, you can customize the Global policy. Let's take a look at the default policy.

1. On the Azure Information Protection blade, click Policies and select the Global Policy item.

2. Review the information and expand the confidential label displayed on the Global Policy blade (see Figure 4-60).

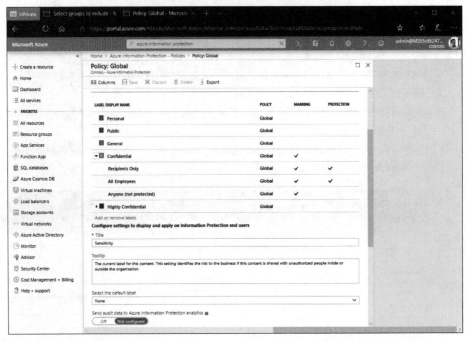

FIGURE 4-60 Configuring the default Global Azure Information Protection Policy

3. To set the default label and prompt the user for justification to set a lower classification label, click the Select The Default Label > General.

4. Toggle the Users Must Provide Justification To Set A Lower Classification Label, Remove A Label, Or Remove Protection option to On.

5. You should explore the policy further by creating a new label for protection, creating visual markers, and creating a condition to prompt the user for classification.

6. If you have made any changes, click Save.

7. For the policy to be available to users, it needs to be published. However, this is no longer a separate step. The warning message reminds you of this. If you are happy to save (and publish) click OK.

Install the Azure Information Protection client

You learned earlier that Windows 10 has the WIP framework built in to the operating system. When you install the Azure Information Protection client, Windows will communicate with Azure and display the labels in Office applications.

To install the Azure Information Protection client, follows these steps:

1. On the client PC, ensure that Office has been installed and the user has signed into the Office application.

2. Close all running Office apps and download the Azure Information Protection client (AzInfoProtection.exe), from the Microsoft download center at *https://www.microsoft.com/en-us/download/details.aspx?id=53018*.

3. Run the Azure Information Protection client and follow the prompts to install it.

4. Open Word and create a new blank document.

5. You should see a Congratulations page with basic instructions. Read the instructions and click Close.

6. After the new document loads, you should see on the Home tab, a new Protection group, with a button named Protect and the Information Protection bar under the ribbon. The bar displays the labels that you saw in the Azure portal as shown in Figure 4-61.

FIGURE 4-61 Using the Azure Information Protection client in Office Word

You should create documents, protect them using Azure Information Protection, and see how labeling works. Try out the other settings and in Excel, PowerPoint, and Outlook that support Azure Information Protection.

Thought experiments

In these thought experiments, demonstrate your skills and knowledge of the topics covered in this chapter. You can find the answers to these thought experiments in the next section.

Scenario 1

At Adatum, you want to be able to provide your users with a number of apps that are available in the Microsoft Store. However, you only want users to be able to view and install specific apps. Your organization has a Microsoft 365 Enterprise E5 subscription.

As a consultant for Adatum, answer the following questions.

1. How could you use the Microsoft Store for Business to help with this requirement?

2. How could you use Intune to help provide more control over this solution?

Scenario 2

At Adatum, it's important that sensitive data does not get inadvertently sent to external users. Your organization has a Microsoft 365 Enterprise E5 subscription.

As a consultant for Adatum, answer the following questions.

1. How could you address this requirement using Microsoft 365 features?

2. What is the specific process that you would need to perform?

3. Are there any other approaches you could take?

Thought experiment answers

This section provides the solutions for the tasks included in the Thought Experiments section.

Scenario 1

1. You could acquire the apps from the Microsoft Store and then publish the apps to a Private Store in Microsoft Store for Business. Users can then browse the Private Store and access the desired apps.

2. You can use Intune to assign acquired apps by synchronizing the Microsoft Store for Business and Intune. The synced apps would show in the Microsoft 365 Device Management portal in the Client Apps—Apps list. You can then assign the apps to specific groups. This means they wouldn't need to use the Store app at all.

Scenario 2

1. You can use Intune to create and enforce a DLP policy.

2. In the Compliance center, you can launch the New DLP policy wizard. You will

   - Define the type of sensitive data you want to protect, such as credit card numbers.

   - Specify where the data resides (locations).

   - Select the option for detecting when content is shared with people outside your organization.

   - Configure the actions to take when sensitive data has been detected.

   - Enable the policy.

3. In addition to an DLP Policy, you can also use Azure Information Protection.

Chapter summary

- You can use Intune to deploy Store apps, Office 365 Suite apps, Web link apps, Built-in apps, Line-of-business apps, and Windows (Win32) apps.

- After configuring an app for deployment, you must remember to assign the app to the appropriate user or device groups.

- You can customize the components of the Office 365 app suite that are available to your Windows 10 users by creating an Office 365 Suite app for Windows 10.

- You can use role assignments in the Microsoft Store for Business to determine what designated users can do within the store.

- You must enable the Microsoft Store for Business Private Store before it can be seen and used by your organization's users.

- To enable Intune to distribute Microsoft Store for Business apps, you must enable Intune as a management tool in the Microsoft Store for Business portal. Also, you must enable synchronization between Microsoft Store for Business and Intune from the Microsoft 365 Device Management portal.

- Offline licensing in the Microsoft Store for Business enables you to distribute apps through your Intune or your internal network infrastructure rather than relying on the Microsoft Store for Business storefront.

- When making apps available in the private Store in Microsoft Store for Business, you can choose to make an app visible to the following: No One, Everyone, or Specific Groups.

- You can sideload LOB apps with Windows 10 by creating a provisioning package with Windows Configuration Designer and using that package to distribute the app.

- You can also sideload apps into Windows images using DISM.exe.

- When enabling kiosk mode, you must specify a user account and an associated app.

- Internet Explorer Enterprise Mode enables you to define which Microsoft browser is used for which specific websites.

- App protection policies enable you to control corporate data when used in protected apps.

- An DLP policy enables you to control and helps to prevent data leakage from your organization.

Index

A

actions, 205
activating, Azure RMS, 279
Active Directory-based activation, 8
AD (Active Directory), Windows Autopilot
 requirements, 20
AD DS (Active Directory Domain Services), 153–154, 217
adding
 apps to Microsoft Store for Business, 236–237
 desktop apps to allowed apps list, 275–277
 Line-of-Business (LOB) apps to enrolled devices,
 228–229
 Log Analytics views to Azure AD, 42
 Office 365 apps to enrolled devices, 224
 scope tags to configuration policies, 129
Add-MpPreference cmdlet, 165
administrative roles (Microsoft Store for Business),
 assigning to users, 230–233
administrative template profiles, deploying, 122–124
administrator role permissions, conditional access
 policies, 110
ADMX-backed policies, 122–124
alerts, for managed devices, 203–204
Android
 app configuration policy, implementing, 268
 app protection policy, 264–265
 device data available in Intune, 105–106
 enrollment, 196–197
 MAM management options, 260–261
annual certificate renewal, 177
applying, provisioning packages, 7–8, 248
apps
 adding to Microsoft Store for Business, 236–237
 Android
 app configuration policy, implementing, 268
 app protection policy, implementing, 264–265
 assigning from the Private Store, 238

AUMID, finding, 252
 deploying, 217, 245–246
 desktop, adding to allowed app list, 275–277
 distributing
 from Intune, 239
 from the Private Store, 236–237
 iOS
 app configuration policy, implementing,
 266–268
 app protection policy, implementing, 261–263
 Line-of-Business (LOB), adding to enrolled devices,
 228–229
 membership types, 242
 Microsoft Store for Business, synchronizing with
 Intune, 240–241
 Office 365, adding to enrolled devices, 224–225
 sideloading, 243–244
 using DISM, 245
 types of, 220–221
 URL, obtaining from Appstore, 222
 UWP, 243
 Windows 10, app protection policy, implementing,
 265–266
 Windows store apps
 adding to enrolled devices, 222–223
 assigning to enrolled devices, 223
Appstore, obtaining URL for apps in, 222
AppX module, Cmdlets, 244
assigning
 apps from the Private Store, 238
 deployment profiles, 25
 device profiles, 126–127
 Microsoft Store for Business administrative roles,
 230–233
 update rings, 58
 Windows store apps to enrolled devices, 223

ATP (Advanced Threat Protection), 167
   capabilities, 167
   requirements, 168
Attack Surface Reduction rules
   configuring, 160–161
   enabling, 160
   implementing, 159–160
audit logs, reviewing, 207
AUMID (application user model ID), finding, 252
authentication, 67
   Azure AD Password Protection, 68–70
   Kerberos tickets, 153–154
   MFA (Multifactor Authentication), 66, 70–73
   Microsoft Authenticator app, 67–68
   picture passwords, 82
   self-service password reset, 70
   Windows Hello, 76–78
automatic enrollment, configuring, 187–188
Azure AD
   assigning device profiles, 126–127
   Commercial ID, obtaining, 38–40
   device enrollment, 192–196
   Device Health, configuring, 40
   enterprise state roaming, 144–146
   joining, 83–88
   Log Analytics views, adding, 42
   with MDM enrollment, 10
   MFA (Multifactor Authentication), 71–73
   Password Protection, 68–70
   registering BYO devices, 87
   routing activity logs to Log Analytics workspace, 38
   self-service password reset, 70
   troubleshooting, 29
   Update Compliance, adding, 38–39
   Upgrade Readiness, configuring, 40
Azure Information Protection, 278
   configuring, 278
   installing, 274–281
   policies, 279–280
Azure RMS (Rights Management), 278, 279

B

backups, performing with USMT, 47
biometrics
   picture passwords, 82
   Windows Biometric Framework, 66, 71

Windows Hello, 76–82
   Windows Hello for Business, 78–79
BitLocker, 66
BYO devices, registering to Azure AD, 87

C

capabilities, Windows Defender Advanced Threat
     Protection, 167
CFG (Control Flow Guard), 158
client options, co-management, 100
cloud services
   importing device hardware information to, 26–28
   MAPS, 173
   Windows Analytics, 210–212
cmdlets
   Add-MpPreference, 165
   AppX module, 244
   Set-MpPreference cmdlet, 164
Columns button, generating inventory reports, 198–200
co-management, 95–96
   client options, 100
   migrating group policy to MDM policies, 98–100
   precedence, implementing, 96–98
   prerequisites, 101
   recommending a strategy, 100
   staged rollout, 101–102
Commercial ID
   adding to devices, 42
   obtaining from Azure, 38–40
compatibility, hardware, 12
CompatibilityAssessment, 37
compliance, monitoring, 212–213. *See also* compliance
     policies
compliance policies, 102–103
   creating, 116
   implementing, 115–116
   managing, 117–118
   network location-based, 113–115
   noncompliant devices, 112
   planning, 110–111
   refresh cycle times, 118, 128
   and regulatory laws, 110
   troubleshooting, 130
conditional access policies, 102–103
   administrator role permissions, 110
   creating, 107–109

creating for MFA, 73
device data available in Intune, 105–106
implementing, 106–109
managing, 109–110
planning, 103–104
conditions, 104
configuration policies
adding scope tags, 129
refresh cycle times, 128
configuring
Attack Surface Reduction rules, 160–161
Azure AD Password Protection, 68–69
Azure Information Protection, 278
device enrollment
device categories, 184–185
device identifiers, 185
enrollment managers, 185
restrictions, 182–184
device profiles, 119
Dynamic Lock, 82–83
enterprise state roaming, 144–146
Intune, automatic enrollment, 187–188
MDM, device enrollment, 176–180
sync settings, 135–139
Windows Defender Advanced Threat Protection, 173
Windows Defender Antivirus, 171–172
Windows Defender Application Control, 168–169
Windows Defender Application Guard, 166–167
Windows Hello, 76–82
Windows Update for Business service
using Group Policy, 57
using Intune, 57–60
Windows Update Service, 55–56
conflicting policies, 118
Controlled Folder Access
folders, adding, 165
implementing, 162–163
protected folders, adding, 165
ControlPolicyConflict, 97
controls, 104
copying to different range, USMT, 46
creating
compliance policies, 116
conditional access policies, 73, 107–109
deployment profiles, 23–24
dynamic service groups, 242–243
endpoint protection profiles, 174–175
MDMWinsOverGP policy, 97–98

picture passwords, 82
provisioning packages, 5–6, 246–247
update rings, 58
Windows Analytics workspace, 38
WIP policies, 274–277

D

default policy for Windows Defender Application
Control, creating, 169
Delivery Optimization, 48
configuring with Microsoft Intune, 49–51
GPO settings, 49
DEP (Data Execution Prevention), 158
deploying
administrative template profiles, 122–124
apps, 217, 245–246
Office 365 ProPlus, 253
administrative control over deployment options,
254–255
using Intune, 255
PowerShell scripts, 7, 124–126
deployment option, selecting, 18
deployment profiles, 22
assigning, 25
creating, 23–24
forcing Autopilot to download, 22
settings, 23
deployment scenarios, Windows Autopilot, 18–19
DeviceHealthProd, 37
devices
actions, 205
adding a Microsoft account, 75
alerts, 203–204
annual certificate renewal, 177
audit logs, reviewing, 207
automatic enrollment, configuring, 187–188
Commercial ID, adding, 42
compliance, monitoring, 212–213
compliance policies
implementing, 115–116
refresh cycle times, 118
compliance settings, 111
enrollment
Android devices, 196–197
Azure AD join during OOBE, 192–193

Azure AD join using Windows Autopilot in user-driven deployment mode, 193–196
configuration options, 179–180
configuring, 176–180
device categories, configuring, 184–185
device identifiers, configuring, 185
enrollment, 186–187
enrollment managers, configuring, 185
iOS devices, 197
MDM-only, 192
requirements, 176
restrictions, configuring, 182–184
terms and conditions, 180–182
Windows, 188–191
hardware information
extracting, 25–26
importing to cloud service, 26–28
inventory reports, 198–199
Columns button, 198–200
exporting results, 200–201
filtering results, 198–200
joining Azure AD, 83–88
MDM-only, 192
monitoring and reporting on managed devices, 202
noncompliant, 112
profiles
configuring, 119
implementing, 122–123
managing, 126–127
planning, 119–120
store apps, adding, 221–222
sync settings, 135–139
upgrading to Windows 10, 30–32
downgrade paths due to license expiration, 33
Windows Analytics, 13–14
DHA (Device Health Attestation), 66
digitally signing apps for Windows Defender Application Control, 169
DISM (Deployment Image Servicing and Management), sideloading apps with, 245
distributing
apps from Intune, 239
apps from the Private Store, 236–237
DLP policies, 268–273
downgrade paths, identifying, 31–32
downloading
Microsoft Assessment and Planning Toolkit, 13
Windows ADK, 4

dynamic deployment, 3
Azure AD with MDM enrollment, 10
manage and troubleshoot provisioning packages, 14–15
provisioning packages, 4–7
applying, 7–8
creating, 5–6
troubleshooting, 15–16
versus traditional deployment methods, 2
transforms, 3
Dynamic Lock, 82–83
dynamic service groups, creating, 242–243

E

EA (Enterprise Agreements), volume activation methods, 8–9
enabling
Attack Surface Reduction rules, 160
Exploit Protection, 157
Intune as MDM authority, 177
Private Store, 233–234
Windows Defender Application Control, 170
Windows Defender Credential Guard, 154
endpoint protection profiles, creating, 174–175
enrollment
Android devices, 196–197
Azure AD join
during OOBE, 192–193
using Windows Autopilot in user-driven deployment mode, 193–196
configuring, 176–180
device enrollment, 186–187
device identifiers, configuring, 185
device inventory reports, 198–199
Columns button, 198–200
exporting results, 200–201
filtering results, 198–200
enabling, 186–187
enrollment managers, configuring, 185
iOS devices, 197
MDM-only, 192
requirements, 176
restrictions, configuring, 182–184
terms and conditions, 180–182
in Windows Analytics, 40–41
Windows devices, 188–191

Enterprise mode, Windows Defender Application Guard, 166
enterprise state roaming, 135, 144–146
error codes, Windows Autopilot, 29–30
evaluating, Windows 10 Enterprise, 12
Exploit Protection
    enabling, 157
    implementing, 157–159
    mitigations, 158
exporting device inventory reports, 200–201
extracting, device hardware information, 25–26

F

features
    updates, 52
    Windows Defender Exploit Guard, 156
filtering inventory reports, 198–200
finding, AUMIDs, 252
folder redirection, 140–141. *See also* KFM (known folder move)
forcing, AutoPilot to download deployment profiles, 22
free trial of Microsoft Azure, 37
functions, of provisioning packages, 4–5

G

gathering Office readiness data, 255–256
GDPR (General Data Protection Regulation), 110
GPO (Group Policy object), 4, 96
    configuring XML file location for Internet Explorer Enterprise Mode, 258–259
    distributing Exploit Protection settings, 158–159
    Network Protection, implementing, 162
    settings, for Delivery Optimization, 49
Gramm-Leach-Bliley Act, 110
Group Policy
    configuring XML file location for Internet Explorer Enterprise Mode, 258–259
    folder redirection, 140–141
    KFM (known folder move), 141–143
    policies supported by, 98
    Windows Defender Credential Guard, enabling, 154
    Windows Update for Business service, configuring, 57

groups
    dynamic service groups, 242–243
    types of in Intune, 241

H

hardware
    compatibility with Windows 10, 12
    Windows Analytics, 13–14
HIPAA (Health Insurance Portability and Accountability Act), 110
Hybrid Azure AD joined devices, 145
hybrid MDM, 102

I

identifying
    hardware requirements for Windows 10, 11–12
    upgrade and downgrade paths, 31–32
images, sideloading apps into, 243
implementing
    Attack Surface Reduction rules, 159–160
    co-management precedence, 96–98
    compliance policies, 115–116
    conditional access policies, 106–109
    Controlled Folder Access, 162–163
    device profiles, 122–123
    Exploit Protection, 157–159
    folder redirection, 140–141
    iOS app protection policy, 261–262
    Network Protection, 162
importing, device hardware information to cloud service, 26–28
installing
    Azure Information Protection, 274–281
    Office 365 ProPlus, 253
Internet Explorer Enterprise mode, 257–258
    configuring websites for Enterprise Mode site lists, 258–259
Intune. *See also* co-management
    activating for Microsoft Store for Business management, 240
    alerts, 203–204
    app management

Line-of-Business (LOB) apps, adding to enrolled devices, 228–229

Office 365 apps, adding to enrolled devices, 224

automatic enrollment, configuring, 187–188

compliance policies, 110–111

configuring Windows Update for Business service, 57–60

ControlPolicyConflict, 97

Delivery Optimization, 49–51

deploying Office 365 ProPlus, 255

device data available in, 105–106

device-configuration profiles, 120

distributing apps from, 239

DLP policies, 268–269

dynamic service groups, creating, 242–243

enabling as MDM authority, 177

group types, 241

MAM, 217, 259

Android app configuration policy, 268

Android app protection policy, 264–265

app protection policy, selecting, 262–263

iOS app configuration policy, 266–268

iOS app protection policy, implementing, 261–262

management options, 260–261

planning, 260

Windows 10 app protection policy, 265–266

managing apps in, 218–220

managing device profiles, 120

MDM, enrollment settings, configuring, 176–180

membership types, 242

monitoring and reporting on managed devices, 202

notifications, 203–204

PowerShell scripts, deploying, 124–126

scope tags, 128–129

store apps, adding to enrolled devices, 221–222

Store apps, viewing, 241

synchronizing with Microsoft Store for Business apps, 240–241

types of apps, 220–221

update rings, creating, 58

Windows Health Attestation reports, 210

Windows Hello for Business, managing, 78–79

inventory reports

Columns button, 198–200

exporting results, 200–201

filtering results, 198–200

MDM, 198–199

iOS

app configuration policy, implementing, 266–268

app protection policy, implementing, 261–262

device data available in Intune, 105–106

devices, enrollment, 197

MAM management options, 260–261

J-K

joining, Azure AD, 83–88

Kerberos tickets, 153–154

KFM (known folder move), 141–143

kiosk mode

enabling with Settings app, 248–250

enabling with Windows Configuration Designer, 250–251

KMS (Key Management Service), 8

L

licensing

Azure AD Password Protection, 68

Store apps, 235

Windows Autopilot requirements, 19

limiting, Microsoft accounts, 75

LOB (Line-of-Business) apps

adding to enrolled devices, 228–229

sideloading, 243

Local Security Authority, 154

Log Analytics, 207

adding views to Azure AD, 42

requirements, 208–209

log entries, Windows Autopilot, 30

LTSC (Long Term Servicing Channel), 31

M

macOS, MAM management options, 260–261

MAK (multiple activation key), 9

malware, 170

monitoring for, 171–172

protecting against, 170–171

MAM (Mobile Application Management), 217, 259

Android apps

configuration policy, 268

protection policy, 264–265

app protection policy, selecting, 262–263
iOS apps
    configuration policy, implementing,
       266–268
    protection policy, implementing, 261–262
management options, 260–261
planning, 260
Windows 10 app protection policy, 265–266
management tasks, MDM, 175
managing
    compliance policies, 117–118
    conditional access policies, 109–110
    device profiles, 126–127
    pilot deployments, 10–11
    in-place upgrades, 36
    updates, 47–48
    user profiles, 131
    Windows Hello for Business, 78–79
MAP (Microsoft Assessment and Planning) toolkit, 36
MAPS (Microsoft Active Protection Service), 173
MDM (Mobile Device Management), 10, 95
    alerts, 203–204
    annual certificate renewal, 177
    device data available in Intune, 105–106
    device enrollment, 192
        Android devices, 196–197
        Azure AD join during OOBE, 192–193
        Azure AD join using Windows Autopilot in user-
          driven deployment mode, 193–196
        configuration options, 179–180
        configuring, 176–180
        device categories, configuring, 184–185
        device identifiers, configuring, 185
        enabling, 186–187
        enrollment managers, configuring, 185
        iOS devices, 197
        requirements, 176
        restrictions, configuring, 182–184
        terms and conditions, 180–182
        Windows devices, 188–191
    device inventory reports, 198–199
        Columns button, 198–200
        exporting results, 200–201
        filtering results, 200–201
    device profiles, planning, 119–120
    endpoint protection profiles, creating, 174–175
    hybrid, 102
    management tasks, 175

monitoring and reporting on managed devices,
    202
    policies, 98–100
    PowerShell scripts, deploying in Intune, 124–126
MDMWinsOverGP policy, creating, 97–98
MDT (Microsoft Deployment Toolkit), 2
membership types (Intune), 242
MFA (Multifactor Authentication), 66, 70
    Azure AD, 71–73
    conditional access policy, creating, 73
Microsoft 365 Device Management portal
    Log Analytics, 207-209
    monitoring device actions, 205
    reviewing device audit logs, 207
Microsoft accounts, 74
    connecting to your device, 75
    limiting the use of, 75
    signing up for, 74–75
Microsoft Assessment and Planning Toolkit,
    downloading, 13
Microsoft Authenticator app, 67–68
Microsoft Azure, free trial, 37
Microsoft Intune. *See* Intune
Microsoft Store for Business
    activating Intune management for, 240
    adding apps to the store, 236–237
    administrative roles, assigning to users,
       230–233
    apps, viewing with Intune, 241
    licensing Store apps, 235
    Private Store
       assigning apps from, 238
       distributing apps from, 236–237
       enabling, 233–234
    signing up for, 229–230
    synchronizing apps with Intune, 240–241
migrating
    group policy to MDM policies, 98–100
    user profiles
       with User State Migration tool, 44–47
       to Windows 10, 44
minimizing, user profile size, 133–134
MMAT (MDM Migration Analysis Tool), 98
monitoring
    device actions, 205
    device compliance, 212–213
    for malware, 171–172
    managed devices, 202-204

N

network connectivity, troubleshooting Windows Autopilot, 28
network location-based compliance policies, 113–115
Network Protection, implementing, 162
networking configuration, Windows Autopilot requirements, 19–20
noncompliant devices, 112
non-deferrable updates, 52
non-Windows devices, enrollment, 196

O

Office 365 apps
adding to enrolled devices, 224–225
suite properties, configuring, 226–227
Office 365 ProPlus
administrative control over deployment options,
254–255
deploying, 253, 255
gathering Office readiness data, 255–256
installing, 253
Readiness Toolkit, 256–257
offline licensing mode, 235
OneDrive for Business, KFM (known folder move),
141–143
online licensing mode, 235
OOBE (Out-Of-Box Experience), 18, 23, 28
opening, support case for Windows Autopilot, 30

P

passwords, self-service password reset, 70
PCmoverExpress, 47
permissions, for PowerShell, 126
picture passwords, creating, 82
pilot deployments
planning, 10–11
Windows Autopilot, 20–21
PIN, configuring for Windows Hello, 79–82
in-place upgrades, managing, 36
planning
compliance policies, 110–111
device profiles, 119–120

MAM, 260
pilot deployments, 10–11
determine hardware compatibility for
Windows 10, 12
identify hardware requirements for Windows 10,
11–12
policies
ADMX-backed, 124
Azure Information Protection, 279–280
compliance
creating, 116
implementing, 115–116
managing, 117–118
network location-based, 113–115
noncompliant devices, 112
planning, 110–111
conditional access, 103–104
administrator role permissions, 110
creating, 107–109
device data available in Intune, 105–106
implementing, 106–109
managing, 109–110
configuration, refresh cycle times, 128
conflicting, 118
default policy for Windows Defender Application
Control, creating, 169
DLP, 268–273
MDM, migrating to, 98–100
MDMWinsOverGP, 97–98
refresh cycle times, 118
scope tags, 128–129
troubleshooting, 130
Windows Defender Application Control, configuring,
168–169
WIP, 274–277
PowerShell scripts
deploying, 7
Intune deployment, 124–126
permissions, 126
prerequisites, for co-management, 101
Private Store
assigning apps from, 238
distributing apps from, 236–237
enabling, 233–234
profiles
administrative template, deploying, 122–124
configuring, 119
device, managing, 126–127

implementing, 122–123
planning, 119–120
scope tags, 128–129
troubleshooting, 130
user, 131
    configuring, 131–133
    minimizing size, 133–134
protecting, data with DLP policies, 268–269
protecting against malware, 170–171
provisioning packages, 4–7
    applying, 7–8, 248
    creating, 5–6, 246–247
    functions, 4–5
    PowerShell scripts, deploying, 7
    troubleshooting, 15–16
    usage scenarios, 15
purchasing roles (Microsoft Store for
        Business), 231

Q

quality updates, 52
quotas, 134

R

ransomware, 170
recommending, co-management strategy, 100
refresh cycle times, for configuration policies, 128
registering, BYO devices to Azure AD, 87
regulatory laws, and compliance policies, 110
reporting, Windows Health Attestation reports, 210
requirements
    for co-management, 101
    for device enrollment, 176
    for Log Analytics, 208–209
    for Windows Autopilot
        AD configuration, 20
        configuration, 20
        licensing, 19
        networking configuration, 19–20
    for Windows Defender Advanced Threat
            Protection, 168
    for Windows Defender Application Guard, 165–166
    for Windows Defender Credential Guard, 154
reviewing device audit logs, 207

S

S Mode, switching devices running Windows 10 in,
        34–35
Sarbanes Oxley Act, 110
scan options for Windows Defender Antivirus, 171
ScanState, 47
SCCM (Systems Center Configuration Manager), 2, 26,
        36, 217. *See also* co-management
scope tags, 128–129
Secure Boot, 66
security. *See also* authentication
    Azure RMS, 278
    Dynamic Lock, 82–83
    Windows 10 features, 65–66
    WIP, 273–274
selecting
    app protection policy, 262–263
    deployment option, 18
self-service password reset, 70
servicing and support, Windows 10, 60–61
Set-MpPreference cmdlet, 164
settings, for deployment profiles, 23
side-by-side migration, 44
sideloading apps, 243-244
    using DISM, 245
    in Windows 10, 243–244
signing up for Microsoft accounts, 74–75
signing up, for Microsoft Store for Business, 229–230
spyware, 170
staged rollout, co-management, 101–102
standalone mode, Windows Defender Application
        Guard, 166
store apps
    adding to enrolled devices, 221–222
    licensing, 235
subscription activation, 8–9
suite properties, configuring for Office 365 apps,
        226–227
switching devices running Windows 10 in S Mode, 34–35
sync settings, configuring, 135–139

T

templates, DLP policies, 269–273
terms and conditions, for device enrollment,
        configuring, 180–182

traditional deployment methods, 2
transforms, for dynamic deployment, 3
Trojan horses, 170
troubleshooting
    policies, 130
    profiles, 130
    provisioning packages, 15–16
    Windows Autopilot, 28–29
        error codes, 29–30
        MDM, 29
trusted apps, adding to Controlled Folder Access, 165
types of apps, 220–221

U

Update Compliance, 63–64
update history, viewing, 61–63
update rings, creating, 58
updates, 47–48
Upgrade Readiness assessment, 42–44
upgrading
    devices to Windows 10, 30–31
        downgrade paths due to license expiration, 33
        identify upgrade and downgrade paths, 31–32
        from Windows 10 in S Mode, 34–36
usage scenarios, for provisioning packages, 15
user profiles
    managing, 131
    migrating to Windows 10, 44
    minimizing size of, 133–134
USMT (User State Migration Tool), 44–45
    backing up files to a network share, 47
    components, 46
    data type accessible by, 45–46
    features, 45
    xml files, 45
UsmtUtils, 47
UWP (Universal Windows Platform) apps, 243

V

viewing
    Store apps with Intune, 241
    Windows 10 update history, 61–63
virtualization-assisted security, 154
viruses, 170
volume activation methods, 8–9

W

WaaSUpdateInsights, 37
WCD (Windows Configuration Designer), 4
Windows 10
    app protection policy, 265–266
    authentication, 67
        MFA (Multifactor Authentication), 70
        Microsoft Authenticator app, 67–68
    block switching out of in S Mode, 36
    Delivery Optimization, 48-51
    Dynamic Lock, 82–83
    Internet Explorer Enterprise mode, 257–258
    kiosk mode
        enabling with Settings app, 248–250
        enabling with Windows Configuration Designer, 250–251
    MAM management options, 260–261
    Microsoft accounts, 74
    migrating user profiles, 44–47
    security features, 65–66
    servicing and support, 60–61
    sideloading apps, 243–244
    subscription activation, 8
    switching out of in S Mode, 35–36
    update history, viewing, 61–63
    updates, 47–48
    Upgrade Readiness assessment, 42–44
    upgrading in S Mode, 34–36
    Windows Update for Business service, 51–53
    Windows Update Service, configuring, 55–56
Windows 10 Enterprise
    evaluating, 12
    subscription activation, 34
Windows ADK, downloading, 4
Windows Analytics, 13–14, 36–37, 210–212
    adding Commercial ID to devices, 42
    components, 37
    Delivery Optimization, GPO settings, 49
    enrolling devices in, 40–41
    Log Analytics, adding views to Azure AD, 42
    routing Azure AD activity logs to Log Analytics workspace, 38
    Update Compliance, 63–64
    Upgrade Readiness, 42–44
    Windows telemetry, 41
    workspace, creating, 38
Windows Autopilot, 17
    Azure AD, troubleshooting, 29

deployment profile, troubleshooting, 28
deployment profiles, 22
     assigning, 25
     creating, 23–24
     settings, 23
deployment scenarios, 18–19
device hardware information
     extracting, 25–26
     importing to cloud service, 26–28
error codes, 29–30
forcing to download deployment profiles, 22
log entries, 30
MDM, troubleshooting, 29
network connectivity, troubleshooting, 28
opening a support case, 30
pilot deployment, 20–21
requirements, 19
     for AD configuration, 20
     for configuration, 20
     licensing, 19
     networking configuration, 19–20
troubleshooting, 28–29
Windows Biometric Framework, 66, 71
Windows Configuration Designer
     deploying apps, 245–246
     kiosk mode, enabling in Windows 10, 250–251
     provisioning packages
          applying, 248
          creating, 246–247
Windows Defender, 153
     Advanced Threat Protection, 167
          capabilities, 167
          configuring, 173
          requirements, 168
     Antivirus, 170-171
          configuring, 171–172
          monitoring for malware, 171–172
          scan options, 171
     Application Control, 168–169
          default policy, creating, 169
          enabling, 170
          signing apps, 169
     Application Guard, 165
          configuring, 166–167
          requirements, 165–166
     Controlled Folder Access, implementing, 162–163
     creating and editing settings with Microsoft 365
          MDM, 174–175
     Credential Guard, 154
          enabling, 154
          requirements, 154

Exploit Guard, 155
     Exploit Protection, implementing, 157–159
     features, 156
Exploit Protection
     Attack Surface Reduction rules, implementing,
          159–160
     Network Protection, implementing, 162
     Security Center portal, 168
     Threat Agent Status, 213–214
Windows devices, enrolling, 188–191
Windows Health Attestation reports, 210
Windows Hello, 76–78
     PIN, configuring, 79–82
Windows Hello for Business, 78–79
Windows Phone 8.1, MAM management options,
          260–261
Windows PowerShell
     Attack Surface Reduction rules, configuring, 160–161
     Controlled Folder Access, configuring, 164
     protected folders, adding, 165
     sideloading aps, 244
     trusted apps, adding, 165
Windows Security app, 156
     Controlled Folder Access, configuring, 164–165
     Exploit Protection, enabling, 157
Windows store apps, adding to enrolled devices,
          222–223
Windows telemetry, 41
     enabling, 42
Windows Update for Business service, 51–53
     configuring
          using Group Policy, 57
          using Intune, 57–60
     options, 54–55
     update management, 53–54
Windows Update Service, configuring, 55–56
WIP (Windows Information Protection), 273–277
wipe-and-load migration, 44
workspace, creating for Windows Analytics, 38
worms, 170
WSUS (Windows Server Update Service), 51

X-Y-Z

xml files
     configuring for Internet Explorer Enterprise Mode,
          258–259
     for USMT, 45

Plug into learning at

MicrosoftPressStore.com

The Microsoft Press Store by Pearson offers:

- Free U.S. shipping

- Buy an eBook, get three formats – Includes PDF, EPUB, and MOBI to use with your computer, tablet, and mobile devices

- Print & eBook Best Value Packs

- eBook Deal of the Week – Save up to 50% on featured title

- Newsletter – Be the first to hear about new releases, announcements, special offers, and more

- Register your book – Find companion files, errata, and product updates, plus receive a special coupon* to save on your next purchase